Fearful Symmetry

Fearful Symmetry

India–Pakistan Crises in the
Shadow of Nuclear Weapons

Sumit Ganguly

and

Devin T. Hagerty

University of Washington Press
Seattle

Published in India by Oxford University Press, New Delhi

© Oxford University Press 2005
The moral rights of the author have been asserted
Database right Oxford University Press (maker)
First published 2005

Published simultaneously in the United States of America by
University of Washington Press
PO Box 50096
Seattle, WA 98145-5096, U.S.A.
www.washington.edu/uwpress

Library of Congress Cataloging-in-Publication Data

Ganguly, Sumit.
    Fearful symmetry : India-Pakistan crises in the shadow of nuclear weapons
    / Sumit Ganguly and Devin T. Hagerty.
        p.   cm.
    Includes index.
    ISBN 0-295-98525-9 (hardback)
    1. India—Foreign relations—Pakistan. 2. Pakistan—Foreign relations—India.
3. Nuclear weapons—India. 4. Nuclear weapons—Pakistan. 5. India—Politics
and government—1977- 6. Pakistan—Politics and government—1988-
I. Hagerty, Devin T. II. Title.
DS450.P18G37 2005
327.5405491'09'045—dc22   2005002816

Typeset in Garamond by Le Studio Graphique, Gurgaon 122 001

For Traci Nagle

For Vivian Grace Hagerty

Contents

Preface

The genesis of this book was a conversation between the authors, on the sidelines of a conference, about the curious phenomenon of non-war in contemporary South Asia. Independently, we had grown increasingly puzzled by the fact that India and Pakistan have managed to avoid a major war during the last few decades, despite several factors that, taken together, lead many analysts to believe that the subcontinent is the most dangerous place on earth: a savage proxy war in Kashmir, periodic crises, meagre diplomatic and economic relations, chronic everyday vituperativeness, and—most worrisome for many observers—the two countries' increasingly intense competition in nuclear weaponization.

Although their limited war in Kashmir continued apace as India and Pakistan emerged as overt nuclear weapon states in the late 1990s and beyond, New Delhi and Islamabad managed to defy the confident predictions of many in the West that major war was all but certain. Why?

Having individually invested an enormous amount of intellectual energy on India–Pakistan relations, the Kashmir dispute, and regional nuclear proliferation, we agreed that the best way to tackle this question was a joint project building upon our previous work. The end result is this book, a genuinely collaborative effort in which we have sought to meld our respective substantive and analytical strengths. Each author drafted those chapters he felt most competent to write (Chapters 1, 3, 5, 6, and 9 for Hagerty; Chapters 2, 4, 7, and 8 for Ganguly). The drafts were then subjected to each other's scrutiny for assessment, comment, and critique. The final product is a truly collective effort, for which we will share in equal measure any accolades or criticisms.

We are deeply grateful for the support, assistance, and good cheer of our editors at Oxford University Press in New Delhi and Michael Duckworth at the University of Washington Press in Seattle. Without their patience, understanding, and critical input this book would not have materialized. We can only hope that their abiding faith in our work will be suitably rewarded. We would also like to extend a word of thanks to Traci Nagle, the Production Editor of *Foreign Affairs* magazine, who generously agreed to copy-edit the initial version of the manuscript. Thanks to her keen eye, a number of errors of fact and interpretation were combed out of the manuscript. All those that remain are the sole responsibility of the authors.

November 2004   Sumit Ganguly
                                                    Bloomington, Indiana

                                                     Devin T. Hagerty
                                                       Washington, DC

1

Introduction

This book is the first comprehensive analysis of Indo-Pakistani crisis behaviour in South Asia's nuclear era, a period extending back roughly two decades. By the word 'comprehensive', we do not mean a study that represents the final and definitive word on India–Pakistan relations from the early 1980s until today. Such an account would necessitate an exhaustive analysis of often very sensitive archival materials, which are not yet—and may never be—available. Instead, we seek to be comprehensive in the sense of covering *all* of the crises, major and minor,[1] that have sundered ties between New Delhi and Islamabad since both countries became nascent nuclear weapon states.[2]

India and Pakistan have now weathered six crises in twenty years, all while engaging in a vigorous nuclear arms competition.[3] In 1984, the Indian government considered launching preventive air strikes to destroy Pakistan's evolving, but as yet disaggregated, nuclear capabilities. In turn, alarmed Pakistani leaders warned that they would respond to such an attack by ordering their own air strikes against India's nuclear facilities, and thereby spread lethal radioactive materials into populous areas. Ultimately, both countries restrained themselves, and they subsequently

reached an agreement not to attack each other's nuclear sites.[4] In 1986–
7, the two countries endured a month-long crisis emanating from India's
'Brasstacks' military exercises, the largest in South Asia's history. Then,
in 1990, India and Pakistan engaged in an intense crisis over the emerging
Kashmir insurgency. Despite large military build-ups, heightened alert
levels, ongoing nuclearization, and mutually fearful perceptions, these
crises, too, were resolved peacefully.[5]

In May 1998, New Delhi and Islamabad each conducted a series of
nuclear explosive tests, creating a spiral of alarm that raised mutual fears
of pre-emptive nuclear strikes and put the two sides' military forces on
high alert.[6] Again, however, military hostilities were avoided. In 1998–
9, Pakistan infiltrated soldiers into the remote Kargil region of Indian
Kashmir, a surprise initiative that sparked a robust Indian military
response—but one carefully limited to the Indian side of the disputed
territory.[7] In late 2001 and 2002, New Delhi responded to an audacious
Pakistani-supported terrorist attack on the Indian parliament by fully
mobilizing its military forces on the international border and the Line
of Control (LoC) in Kashmir.[8] After Islamabad responded in kind, an
estimated one million Indian and Pakistani troops were poised on high
alert along the entire Indo-Pakistani frontier. Armoured formations stood
ready to launch offensive strikes deep into the opponent's territory, and
short-range ballistic missiles were moved to border areas.[9] By the time it
was defused in autumn 2002, this latest crisis had generated the largest
South Asian military build-up since the 1971 Indo-Pakistani war.[10]

All but one of these six crises were resolved peacefully, and the 1999
Kargil war was purposefully contained within the disputed territory of
Kashmir. This book attempts to answer one central question: what
accounts for the fact that India and Pakistan have avoided a major war
over the past two decades, despite profound mistrust, chronic everyday
tensions, an intractable political conflict over Kashmir, a prior history
of three Indo-Pakistani wars, and the gradual but steady refinement of
both sides' nuclear weapon capabilities—all of which in combination
suggest to many analysts that South Asia is ripe for war, even nuclear
war?[11] While we believe that previous studies of one or a few of these
crises have been extremely valuable in creating new knowledge, we feel
equally strongly that stepping back and surveying the broader landscape

of *every* Indo-Pakistani crisis under the 'shadow of mutual destruction'[12] can expose patterns of behaviour that might otherwise be missed.

Theoretical Perspective and Levels of Analysis

We write from a theoretical perspective most aptly characterized as 'mere realism'.[13] Over the past twenty-five years, the realist international relations paradigm has been dissected into an increasingly complex array of competing 'realisms', each with its own particular 'take' on international political dynamics. While some of these theoretical refinements are useful and generate productive new insights, it increasingly seems that we may be missing the forest for the trees. Although neither author of this book considers himself to be a dyed-in-the-wool realist of any particular denomination, we do find that in the analysis of India-Pakistan relations over a relatively long period of time, 'mere realist' assumptions tend to be more useful than those of any other paradigm in international relations theory.[14] For the purposes of this book, then, these are the core assumptions:

- The state is the main actor in international politics, 'in that the nature of the state and the pattern of relations among states are the most important determinants of the character of international relations at any given moment.'[15]
- The international system is anarchical: 'the state is the repository of political power and...there is no authority above the state capable of imposing moral behaviour on it.' In pursuing their ends, states, therefore, have a 'right of self-help'.[16]
- Power is the most important variable in relations between states. 'International politics, like all politics, is a struggle for power.' States do not necessarily maximize their power, but they are always conscious of their relative power position.[17]
- States interacting under anarchy tend to balance power against other states. The term 'balance of power' refers to the existing distribution of capabilities across the system, be it multipolar, bipolar, or unipolar.[18]

- Moral standards—laws, rules, and norms—influence international politics,[19] but the moral code at any given time depends on the existing balance of power; great powers make the rules.[20] When forced to choose between power and norms, states tend to choose power.[21]

In addition to laying their philosophical cards on the table, international relations scholars should also be attentive to the 'level-of-analysis' problem. This refers to the challenge of identifying, distinguishing between, and assigning relative weight to causal factors originating from human nature, domestic political systems, the international system itself, or any other level of analysis that seems advisable.[22] In this study, we focus mainly on Kenneth Waltz's third and second images: the international system and the Indian and Pakistani domestic political systems.[23]

During the period under analysis, the early 1980s to the early 2000s, the international system underwent a transformation from bipolarity to unipolarity.[24] This shift is often portrayed as having been sudden, with most scholars dating the change to November 1989, when the Berlin Wall was torn down, or to December 1991, when the Soviet Union went out of business. Instead, we prefer to view the past two decades as a period of time during which the international system was gradually but inexorably *unipolarizing*.[25] In retrospect, the relative power of the Soviet Union was demonstrably declining, at least since the death of Leonid Brezhnev in 1982. Brezhnev was succeeded by two tired, old-guard Communists who exemplified the exhaustion of the Soviet system. From today's vantage point, the ill-fated Soviet occupation of Afghanistan (1979–89) seems like the last gasp of a decrepit empire. By the time Mikhail Gorbachev arrived on the scene in 1985, Afghanistan was acknowledged to be Moscow's 'bleeding wound'; and, while Gorbachev's reforms were ultimately intended to strengthen the Soviet Union, their initial impact was to hasten the country's relative decline. Meanwhile, the 1980s saw the United States (US) reasserting itself internationally following the post-Vietnam malaise of the Ford and Carter presidencies. As the Soviets began to retrench from their European and Asian zones of influence in the second half of the decade, the US pressed its advantage under the second Reagan and George H.W. Bush administrations. By the time Bill Clinton was elected president in 1992, the world had become unipolar,[26] but the transformation from bipolarity was not as sudden as it is often depicted.

From the perspectives of the governments in New Delhi and Islamabad, the period under examination in this book was one in which the unfolding process of *unipolarization* seemed even more pronounced. For much of the Cold War, India and Pakistan could leverage US–Soviet acrimony into military, economic, and diplomatic support from Moscow and Washington; until the 1980s, global bipolarity was reflected microcosmically in South Asia. However, as unipolarization gained momentum, Washington increasingly took on the role of a 'security facilitator' in the region. Thus, while the Soviet Union was a significant regional player in the Indo-Pakistani wars of 1965 (brokering the 1966 Tashkent peace agreement) and 1971 (signing a mutual security treaty with India), Moscow's influence began to wane by the early 1980s. Although New Delhi chose not to condemn the Soviet occupation of Afghanistan in official terms, Indian Prime Minister Indira Gandhi and her closest advisers were known privately to be disconcerted by Moscow's aggression in the region. India's distancing from a declining Soviet Union continued after Mrs Gandhi's death in 1984. Her son and successor, Rajiv Gandhi, realized that speeding up India's economic development would require substantial infusions of technological assistance, an area in which it was increasingly apparent that the US was outpacing the Soviet Union. The net result of global unipolarization from the early 1980s onwards was that the US came to play an increasingly influential and uncontested role in Indo-Pakistani relations during the crises we analyse in the empirical chapters of this book. Indeed, by the 1990s, the triangular relationship between Washington, Islamabad, and New Delhi constituted the core architecture of South Asian international security affairs.

We also focus on the Indian and Pakistani domestic political systems during the relevant crises. The lens through which we view second-image dynamics is the concept of grand strategy. If military strategy is the 'art of distributing and applying military means to fulfil the ends of policy',[27] then grand strategy is the art of using *all* of a state's means—military, diplomatic, covert, economic, etc.—for this purpose. 'Military strategy is mainly the province of generals. Grand strategy is mainly the purview of statesmen.'[28] Or, as one scholar puts it, grand strategy is the 'state's theory about how it can best "cause" security for itself'.[29] In so theorizing, the state tries to reconcile its capabilities with its vital interests through the 'full package of domestic and international policies designed to increase national power and security.'[30] Because the grand strategic imperative arises directly out of the condition of anarchy in international politics, it links the second and third images:

The history, geography, and culture of each country on our planet are unique—just as each war is different, and each battle particular unto itself—but there are always some unifying elements, deriving from our common humanity. One of them is the demand placed upon the *polities* of this world, whether ancient empires or modern democracies, to devise ways of enabling them [*sic*] to survive and flourish in an anarchic and often threatening international order that oscillates between peace and war, and is always changing.[31]

Another analyst elaborates on the connection between anarchy and grand strategy—and, implicitly, the second and third images: 'So long as technology, geography, and economy make it possible for states to aggress against one another, and so long as there is no international authority to protect those satisfied with the status quo and to punish those who violate it, states will be strongly encouraged to take steps to protect themselves from one another. These steps are all part of a state's grand strategy.'[32]

Grand strategy is as much a peacetime as a wartime preoccupation, which makes it an ideal conceptual lens through which to study crises. Two scholars call grand strategy the 'modern equivalent of what was, in the seventeenth and eighteenth centuries, called *ragione di stato* or *raison d'état*. It is the rational determination of a nation's vital interests, the things that are essential to its security, its fundamental purposes in its relations with other nations, and its priorities with respect to goals.'[33] Grand strategy is the highest level of strategy, 'where all that is military happens within the much broader context of domestic governance, international politics, economic activity, and their ancillaries.'[34] Grand strategy is, therefore, 'not merely a concept of wartime', but 'an inherent element of statecraft at all times'. Indeed, a well-conceived grand strategy would so integrate the 'policies and armaments of that nation that the resort to war is either rendered unnecessary or is undertaken with the maximum chance of victory'.[35] Ideally, the state's grand strategy is so successful that it 'alleviates any need for violence'.[36]

Thus far, we have used the term 'grand strategy' only in its instrumental sense—that is, as the purposeful product of decisionmakers trying to devise a 'coherent architecture for the conduct of statecraft'.[37] However, whereas some states' grand strategies are the result of conscious design, others' can only be inferred from the totality of their diplomatic, military, economic, covert, and other policies. As one strategist notes, 'very few of the states that participate in international politics have a thought-out grand strategy of their own.'[38] In this case, scholars 'may be guided by the conceptualization in [their] attempt to ferret out the grand strategy of a state'.[39] To say that a country 'has no grand strategy' is a *non sequitur*. In both its instrumental and inferred senses, grand strategy's essence is its long-term nature and its imperviousness to the everyday events of international politics and even changes in government. Grand strategies are modified—consciously or otherwise—only in response to fundamental transformations in the context of international politics, like the world wars and the unipolarization process of the 1980s and 1990s.

Propositions

Our analysis of Indo-Pakistani crises is guided by three propositions, each of which is derived from a more general body of international relations theory: unipolarity theory, nuclear deterrence theory, and conventional deterrence theory. We chose these theoretical perspectives because they seemed potentially to offer the most fruitful explanations of our central puzzle: why have the six India–Pakistan crises in the last two decades been resolved short of major war?[40]

1. *Unipolarity theory* is the least-developed body of theory we use, both because the condition of global unipolarity is so new, and because the main proponents of polarity theory in general—neorealists—have been loath even to accept unipolarity as a theoretical possibility of any significance.[41] Like all structural theory, unipolarity theory maintains that relations between states are significantly shaped by the distribution of capabilities between the great powers. For theorists writing in this

vein, 'a principal foreign policy challenge' for states in today's post-bipolar era 'is to adjust their strategies to the emergence and possible endurance of a unipolar distribution of power'.[42] However, as with multipolarity and bipolarity, there is no realist consensus on the exact influence of unipolarity on state behaviour. The mere realist perspective outlined earlier suggests that analysis rooted exclusively in the third image—the structure of the international system—is not sufficient to yield definitive predictions about unipolarity's effects; second-image characteristics, such as the nature of the 'sole pole's'[43] political system, are also crucial.[44] Theorists tend to agree that the US today is a relatively benevolent sole pole.[45] In such a case, the global order is 'organized around asymmetrical power relations, but the most overtly malign character of domination is muted.'[46] Indeed, empirical findings in the unipolarity research programme indicate that Washington's influence on weaker states is, in the main, beneficial: 'Some authors argue that there is a demand for American power.' US security commitments 'help overcome regional security dilemmas in Europe, Asia, and the Middle East', and the US economy 'provides an essential market for exports. The security and economic costs and benefits of the current unipolar order must be compared with the costs and benefits of whatever order might emerge from a return to a [bipolar or multipolar] balance of power.'[47] In this view, then, the international system's relatively benign sole pole—the US—has become the new global security facilitator. This observation generates our first proposition:

The Indian and Pakistani governments, despite compelling incentives to attack one another during the crises under examination, were dissuaded from doing so by timely and forceful US intervention.

2. *Nuclear deterrence theory* is a voluminous body of work from which we derive our second proposition.[48] The foundational insight of nuclear deterrence theory is that states possessing nuclear weapons avoid direct military conflict with one another for fear of escalation to the use of nuclear weapons—and of the mass death, suffering, and destruction nuclear use would cause.[49] While unipolarity theory arose from the Cold War's end, nuclear deterrence theory grew out of the creation of nuclear weapons during World War II, and the subsequent arms race between the US and the Soviet Union. Scholars have typically argued that effective

nuclear deterrence rests on three foundations: reliable nuclear capabilities, the resolve to use them if necessary, and the credibility of nuclear threats that results from combining capabilities and resolve. As the US and the Soviet Union moved towards a very rough nuclear parity in the 1960s, theorists began to examine the requirements of credibility more closely. Their work gave rise to what would eventually become nuclear-deterrent orthodoxy: the need for nuclear weapon states to develop secure second-strike capabilities, that is, weapons that could withstand an incoming first strike, and be launched against the enemy in retaliation. Classical nuclear deterrence theory was subsequently refined by McGeorge Bundy, US President John F. Kennedy's national security advisor and a participant in the Cuban Missile Crisis of 1962. Coining the term 'existential deterrence', Bundy maintained that nuclear weapons deter war not because those who possess them make complex calculations about the adversary's capabilities, resolve, and credibility, but simply because the weapons *exist* on both sides and might be used in a war whether national leaders intend to use them or not.[50] From nuclear deterrence theory, we derive our second proposition:

The Indian and Pakistani governments, despite compelling incentives to attack one another during the crises under examination, were dissuaded from doing so by the fear that war might escalate to the nuclear level.

3. *Conventional deterrence theory*,[51] in particular John Mearsheimer's seminal work,[52] provides the theoretical context for our third proposition. Mearsheimer distinguishes between two conventional military strategies: the attrition strategy, in which 'the attacker is primarily concerned with overwhelming a stubborn defense in a series of bloody set-piece battles', and the blitzkrieg strategy, which uses armour to drive deep into enemy territory without bogging down in major engagements. According to Mearsheimer's theory, 'if a potential attacker believes that he can launch a successful blitzkrieg, deterrence is very likely to fail.' On the other hand, 'if a potential attacker believes that he can secure a decisive victory only by means of an attrition strategy, deterrence is very likely to obtain.'[53] From Mearsheimer's conventional deterrence theory, we deduce our third proposition:

The Indian and Pakistani governments, despite compelling incentives to attack one another during the crises under examination, were dissuaded from doing so by their lack of sufficient conventional military superiority to pursue a successful blitzkrieg strategy.

Why This Book?

India and Pakistan remain embroiled in one of the world's most intractable political disputes. While the characterization of South Asia as the most 'dangerous place in the world' is exaggerated, Indo-Pakistani relations do rank with Israeli-Palestinian affairs, China–Taiwan issues, and the North Korean–South Korean conflict as global problems of first-order significance. As with these other three disputes, there seems to be no ready solution to the India–Pakistan quarrel that would meet the legitimate demands of all concerned parties in a just and security-generating way. In addition, nuclear weapons loom larger in the Indo-Pakistani conflict than they do in West Asia, the Taiwan Strait, or the Korean peninsula. While the other areas are characterized by nuclear asymmetry—with only one party to the dispute possessing nuclear weapons—South Asia has evolved into a region marked by a very rough symmetry of nuclear capabilities between the main actors.[54]

New Delhi and Islamabad have engaged in a fitful but sustained nuclear weapons competition since 1972. India tested its first nuclear device in 1974 and since then, has indigenously refined its weapon and delivery capabilities. Pakistan embarked on a clandestine nuclear development programme in the 1970s, and has successfully imported technologies that have allowed it to achieve a degree of nuclear parity with India.[55] South Asia's nuclear competition came to a head in May 1998, when India and Pakistan conducted underground nuclear explosive tests and announced their arrival as overt nuclear weapon states. Today, both New Delhi and Islamabad are believed to possess relatively small numbers of nuclear weapons deliverable against the other by aircraft and ballistic missiles. It is in this context that the stakes of the Indo-Pakistani political dispute are perhaps higher than anywhere else in the world.[56]

To date, we have several valuable accounts of various aspects of the contemporary India–Pakistan security competition, including the evolution of the Indian nuclear weapons programme,[57] contemporary

Indian nuclear doctrine,[58] the Kashmir dispute,[59] the four Indo-Pakistani wars,[60] and Indo-Pakistani nuclear dynamics during the 1986–7 and 1990 crises.[61] However, there has been no comprehensive study of Indian and Pakistani crisis behaviour during South Asia's nuclear era. This book will also be the first to take systematic account of the US role in South Asia's security dynamics over the last two decades, in a context of unipolarization. In some cases, the US has helped to lower tensions by providing information in a timely fashion to both parties. On other occasions, the US has been inordinately hasty in sounding the tocsin about the prospects of war. Careful analysis of South Asia's nuclear-shadowed crises can help to ensure that future US policies are more consistently effective.

Main Arguments and Organization

Our main overall conclusion is that the nuclear-deterrence proposition provides the strongest explanation for the absence of major war in the region over the last two decades, especially in the four crises beginning with that of 1990. US intervention in the form of crisis management sometimes played a secondary, but important, role—particularly in 1990, 1999, and 2001–2. Washington was most influential during the Kargil war of 1999, when the Clinton administration resolutely eased Pakistani leaders into ceasing their ill-fated incursion into Indian Kashmir. At other times, US policies were neither timely nor forceful; indeed, they were occasionally counterproductive, as was the case in 1984. This conclusion has significant policy ramifications that we will discuss in the concluding chapter. The weakest of our three propositions turned out to be the one concerning conventional deterrence, not because the theory underlying it is flawed, but because India nearly always had sufficient conventional military capabilities to inflict a devastating blitzkrieg against Pakistan, except in 1986–7, and consistently chose a different course of action. This strongly suggests that the nuclear-deterrence factor generally trumped conventional deterrence as a source of crisis resolution.

The rest of the book is organized in the following way. Chapter Two is a brief history of Indo-Pakistani behaviour during the three wars in

South Asia's pre-nuclear history. It is meant as a 'baseline' for comparatively examining Indian and Pakistani decisionmaking during the nuclear era under consideration here. Chapters Three through Eight are detailed case studies of the India–Pakistan crises of 1984, 1986–7, 1990, 1998, 1999, and 2001–2. Chapter Nine concludes the book by summarizing our findings, elaborating on our main arguments, examining South Asia's nuclear dynamics today, and making recommendations for US policy. Our primary conclusion in this regard is that, although the United States has a severely limited degree of influence on Indian and Pakistani decisionmaking concerning nuclear weapons, Washington can do a much better job of addressing the underlying political conflicts between New Delhi and Islamabad, particularly over Kashmir. In the book's final section, we outline a concrete, step-by-step blueprint for exercising American influence towards a more positive and productive Indo-Pakistani relationship.

Notes

[1] Glenn Snyder and Paul Diesing define a crisis as a 'sequence of interactions between the governments of two or more sovereign states in severe conflict, short of actual war, but involving the perception of a dangerously high probability of war.' The crisis is an 'intermediate zone between peace and war', a 'sort of hybrid condition, neither peace nor war, but containing elements of both and comprising the potential for transformation from peace to war.' See their *Conflict among Nations: Bargaining, Decision Making, and System Structure in International Crises* (Princeton: Princeton University Press, 1977), pp. 6, 10.

[2] Previous studies have analysed one or more of these crises, but none has covered them all. These works include: Sumit Ganguly, *Conflict Unending: India–Pakistan Tensions since 1947* (New York: Columbia University Press, and Washington, DC: Woodrow Wilson Center Press, 2001); Devin T. Hagerty, *The Consequences of Nuclear Proliferation: Lessons from South Asia* (Cambridge: MIT Press, 1998); Kanti P. Bajpai, P.R. Chari, Stephen P. Cohen, Pervaiz Iqbal Cheema, and Sumit Ganguly, *Brasstacks and Beyond: Perception and Management of Crisis in South Asia* (New Delhi: Manohar, 1995); and P.R. Chari, Pervaiz Iqbal Cheema, and Stephen P. Cohen, *Perception, Politics and Security in South Asia: The Compound Crisis of 1990* (London: RoutledgeCurzon, 2003).

[3] Most of the literature on nuclear proliferation considers the transition to nuclear weapons to be especially dangerous. See Hagerty, *Consequences of Nuclear Proliferation*, pp. 9–37.

[4] George Perkovich, *India's Nuclear Bomb: The Impact on Global Proliferation* (Berkeley: University of California Press, 1999), pp. 276–7.

[5] Ganguly, *Conflict Unending*, pp. 79–100; Hagerty, *Consequences of Nuclear Proliferation*, pp. 91–170.

[6] Sumit Ganguly, 'India's Pathway to Pokhran II: The Origins and Sources of India's Nuclear Weapons Program', *International Security*, vol. 23, no. 4 (Spring 1999), pp. 148–77; Devin T. Hagerty, 'South Asia's Big Bangs: Causes, Consequences, and Prospects', *Australian Journal of International Affairs*, vol. 53, no. 1 (April 1999), pp. 19–29.

[7] Ganguly, *Conflict Unending*, pp. 114–33. The Kargil war was only the second instance of direct military conflict between two nuclear weapon states, the other being the Soviet-Chinese border fighting in 1969. On the latter, see Lyle J. Goldstein, 'Do Nascent WMD Arsenals Deter? The Sino-Soviet Crisis of 1969', *Political Science Quarterly*, vol. 118, no. 1 (Spring 2003), pp. 53–79.

[8] The LoC, created by the Simla Agreement of July 1972, divides Indian- and Pakistani-held Kashmir. For the agreement's text, see Ganguly, *Conflict Unending*, pp. 168–9.

[9] A senior US intelligence analyst with years of regional experience told one of the authors in early June 2002 that he estimated the chances of war on the Subcontinent at '100 per cent'.

[10] Devin T. Hagerty, 'US Policy and the Kashmir Dispute: Prospects for Resolution', *India Review*, vol. 2, no. 3 (July 2003), pp. 83–110.

[11] On the eve of his 2000 visit to India and Pakistan, US President Bill Clinton famously termed the subcontinent 'the most dangerous place in the world today'. Jane Perlez, 'US and India, Trying to Reconcile, Hit Bump', the *New York Times*, 22 March 2000. In 1996, *The Economist* called South Asia 'the likeliest place for a[n atomic] bomb to be detonated in anger.' See 'A Test Ban for All', *The Economist* (editorial), 6 July 1996, pp. 20–2. In 1993, US director of central intelligence James Woolsey testified before Congress that 'the arms race between India and Pakistan poses perhaps the most probable prospect for future use of weapons of mass destruction, including nuclear weapons.' House Committee on Foreign Affairs, Subcommittee on International Security, International Organizations and Human Rights, *US Security Policy vis-à-vis Rogue Regimes*, 103rd Cong., 1st Sess., 28 July 1993. A 1989 *Washington Post* editorial called South Asia 'the likeliest place in the world for a nuclear war'. See 'The Next Nuclear War', *Washington Post*, 13 October 1989.

[12] This term is taken from Robert Jervis, *The Meaning of the Nuclear Revolution: Statecraft and the Prospect of Armageddon* (Ithaca: Cornell University Press, 1989), p. 79.

[13] This notion is borrowed from C.S. Lewis, whose book *Mere Christianity* (New York: Collier, 1952) outlined 'an agreed, or common, or central, or "mere" Christianity', (p. viii) as opposed to a schismatic faith with many different denominations.

[14] For example, three prominent bodies of the 'liberal' international relations paradigm—economic interdependence theory, democratic peace theory, and neoliberal institutionalist theory—would seem to offer little intellectual purchase in the analysis of Indo-Pakistani relations. New Delhi and Islamabad have minimal economic linkages, Pakistan has never been a liberal democracy, and international institutions have hardly influenced Indo-Pakistani relations. On liberal international relations theory, see Michael W. Doyle, *Ways of War and Peace: Realism, Liberalism, and Socialism* (New York: Norton, 1997), pp. 205–300. Constructivist theories might be useful in explaining the sources of *enmity* between India and Pakistan, but they would seem to have difficulty explaining why India and Pakistan have avoided major war during South Asia's nuclear era.

[15] Robert Gilpin, *War and Change in World Politics* (Cambridge: Cambridge University Press, 1981), p. 18. See also Kenneth N. Waltz, *Theory of International Politics* (New York: Random House, 1979), p. 94.

[16] Edward Hallett Carr, *The Twenty Years' Crisis, 1919–1939: An Introduction to the Study of International Relations*, 2nd edition (New York: Harper and Row, 1964 [1946]), pp. 160–1. Also see Kenneth N. Waltz, *Man, the State and War: A Theoretical Analysis* (New York: Columbia University Press, 1959), pp. 160, 238.

[17] The quotation is from Hans Morgenthau, *Politics among Nations: The Struggle for Power and Peace*, 4th edition (New York: Knopf, 1967), p. 25. Also see Gilpin, *War and Change*, p. 214; Carr, *Twenty Years' Crisis*, p. 102. On states not maximizing their power, see Arnold Wolfers, *Discord and Collaboration: Essays on International Politics* (Baltimore: Johns Hopkins University Press, 1962), p. 72; Waltz, *Man, the State and War*, p. 206; Gilpin, *War and Change*, pp. 19–20, 51, 92.

[18] Waltz, *Man, the State and War*, p. 205; Waltz, *Theory of International Politics*, p. 118; Morgenthau, *Politics among Nations*, p. 161; Gilpin, *War and Change*, p. 86. Waltz writes, 'A balance of power may exist because some countries consciously make it the end of their policies, or it may exist because of the quasi-automatic reactions of some states to the drive for the ascendancy of other states.' *Man, the State and War*, p. 208.

[19] Morgenthau, *Politics among Nations*, pp. 16, 22, 211–5; Carr, *Twenty Years' Crisis*, pp. 146–69.

[20] Gilpin, *War and Change*, pp. 28–9, 34–5; Morgenthau, *Politics among Nations*, p. 3.

[21] Wolfers, *Discord and Collaboration*, p. 16; Carr, *Twenty Years' Crisis*, p. 59.

[22] Waltz's *Man, the State and War* is the now-classic statement of the three-image conception of international relations. Waltz identified the anarchy of the international system itself as the permissive cause of war and located the immediate causes of particular wars in the nature of states and in human nature. Other organizing frameworks identify more or fewer levels of analysis. Notable among these is J. David Singer's two-image conception, which emphasizes causal factors operating at the international and domestic levels. See his 'The Level-of-Analysis Problem in International Relations', in Klaus Knorr and Sidney Verba (eds), *The International System: Theoretical Essays* (Princeton: Princeton University Press, 1961), pp. 77–92. As Singer argues, 'the problem is not really one of deciding which level is most valuable to the discipline as a whole and then demanding that it be adhered to from now unto eternity. Rather, it is one of realizing that there *is* this preliminary conceptual issue and that it must be temporarily resolved prior to any given research undertaking' (p. 90).

[23] On the importance of judiciously combining second- and third-image analysis, see Waltz, *Man, the State and War*, pp. 231–2, 238. As Waltz writes on p. 238, the third image is a 'theory of the conditioning effects of the state system itself.' But we 'still have to look to motivation and circumstance in order to explain individual acts.'

[24] Bipolarity refers to a system in which two roughly power-equivalent states enjoy greater capabilities than every other country; unipolarity is a configuration in which one major power towers above the rest. For examinations of the implications of global unipolarity, see Ethan B. Kapstein and Michael Mastanduno (eds), *Unipolar Politics: Realism and State Strategies After the Cold War* (New York: Columbia University Press, 1999); and G. John Ikenberry (ed.), *America Unrivaled: The Future of the Balance of Power* (Ithaca: Cornell University Press, 2002).

[25] Neorealism, with its faith in the automaticity of balancing behaviour, has a hard time with the notion of open-ended unipolarization. This has led to a degree of ambiguity in neorealist interpretations of bipolarity's demise. In 1991, Kenneth Waltz—neorealism's founding father—indicated that bipolarity had passed: 'So long as the world *was* bipolar, the United States and the Soviet Union held each other in check. With the crumbling of the Soviet Union, no country or set of countries can presently restore a balance.' Kenneth N. Waltz,

'America as a Model for the World? A Foreign Policy Perspective', *PS: Political Science and Politics*, vol. 24, no. 4 (December 1991), p. 669. (Emphasis added.) In 1993, however, Waltz back-pedalled, claiming that 'bipolarity endures, but in an altered state'. Kenneth N. Waltz, 'The Emerging Structure of International Politics', *International Security*, vol. 18, no. 2 (Fall 1993), p. 52. Then, in 1997, Waltz wrote: 'Multipolarity is developing before our eyes: To all but the myopic, it can already be seen on the horizon. Moreover, it is emerging in accordance with the balancing imperative.' Kenneth N. Waltz, 'Evaluating Theories', *American Political Science Review*, vol. 91, no. 4 (December 1997), p. 915. More recently, Waltz has written that 'on the demise of the Soviet Union, the international political system became unipolar.' Kenneth N. Waltz, 'Structural Realism after the Cold War', in Ikenberry, *America Unrivaled*, p. 52. Tellingly, while the terms 'polarity', 'bipolarity', 'multipolarity', and 'tripolarity' appear in the index to *Theory of International Politics*, 'unipolarity' does not. In contrast to neorealism, in which two 'is the smallest number in a self-help system', (*Theory of International Politics*, p. 136), mere realism is agnostic as to the sustainability of unipolarity, which it views as being contingent on developments at every level of analysis in international politics.

²⁶ For the purposes of our analysis, it is necessary to distinguish between the concepts of unipolarity and hegemony. As used herein, unipolarity refers simply to a given distribution of power in the international system. It is neutral as to the intentions of the system's sole great power. Hegemony has numerous meanings in the literature, some of which are value-loaded. Because of that, we avoid using the term. John Mearsheimer's definition illustrates the importance of the great power's intentions in the concept of hegemony: 'Under a hegemony there is only one major power in the system. The rest are minor powers that cannot challenge the major power, *but must act in accordance with the dictates of the major power.*' 'Back to the Future: Instability in Europe After the Cold War', *International Security*, vol. 15, no. 1 (Summer 1990), p. 13. (Emphasis added.) Readers should not infer from our use of the term 'unipolarity' that we believe the United States can simply impose its will on secondary states. All hegemons are unipolar great powers, but not all unipolar great powers are hegemons.

²⁷ B.H. Liddell Hart, *Strategy*, 2nd revised edition (New York: Praeger, 1967), p. 335.

²⁸ John M. Collins, *Grand Strategy: Principles and Practice* (Annapolis: Naval Institute Press, 1973), p. 15.

²⁹ Barry R. Posen, *The Sources of Military Doctrine: France, Britain, and Germany Between the World Wars* (Ithaca, New York: Cornell University Press, 1984), p. 13.

[30] Thomas J. Christensen, *Useful Adversaries: Grand Strategy, Domestic Mobilization, and Sino-American Conflict, 1947–1958* (Princeton: Princeton University Press, 1996), p. 7.

[31] Paul Kennedy, 'Grand Strategy in War and Peace: Toward a Broader Definition', in Paul Kennedy (ed.), *Grand Strategies in War and Peace* (New Haven: Yale University Press, 1991), p. 6.

[32] Posen, *Sources of Military Doctrine*, p. 16. Also see Richard Rosecrance and Arthur A. Stein, 'Beyond Realism: The Study of Grand Strategy', in Richard Rosecrance and Arthur A. Stein (eds), *The Domestic Bases of Grand Strategy* (Ithaca: Cornell University Press, 1993), p. 20.

[33] Gordon A. Craig and Felix Gilbert, 'Reflections on Strategy in the Present and Future', in Peter Paret (ed.), *Makers of Modern Strategy: from Machiavelli to the Nuclear Age* (Princeton: Princeton University Press, 1986), p. 869.

[34] Edward N. Luttwak, *Strategy: The Logic of War and Peace* (Cambridge: Harvard University Press, 1987), p. 70.

[35] Edward Mead Earle, 'Introduction', in Edward Mead Earle (ed.), *Makers of Modern Strategy: Military Thought from Machiavelli to Hitler* (Princeton: Princeton University Press, 1943), p. 8.

[36] Collins, *Grand Strategy*, p. 15.

[37] Gregory D. Foster, 'A Conceptual Foundation for the Development of Strategy', in James C. Gaston (ed.), *Grand Strategy and the Decisionmaking Process* (Washington, DC: National Defense University Press, 1992), p. 60.

[38] Luttwak, *Strategy*, p. 178; also see Bernard Brodie, *War and Politics* (New York: Macmillan, 1973), pp. 358–65.

[39] Posen, *Sources of Military Doctrine*, p. 13.

[40] We rejected other theoretical perspectives because they seemed not to offer compelling explanations of Indian and Pakistani restraint during crises. These include liberalism and constructivism, for the reasons described in note 14. And, while we appreciate the insights of several other bodies of theory, including bureaucratic politics models, learning theory, and organization theory, we judged them to be incapable of explaining the broad pattern of India–Pakistan peace over the previous two decades.

[41] Again, because of their belief in the automaticity of balancing behaviour in international political life, neorealists expect unipolarity to be fleeting. See note 25.

[42] Michael Mastanduno and Ethan B. Kapstein, 'Realism and State Strategies After the Cold War', in their *Unipolar Politics*, p. 5. For an impressive graphical depiction of US global dominance, see William C. Wohlforth, 'US Strategy in a Unipolar World', in Ikenberry, *America Unrivaled*, p. 105.

[43] The term is William C. Wohlforth's: 'The Stability of a Unipolar World', *International Security*, vol. 24, no. 1 (Summer 1999), p. 40.

[44] The early conclusion of many scholars is that unipolarity is thus far shaping state behaviour 'in ways not anticipated by Waltz's balance-of-power theory. Instead of responding by balancing, states are adjusting in various ways to the reality of a US-centered international system.' Mastanduno and Kapstein, 'Realism and State Strategies', p. 15. William Wohlforth puts this more bluntly: 'The absence of balancing among the great powers is a fact.' See his 'US Strategy in a Unipolar World', p. 98. Mere realism generates an interesting question: Would states be acting in the same way—bandwagoning—if the Soviet Union, a less benign 'sole pole', had won the Cold War?

[45] See the numerous chapters in Kapstein and Mastanduno, *Unipolar Politics*, and Ikenberry, *America Unrivaled*.

[46] G. John Ikenberry, 'Introduction', in Ikenberry, *America Unrivaled*, p. 9.

[47] Ibid., p. 5. For an application of this argument to Asia, see Michael Mastanduno, 'Incomplete Hegemony and Security Order in the Asia-Pacific', in Ikenberry, *America Unrivaled*, pp. 181–210.

[48] Classics of the field include Bernard Brodie (ed.), *The Absolute Weapon: Atomic Power and World Order* (New York: Harcourt, Brace, 1946); Bernard Brodie, *Strategy in the Missile Age* (Princeton: Princeton University Press, 1959); Thomas C. Schelling, *The Strategy of Conflict* (New York: Oxford University Press, 1965); Thomas C. Schelling, *Arms and Influence* (New Haven: Yale University Press, 1966); Robert Jervis, *The Meaning of the Nuclear Revolution: Statecraft and the Prospect of Armageddon* (Ithaca: Cornell University Press, 1989); and Kenneth N. Waltz, 'Nuclear Myths and Political Realities', *American Political Science Review*, vol. 84, no. 3 (September 1990), pp. 731–45.

[49] This does not imply, of course, that deterrence of war is the *only* conceivable consequence of nuclear weapons. Analysts have long recognized that nuclear weapons can also create a protective umbrella under which states could pursue their political conflicts at levels of violence below the conventional and nuclear thresholds. See Glenn Snyder, 'The Balance of Power and the Balance of Terror', in Paul Seabury (ed.), *The Balance of Power* (San Francisco: Chandler, 1965), pp. 184–201. This 'stability-instability' paradox has been relevant in South Asia's nuclear era, as will be discussed in Chapter Seven.

[50] Bundy memorably phrased the existential deterrent effect of nuclear weapons this way: 'It is one thing for military men to maintain our deterrent force with vigilant skill, and it is quite another for anyone to assume that their necessary contingency plans have any serious interest for political leaders. The object of political men—quite rightly—is that these weapons should never be

used. I have watched two Presidents working on strategic contingency plans, and what interested them most was simply to make sure that none of these awful events would occur.' McGeorge Bundy, 'To Cap the Volcano', *Foreign Affairs*, vol. 48, no. 1 (October 1969), p. 12. For more on existential nuclear deterrence, see McGeorge Bundy, 'The Bishops and the Bomb', *New York Review of Books*, 16 June 1983, p. 4; McGeorge Bundy, 'Existential Deterrence and Its Consequences', in Douglas MacLean (ed.), *The Security Gamble: Deterrence Dilemmas in the Nuclear Age* (Totowa, N.J.: Rowman and Allanheld, 1984), pp. 3–13; McGeorge Bundy, *Danger and Survival: Choices About the Bomb in the First Fifty Years* (New York: Random House, 1988), pp. 391–462.

[51] Classics include Glenn H. Snyder, *Deterrence and Defense: Toward a Theory of National Security* (Princeton: Princeton University Press, 1961); Alexander George and Richard Smoke, *Deterrence in American Foreign Policy: Theory and Practice* (New York: Columbia University Press, 1974); Patrick Morgan, *Deterrence: A Conceptual Analysis* (Beverly Hills: Sage Publications, 1977); and Robert Jervis, Richard Ned Lebow, and Janice Gross Stein, *Psychology and Deterrence* (Baltimore: Johns Hopkins University Press, 1985).

[52] John J. Mearsheimer, *Conventional Deterrence* (Ithaca, New York: Cornell University Press, 1983).

[53] Mearsheimer, *Conventional Deterrence*, pp. 34–6, 53, 63–4.

[54] All other things being equal, India would far outpace Pakistan in nuclear weapons and delivery capabilities. However, China has played the role of 'nuclear equalizer' in the South Asia region, having supplied Pakistan with—at a minimum—nuclear warhead design information and nuclear-capable ballistic missiles. For details, see Joseph Cirincione with Jon B. Wolfsthal and Miriam Rajkumar, *Deadly Arsenals: Tracking Weapons of Mass Destruction* (Washington, DC: Carnegie Endowment for International Peace, 2002), pp. 148–52.

[55] This is not to suggest that India and Pakistan are nuclear peers; New Delhi's existing and potential nuclear weapon capabilities are clearly superior in quantitative terms. Qualitatively, Pakistan's nuclear programme is probably more advanced than India's in some respects, particularly in the area of mating nuclear warheads with ballistic missiles. Pakistan's sophistication in this area is attributable to its proliferation links with China and North Korea. See Cirincione, *Deadly Arsenals*, pp. 213–4. In this context, 'parity' refers to both sides possessing sufficient capabilities to inflict enormous damage on the other, if the nuclear threshold were breached.

[56] This makes it all the more striking that general work on the state of international affairs—as opposed to studies done by South Asianists—still relegates the subcontinent to backwater status in the regional pecking order. For examples,

see Kapstein and Mastanduno, *Unipolar Politics*; and Ikenberry, *America Unrivaled*.

[57] Perkovich, *India's Nuclear Bomb*; Raj Chengappa, *Weapons of Peace: The Secret Story of India's Quest to Be a Nuclear Power* (New Delhi: Harper Collins, 2000).

[58] Ashley J. Tellis, *India's Emerging Nuclear Posture: Between Recessed Deterrence and Ready Arsenal* (Santa Monica, California: RAND Corporation, 2001).

[59] Sumit Ganguly, *The Crisis in Kashmir: Portents of War, Hopes of Peace* (Washington, DC: Woodrow Wilson Center Press, and Cambridge: Cambridge University Press, 1997); Victoria Schofield, *Kashmir in Conflict: India, Pakistan, and the Unending War* (London: I.B. Tauris, 2003); Robert G. Wirsing, *India, Pakistan, and the Kashmir Dispute: On Regional Conflict and Its Resolution* (New York: St. Martin's Press, 1994); Robert G. Wirsing, *Kashmir in the Shadow of War: Regional Rivalries in a Nuclear Age* (Armonk, New York: M.E. Sharpe, 2003).

[60] Ganguly, *Conflict Unending*.

[61] Hagerty, *Consequences of Nuclear Proliferation*.

2

Wars Without End?

Few regional conflicts across the globe are fraught with the level of complexity as the Indo-Pakistani conflict over the disputed territory of Jammu and Kashmir.[1] This conflict has contributed to, at least, four wars and numerous crises since the emergence of India and Pakistan as independent states in the wake of the collapse of the British Indian empire in 1947. Diplomatic efforts to resolve the conflict have involved extensive multilateral as well as bilateral negotiations, but none of these has made significant headway.[2] Nor has the repeated resort to force or the threat of the use of force brought the conflict any closer to resolution. The initially opaque and subsequently transparent acquisition of nuclear weapons by India and Pakistan has further complicated the dynamics of conflict in the region.

This chapter will briefly summarize the origins of the conflict, provide succinct overviews of all four wars, and develop and discuss some general propositions about the experiences of war in the region. It will conclude with an analysis of the social, political, and military-technological changes that are currently underway in the region and are likely to influence the future course of Indo-Pakistani conflict. An assessment of the prior context of conflict between India and Pakistan will provide the necessary basis for understanding and analysing the series of crises that are examined later in this book.

An Unresolved War

The origins of the Indo-Pakistani conflict over the disputed territory of Jammu and Kashmir are complex, rooted in the process of British colonial

withdrawal from the subcontinent. In the late 1940s when the two
competing nationalist movements for India and Pakistan failed to reach
accommodation, Britain decided to partition its Indian empire.[3] As
partition approached, Viceroy Lord Mountbatten, the last representative
of the British Crown in India, had to confront a critical issue: the
principles along which the empire would be divided. His solution to
this: to accommodate the demand for the creation of Pakistan, as a
homeland for the Muslims of the subcontinent, predominantly Muslim
areas of British India which were geographically contiguous would
become Pakistan. Thus the new state of Pakistan was formed with two
flanks, eastern and western, separated by 1500 miles of the new states of
India. However, in addition to enunciating the principle that would
lead to the division of British India, he also had to confront the problem
of the 'princely states'. These states had accepted the tutelage of the British
Crown under the terms of the doctrine of 'paramountcy' under which
they acknowledged the Crown as the 'paramount' authority in the
subcontinent. In practical terms, this meant that they were nominally
independent as long as they had accepted the prerogatives of the Crown
to determine their policies in the areas of defence, foreign affairs, and
communications.[4] With the advent of independence, Mountbatten
decreed that these states would have two choices: they could join either
India or Pakistan. The option of independence was ruled out on the
grounds that such a policy would contribute to the balkanization of the
subcontinent.[5]

The state of Kashmir posed a distinct problem.[6] It had a
predominantly Muslim population but a Hindu ruler, and it abutted
both emergent states India and Pakistan.[7] Both India and Pakistan, for
markedly different reasons, sought to incorporate Kashmir into their
emergent domains. For India, incorporating Kashmir was important
because possessing Kashmir, a Muslim-majority state, would demonstrate
India's fundamental commitment to civic, secular nationalism and that
a Muslim-majority state could thrive within a secular polity.[8] For Pakistan,
envisioned and created as a homeland for the Muslims of South Asia,
the possession of Kashmir was equally significant. Pakistani decision-
makers believed that Pakistan's identity would remain incomplete without

the incorporation of Kashmir. Simply stated, Pakistan's claim to Kashmir was irredentist.[9]

The Hindu monarch of Jammu and Kashmir, Maharaja Hari Singh, did not wish to join either India or Pakistan; he wanted to remain independent. He preferred not to join India because he feared that the socialist propensities and democratic commitments of its first Prime Minister, Jawaharlal Nehru, would lead to a drastic curtailment of his powers and prerogatives. On the other hand, as a Hindu monarch who had done little to better the lives of his Muslim subjects, he was loath to join Pakistan.[10] Thus, after the formal ceremonies of independence of Pakistan and India, Maharaja Hari Singh refused to accede to either state. He did, however, sign a Standstill Agreement with Pakistan, which made provisions for the continuation of normal trade and commercial relations. Despite the existence of the Standstill Agreement, allegations exist that Pakistan failed to supply the kingdom with coal and other essential supplies as winter approached.

Matters worsened for the kingdom in early October 1947 when a tribal rebellion broke out in Poonch in the southwestern reaches of the state, while the maharaja was still vacillating on the question of accession. Within weeks the tribals, now assisted by regular troops from the Pakistani Army, reached the outskirts of Srinagar.[11] The maharaja now in a state of panic, appealed to India for assistance. Prime Minister Nehru agreed to provide assistance to Hari Singh only if two conditions were met: he would have to accede to India, and Sheikh Mohammed Abdullah, the leader of the largest secular and popular political organization in the state, would have to give his imprimatur to the Instrument of Accession.[12] Nehru's insistence on Abdullah's support was far from trivial; although it was within the Maharaja's legal purview to accede to India, Sheikh Abdullah's support was critical for providing a mantle of legitimacy to the accession decision. On 26 October, once the maharaja had signed the Instrument of Accession and Abdullah had granted his approval, Indian troops were airlifted into Kashmir.[13] The Indian troops managed to stop the tribal incursion, but not before the rebels had managed to secure about a third of the former princely state.

From the Cease-Fire Line
to the Breach of the Line of Control

This first Indo-Pakistani war ensued without a formal declaration of war. As already discussed earlier in this chapter, the road to this war was complex and convoluted, and is the subject of much polemical debate.[14] What is not in question is that during the late fall and early winter of 1947, the Indian Army and the rebels, supported by elements of the Pakistani Army, fought a series of pitched battles, with both sides incurring significant losses. The initial force that the Indian Army deployed in Kashmir was the 161st Infantry Brigade. This brigade succeeded in hobbling the Pakistani-backed forces, among whose ranks were Hazara and Afridi tribesmen from the northern areas of Jammu and Kashmir state, paramilitary forces such as the Muslim League National Guards, and even regular Pakistani military personnel disguised as local tribesmen.[15]

After their induction into Kashmir, the Indian forces took the better part of two weeks to launch a significant counter-attack, relying on both infantry and armoured units. Their first major success came around 7 November when they managed to secure Srinagar airfield. They, then, pushed on to capture the town of Baramula, and on 13 November managed to seize the town of Mahura. By December 1947, the Indian forces were losing some of their military momentum owing to a general lack of supplies and the inadequacy of equipment for sustaining combat at high altitudes. More to the point, many troops had been rapidly airlifted from the plains and they had little or no preparation for or training in high-altitude warfare.[16]

In December, the opposing 'Azad Kashmir' (literally, 'free Kashmir') forces successfully exploited the Indian weaknesses, forcing the Indian Army into a tactical retreat. Consequently, it was not until the next spring that the Indians managed to launch a counter-offensive. With the launch of this counter-offensive, the regular Pakistani Army became directly involved in the conflict in support of the 'Azad Kashmir' forces. As the Indian Army started to make further territorial gains in the late spring, several units of the Pakistani Army entered the battlefield. The Pakistani Army concentrated a parachute brigade, two field artillery regiments, and a medium artillery battery west of the city of Jammu. These emplacements enabled the Pakistanis to threaten the slender but critical links between Amritsar (a key city in the Indian state of Punjab) and Jammu, Pathankot, and Poonch in the state of Jammu and Kashmir.

In late spring, the Indian political leadership concluded that the conflict would drag on indefinitely unless Pakistani military support for the insurgents was stopped. To accomplish this, India would have to dramatically expand the scope of the conflict. Unfortunately, it had neither the military resources nor the requisite political will to pursue such a goal. Additionally, India's political leadership was aware that it would find itself at a significant political disadvantage if it pressed military operations into Pakistan-controlled Kashmir. Sheikh Abdullah's popularity was confined mostly to the Kashmir Valley; he commanded little support in Mirpur, Poonch, Muzaffarabad, Gilgit, and Baltistan. Worse still, in Mirpur and parts of Poonch, his old rival, the pro-Pakistani activist Yusuf Shah, wielded considerable influence amongst the Muslim population.[17] Accordingly, Indian decision-makers, on the advice of Lord Mountbatten, referred the dispute to the United Nations (UN) Security Council for resolution under Chapter Six of the UN Charter, which deals with threats to international peace and security. At the UN India adopted a singularly legalistic stance, wheras Pakistan took a very deft political approach. While the Indian delegate, Sir S. Gopalaswamy Iyengar, focused on the legal issue of Pakistan's support for the insurgents, the Pakistani delegate Sir Mohammed Zafrullah Khan turned the discussion to India's putative maltreatment of its Muslim minority following partition, and India's absorption of the Muslim-ruled states of Junagadh and Hyderabad.[18]

It has now been well documented that the actions of the UN Security Council were far from dispassionate. Indeed, there is considerable evidence that the British government and subsequently the US government played distinctly partisan roles in the debates on the Kashmir question.[19] In any event, the Security Council passed two critical resolutions, one on 20 January 1948, and the other on 21 April 1948. These two resolutions created a three-member commission (expanded to five by the second resolution) to report on the conditions prevalent in Jammu and Kashmir, and to then suggest means for mediating an end to the dispute. They also called on Pakistan to withdraw its forces from Kashmir, enjoined India to reduce its troop presence in the state consistent with the minimum necessary for the maintenance of law and order, and called for a plebiscite to determine the wishes of the Kashmiri population. Neither India nor Pakistan carried out the mandate of the commission, and the issue languished for the next two decades in the Security Council.[20] The issue would once again, surface in the aftermath of the disastrous Sino-Indian border war of 1962, when under considerable Anglo-American pressure, India opened bilateral talks with Pakistan to try and bring a resolution to the Kashmir dispute.

Enter the Dragon: The Sino-Indian Border War

The British imperial withdrawal had created disputes between India and China, too. During colonial rule in the subcontinent, the British had sought to extend the frontiers of their empire to the northernmost parts of the Indian subcontinent. However, the limits of cartography in the vast, inhospitable Himalayan range had prevented a precise delineation of the empire's and subsequently India's, northern borders.[21]

In the aftermath of the Communist Chinese revolution of 1949, and the takeover of Tibet in 1950, India, seeking to avoid a confrontation with the People's Republic of China (PRC), quickly adopted a policy of appeasement towards its huge northern neighbour.[22] To this end, India quickly ceded its extra-territorial rights in Tibet and sought to avoid a confrontation with China. Such a strategy accorded well with Prime Minister Nehru's domestic policy goals and his internationalist objectives. Domestically, he wanted to limit defence expenditures and concentrate India's limited economic resources on the gigantic tasks of poverty alleviation and the promotion of economic prosperity. He was also acutely concerned about the dangers of Bonapartism in a new nation and about the militarization of Indian society.[23]

Despite Nehru's attempts to woo the Chinese Communist leadership, differences soon surfaced about the delineation of India's northern Himalayan borders. Initially, Nehru, seeking to avoid inflaming right-wing political opposition, failed to alert the Indian parliament about Chinese claims over what he and his advisors deemed to be Indian territory. However, after important border clashes at the Kongka Pass and Longju in 1958, the dispute spilled into the open. Many Indian parliamentarians, who had been kept uninformed about these territorial claims and about Chinese road-building activities across what was believed to be Indian territory, now adopted intransigent positions in parliament, sharply limiting Nehru's room for political manouevre. In a last-minute attempt to avoid an all-out military confrontation with China, Nehru invited the Chinese premier, Zhou Enlai to New Delhi for talks in 1960. Unfortunately, these talks broke down as Nehru's cabinet colleagues showed no inclination to compromise.

In an attempt to demonstrate India's resolve to defend what its leadership considered to be Indian territory, India embarked upon what was referred to as the 'forward policy'. The 'forward policy' involved sending small pickets of lightly-armed troops into areas that the Chinese had claimed. In the words of a senior military officer who had been involved in the implementation of the 'forward policy', it had 'neither teeth nor tail'[24]: it lacked the requisite firepower to inflict any serious costs on the Chinese forces and it also did not possess adequate logistical support. The policy amounted to a flawed attempt to pursue a strategy of compellence—the threat of the use of force to induce an adversary to undo a hostile act.[25]

The Chinese regime reacted sharply to the forward policy and repeatedly warned India that it saw this strategy as a hostile posture. The Indian political leadership, nevertheless, refused to abandon this strategy. In October 1962, the Chinese People's Liberation Army (PLA) struck without warning along a number of key Himalayan salients, catching the Indian Army completely unprepared. In most arenas the Indian forces, despite attempts at stiff resistance, were forced to retreat. The war proved to be a complete military debacle for India.[26]

The immediate aftermath of the Sino-Indian war saw the most dramatic shift in Indian security and defence policies. Though its leaders refused to abandon the principles of non-alignment, they nevertheless recognized the signal importance of military strength to secure India's borders and guarantee its national security. Accordingly, India embarked upon a significant military modernization programme that sought to create a forty-five squadron air force equipped with supersonic aircraft, an army with a manpower ceiling of a million men under arms, including ten divisions trained and equipped for high-altitude warfare, and a modest effort at naval modernization.[27]

There is little question that these changes in military organization, strategy, and capabilities were directed towards a possible future threat from the China. Indian decision-makers, quite understandably preoccupied with the Chinese threat, remained oblivious to the possible misgivings that India's significant programme of military modernization might generate in Pakistan. Thus, the Indian effort at military modernization unwittingly created a 'security dilemma' for Pakistan. Pakistani decision-makers themselves became obsessed with the potentially adverse consequences for their strategic interests and security concerns. They became increasingly convinced that their ability to wrest Kashmir from India through the use of force would inevitably decline as India's military capabilities expanded in the foreseeable future. Many of the military capabilities that India was acquiring, though designed to cope with the looming Chinese threat, could just as well be used to counter Pakistani capabilities. More to the point, the military regime of Mohammed Ayub Khan also exploited this growth in Indian military capabilities to highlight Pakistan's possible vulnerabilities. The perceived threat from India and the closing window of opportunity proved to be important motivations behind Pakistan's politico-military strategy to destabilize the Indian-controlled portions of Jammu and Kashmir, and then to embark on a second war against India in September 1965.[28]

Warring Yet Again: The Kashmir Conflict of 1965

In the aftermath of the Sino-Indian border war, the US and the United Kingdom (UK) placed substantial pressure on New Delhi to open bilateral negotiations with Pakistan to try and resolve the Kashmir problem. India, beholden to both the US and the UK for military assistance and diplomatic support after the traumatic 1962 border war, agreed to these bilateral negotiations. Despite several rounds of talks, the two sides failed to reach a working accommodation.[29]

The failure of multilateral negotiations, the collapse of the bilateral talks, and India's re-armament in the wake of the 1962 border war with

China convinced Pakistani decision-makers that the 'window of opportunity' to obtain all of Kashmir was rapidly closing. Furthermore, India's attempts to alter the status of the disputed state through the passage of a series of legislative directives led Pakistanis to fear that their legal claim to Kashmir was also eroding.[30] Accordingly, the Pakistani politico-military elite designed a strategy, 'Operation Gibraltar', which involved fomenting a rebellion in Indian-controlled Kashmir, and then sending in regular Pakistani Army units to seize the territory in a short, sharp war.

Pakistan's plans went awry from the outset. Although anti-Indian sentiment did exist in the Valley, such resentment against the shortcomings of Indian rule did not automatically translate into widespread support for Pakistan. Consequently, when the irregular Pakistani forces entered the Valley and sought the support of the local population to destabilize the state, they were not promptly greeted with warmth and support. Instead, members of the local population turned in some of the intruders to the Kashmiri authorities.

This loss of tactical surprise notwithstanding, the Pakistanis pressed ahead with their plans. On 14 August, Pakistani regular forces made a major incursion across the Cease-Fire Line (CFL) near the 'Azad Kashmir' town of Bhimbar. The very next day, the Indian Army retaliated by crossing the CFL. The Pakistanis counter-attacked and shelled Indian positions at Tithwal, Uri, and Poonch. This counter-attack generated a strong Indian response in the form of a thrust into 'Azad Kashmir'.

To cope with the Indian incursion into 'Azad Kashmir', the Pakistani Army launched 'Operation Grand Slam' on 31 August and 1 September in southern Kashmir. This military operation, spearheaded by some seventy tanks and two infantry divisions, caught the Indians by surprise. However, they responded with alacrity and called in air support. Within an hour and a half, the Indian Air Force (IAF) had attacked the advancing Pakistani forces. Faced with Indian air attacks, the Pakistanis also called in their air assets. For the remainder of this war, both sides made extensive use of air operations in support of their ground forces.

On 5 September, the village of Jaurian, some 14 miles within Indian-controlled territory, fell to advancing Pakistani forces. With the capture of Jaurian, the Pakistani forces were now in a position to proceed directly to the town of Akhnur. If they succeeded in capturing Akhnur, they would be in a position to seal off Jammu and Kashmir from the rest of India. The Indian military had made a prior determination that the terrain near Akhnur was not suitable for mounting an effective defence. Accordingly, they decided to escalate the conflict horizontally. On 6 September, Indian forces attacked across the international border near the key Pakistani city of Lahore in the state of Punjab. Almost immediately, they also launched another powerful attack towards the town of Sialkot, a major railway and road centre in Punjab. These two concerted attacks forced the Pakistanis to relieve the military pressure that they had been exerting on Akhnur.

The Indian thrust towards Lahore was quite successful as the advancing forces managed to capture several villages along the way. An actual assault on the city of Lahore was hobbled, however, by the Ichogil irrigation canal on the outskirts of the city. Fearing exactly such an attack, the Pakistani forces had blown up the bridges across the canal.

In an attempt to draw the Indian forces away from Lahore the Pakistanis launched a counteroffensive at Khem Karan in Punjab. The Pakistani First Armoured Division, composed of some 125 to 150 tanks, led this attack. Through aerial reconnaissance, however, the Indian Army had obtained prior warning of this impending attack. Accordingly, it had called in its Second Armoured Brigade, composed of British-built Centurion tanks. Emplaced in a horseshoe fashion, they laid in wait for the Pakistani Patton tank column to enter firing range. The greater firepower of the American-manufactured Pakistani Pattons proved to be of little use when caught in this ambush of punishing fire from three sides.

A second major tank battle took place in the Sialkot sector. This battle proved to be a significant engagement involving close to 600 tanks. From the Indian standpoint, the outcome of this conflict was inconclusive as their forces failed to capture the city of Sialkot.

The eastern front saw very little action in 1965. The Pakistanis had focused their efforts on seizing Kashmir, and the Indian political leadership under Prime Minister Lal Bahadur Shastri had made a political decision not to extend the war into the eastern sector because it had hoped not to squelch the incipient but growing political disenchantment with West Pakistani domination in East Pakistan. A Pakistani military strategy that had long claimed that the 'defence of the east lies in the west' also facilitated the Indian politico-military decision not to pursue significant war aims in the eastern sector. The Pakistani decision to leave East Pakistan to the sufferance of the Indian military, combined with India's choice not to inflict costs in the east, led the Bengali population of East Pakistan to correctly conclude that their security was of limited concern to their West Pakistani counterparts.

Prior scholarship has suggested that by mid-September, the war was rapidly reaching a stalemate. By this time, too, both parties were under intense pressure from the US and the UK to terminate the conflict. Accordingly, on 21 September India accepted the UN Security Council cease-fire resolution that had been passed the day before and Pakistan followed suit on 22 September thereby bringing the hostilities to an end.

In the post-1965 period, the US showed scant interest in promoting a renewed dialogue between the warring parties. Among other matters, the Johnson administration was becoming increasingly preoccupied with the prosecution of the war in Vietnam, and was also disheartened with past American efforts to promote Indo-Pakistani accord. The American withdrawal from the affairs of the subcontinent enabled the Soviets to enter the breach. Leonid Brezhnev invited Prime Minister Shastri and President Ayub Khan to meet him in January 1966, at the then Soviet Central Asian city of Tashkent. Under the terms of the Tashkent Agreement that Brezhnev brokered, the two sides agreed to abjure the use of force to settle the Kashmir dispute and to return the borders to the status quo ante. The meeting did not address the final settlement of the dispute over Kashmir, however.

From Civil to Interstate War

Unlike the two previous conflicts of 1947–8 and 1965, the 1971 war was not fought over the question of Kashmir. Instead, this war stemmed from the exigencies of Pakistani domestic politics.[31] Long-simmering internal tensions between the two wings of Pakistan came to the fore after the failure of power-sharing arrangements in the wake of the 1970 Pakistani national election. The two principal political parties and their respective leaders, the Pakistan People's Party (PPP) of Zulfiqar Ali Bhutto and the Awami League (AL) of Sheikh Mujibur Rehman, representing the two wings of the Pakistani state, deadlocked over the vexed subject of political representation. The Punjabi-dominated Pakistani military, though ostensibly a neutral observer, tended to side with Bhutto and was loath to cede significant authority to the AL and the East Pakistanis. When protracted negotiations broke down and Rehman and his supporters increasingly toyed with the possibility of secession, in late March 1971, the Pakistani military began a harsh crackdown against all possible dissidents among the Bengali population of East Pakistan.[32] Shortly thereafter, a steady stream of refugees fled into India's northeastern states and into the adjoining Indian state of West Bengal. Within a couple of months, the total refugee population had numbered to close to ten million.

By early May 1971, the Indian political leadership under Prime Minister Indira Gandhi had concluded that it was cheaper to resort to war against Pakistan than to absorb the refugees into India's already turgid population. Accordingly, in consultation with her close advisors, she devised a strategy to arrange for a return of the refugees to East Pakistan, and to sever that portion of the Pakistani state from its western counterpart.

Nevertheless, she initially sought to rally a diplomatic solution to the crisis while preparing the military option. In the event, when diplomatic efforts to resolve this crisis failed, the military option was already in place.[33] Among other matters, to discourage China from opening a second front to support its Pakistani ally, she actively courted the Soviet Union and signed with it a treaty of 'peace, friendship and cooperation' in August 1971. One of the key clauses of this treaty called on both sides to consult with, and assist the other in the event of a threat to either's national security.[34]

India's military plans for an eventual war with Pakistan included the support, training, and arming of the 'Mukti Bahini' (literally, 'liberation force') composed of disaffected officers from the Pakistani Army and other men of Bengali origin. Despite Pakistan's vigorous protests, India provided substantial support to this organization. The 'Mukti Bahini' profited from Indian support wreaking considerable havoc across East

Pakistan during the late summer of 1971, and thereby weakening the Pakistani Army's ability to face an Indian military onslaught later that year.

Unable to deal with the growing strength of the insurgents within East Pakistan and frustrated with India's continuing support to these rebels, Pakistan launched an air strike at India's northern military bases on 3 December 1971.[35] The IAF, which was already on alert, responded within a day, striking a number of key West Pakistani air bases in Sargodha, Karachi, and Islamabad. Within days, the IAF had established complete air superiority over Pakistan.

The Indian Navy, which had seen limited action during the 1965 war, undertook a series of bolder actions in the 1971 war. As the air force attacked key targets within Pakistan, including Karachi, the navy carried out a bombardment of Karachi, Pakistan's principal port.[36] In addition, the Indian Navy's Soviet-built *Osa*-class missile boats attacked Pakistani oil storage facilities at Jewani and Gawadar on the Makran coast near the Iranian border. By mid-December, the Indian Navy had established a virtual naval blockade between the two wings of Pakistan.

The land war was most significant in the eastern sector, particularly because India had few military objectives in the west. The forces that attacked in the east were drawn almost solely from the army's Eastern Command headquartered in Calcutta. The striking force was composed of six divisions, including the 8th, 23rd, and 57th Army divisions. These were aided by bridge-building platoons and eight infantry battalions of the Mukti Bahini. The Indian thrust into East Pakistan was directed at two critical targets, the headquarters of the Pakistani 14th Division at Ashuganj and that of the 39th Division at Chandpur. As these land attacks took place the IAF made quick work of the small Pakistani Air Force contingent in East Pakistan and put the Dacca (later Dhaka) airfield out of commission.

By 6 December, the Indian military, working with the Mukti Bahini, had established two possible routes for a final assault on Dhaka: one from the east across the Meghna River, and the other from the north from the Indian state of Meghalaya. The initial Indian thrust towards the Meghna was hampered because retreating Pakistani forces had blown up the bridges across the river. Nevertheless, the Indian troops made an unopposed crossing using local craft and helicopters. By 8 December these forces had reached the outskirts of Dacca. In the meanwhile, the northern flank had already managed to reach Dacca, having bypassed a Pakistani infantry brigade. On 11 December Indian paratroop units reinforced the advancing formation, and on 12 December, in a fierce battle, they managed to defeat the Pakistani brigade bypassed earlier. By 13 December the Indian forces were poised for a final assault on Dacca. This ensued on 16 December after Lieutenant General Jagjit Singh Aurora, the commanding officer of Eastern Command, rejected the offer of a conditional cease-fire from his Pakistani counterpart, General A.A.K. Niazi. On 16 December, the Pakistani forces were easily routed and the Indians entered Dacca. On 17 December, Prime Minister Indira Gandhi ordered a unilateral cease-fire. The same day President Yahya Khan ordered the Pakistani forces to lay down their arms, bringing the 1971 war to an end.

As the war was drawing to a close, the Nixon administration, in an attempt to demonstrate the reliability of its commitment to the Yahya Khan regime, sent in a naval task force led by the U.S.S. Enterprise from its station off the coast of Vietnam towards the Bay of Bengal. The stated purpose of this task force was to rescue any American civilians trapped in Dacca. By the time the task force reached the outer fringes of the bay, the war was over.

The then US national security advisor, Henry Kissinger, later claimed that Nixon had sent in the task force to prevent India from dismembering West Pakistan. No evidence has yet been unearthed which suggests that India had any such plans in the first place. Kissinger's propensity to see every regional conflict through the lenses of superpower designs led him to believe that India was acting in concert with the Soviet Union to try and vivisect Pakistan, an American ally.

In the aftermath of the war, India and Pakistan agreed to hold bilateral talks. These talks, held in May 1972 in the Indian hill station of Simla, led to the repatriation of some 90,000 Pakistani prisoners of war, a reiteration of the prior agreement to settle the Kashmir dispute without resort to the use of force, and a decision to convert the nomenclature of the Cease-Fire Line in Kashmir to the Line of Control reflecting the dispositions of troops after the 1971 war. Once again, the question of the final settlement of the Kashmir dispute was addressed but not reached at Simla. (Indian and Pakistani interlocutors disagree about whether or not Prime Minister Bhutto had made a tacit commitment to settle the Kashmir dispute along the LoC.[37])

The Experiences of War

A number of generalizations can be teased out from the experiences of war between India and Pakistan.[38] Despite the extraordinary passion that significant segments of the general populace in India and Pakistan, not to mention their political elites, attached to the Kashmir dispute, all the wars, with the possible exception of the 1971 war, were fought for limited aims. Pakistan, as the revisionist state in the region, sought to dislodge India from Kashmir. However, it did not seek to unravel the Indian state and did not harbour visions of wider territorial conquest. India, though determined not to concede ground on Kashmir, also did not pursue strategies of territorial aggrandizement.[39] Even in the 1971 war, while India clearly sought and successfully managed to break up Pakistan through its intervention in the East Pakistan crisis, it did not seek to hive off and incorporate any part of Pakistan into its own domain.

Limitations on firepower also placed important constraints on Indian and Pakistani war aims. In all the three wars discussed here, neither side possessed the requisite firepower, mechanized units, and logistical capabilities to sustain long, penetrative military campaigns. Neither of the two countries, particularly not Pakistan, possessed a significant military-industrial base capable of supplying a protracted military campaign.[40] Limited financial resources further hobbled their military capabilities. Finally, in the case of Pakistan, which was acutely dependent on foreign military supplies, especially from the US, arms embargoes had a disproportionately adverse impact on its war-making capabilities. Both in 1965 and 1971, a US arms embargo on the subcontinent following the outbreak of Indo-Pakistani hostilities dramatically curbed Pakistan's ability to wage war.

These constraints on firepower, in turn, helped limit the number of battle deaths in these wars. In the 1999 conflict near Kargil, casualties were substantially higher because such constraints were loosened.

Yet another striking feature of these conflicts involved the willingness of military commanders to adhere to mutually agreed-upon constraints on the use of force. Two episodes, in particular, deserve to be highlighted. The first episode involved Indian and Pakistani restraint in the use of airpower during the Rann of Kutch conflict that preceded the 1965 war. The use of airpower would have resulted in widespread casualties on both sides because of the desert-like terrain of the Rann, where only scrubland vegetation afforded little protection for troops. To prevent the slaughter of each other's infantry, Air Marshal Asghar Khan of Pakistan contacted his counterpart, Air Marshal Arjan Singh, and the two arrived at an informal accord not to use airpower in the Rann of Kutch. Both parties scrupulously adhered to this agreement.[41] When full-scale war later broke out, a more formal agreement on the use of airpower was reached when Air Marshal Arjan Singh and his counterpart, Air Marshal Asghar Khan reached an understanding that neither side would purposely bomb civilian populations.[42] This agreement, which was arrived at without the explicit consent of higher political authorities, held throughout the course of the war.

These restraints on the conduct of hostilities were possible because of the existence of a range of personal contacts and professional ties between key military commanders. Senior military officers in the Indian and Pakistani armed forces had not only been members of the British colonial forces but had fought alongside one another in World War II. Consequently, it was possible for them to reach both tacit and informal agreements and adhere to these commitments even in the midst of war.

Their common military and professional training also played an important role in shaping the course of the first three wars. None of these wars saw significant tactical or strategic innovations, the armies relied mostly on set-piece battle tactics, and the senior commanders drew upon their battlefield experiences of World War II and adapted them to the field conditions of South Asia.

Towards a More Sanguinary Future?

Any future Indo-Pakistani conflicts are unlikely to resemble the past, however. The informal ties and contacts that enabled senior military officers on both sides to agree on mutual restraints no longer exist. The generation of military officers that was steeped in the common British traditions of warfighting and strategic thought has passed from the scene. The officers who now peer at each other across the highly militarized Indo-Pakistani border have had little or no contact with each other. Consequently, they lack the ability to reach informal accords before or after the onset of a conflict.

The two armed forces also possess far greater conventional firepower than they did in the past. Consequently, their ability to inflict damage has increased dramatically. Both militaries now also have greater mechanized capabilities, enabling them to carry the conflict across each other's borders.

Changes in strategic doctrines have accompanied the acquisition of these military capabilities. Both military establishments have embraced offensive military doctrines for a number of years. Neither side plans on fighting a mere holding action; instead each hopes to carry the conflict across its borders into the adversary's frontyard.

The most striking change, however, has been the overt nuclearization of the region. In May 1998, the two countries became overtly nuclear-armed states. Even prior to the open nuclearization of the region, once both parties recognized that the other possessed nuclear weapons, the 'stability–instability' paradox came into play.[43] Briefly stated this proposition holds that the mutual possession of nuclear weapons in an adversarial context gives both parties a strong interest in avoiding resort to full-scale war for fear of escalation to the nuclear level. However, the mutual recognition of the danger of large-scale conflict also leads states to undertake probing actions at lower levels of conflict in the expectation that the risks of such probes are both controllable and calculable.[44] The nuclear weapons provide stability on the macro level, but instability at the micro level.

The most vivid illustration of this principle was the decision of the Pakistani military to undertake military action in Kargil in May 1999. The only significant strategic benefit of this military action, had it succeeded, would have been to cut off one of India's key access routes to the northernmost areas of Kashmir in Ladakh, and thence to the disputed Siachen Glacier.[45] The choice of the routes of incursion was hardly accidental. Apart from threatening the highway, the action would not have placed any vital Indian political or military assets at great risk. The Pakistani politico-military leadership, no doubt cognizant of the risk of initiating a conflict with India that had the potential for escalation, chose to make an incursion in areas of no fundamental strategic or military value.

By the same token, it is important to emphasize that unlike in the 1965 war when India resorted to horizontal escalation within the span of one week, in the Kargil conflict the Indian politico-military leadership carefully confined the ambit of conflict to the areas where the Pakistani forces breached the LoC. Both sides, in effect, understood the consequences of the nuclear revolution and acted with a degree of circumspection to avoid the expansion of the conflict to a wider or higher level.

Finally, yet another factor may transform the dynamics of conflict between India and Pakistan. In the past several years, especially after it embarked upon a process of economic liberalization in 1991, India has been growing at about six per cent annually. Even with a modest momentum in economic reforms, it should be able to sustain that rate of growth. These higher growth rates, in turn, enable India to divert greater resources to defence spending, thereby widening the gap between Pakistan and itself.

Pakistan's economy, which faces significant structural problems and bottlenecks, will be incapable of growing at a similar pace in the foreseeable future. Consequently, Pakistan's ability to cope with increased Indian defence spending will degrade over time. By the same token it will be unable, at least on its own, to match India's increasing technical sophistication. For example, in an attempt to undermine Pakistan's sense of impunity to act in Kashmir, thanks to its possession of nuclear weapons, India is now seeking to acquire airborne warning systems and ballistic missile defences from Israel.[46] The acquisition of such capabilities is clearly directed at degrading Pakistan's reliance on nuclear weapons to blackmail India on Kashmir.

Despite these military-technological changes that are underway, will the caution that characterized the Kargil conflict prevail indefinitely in Indo-Pakistani crises? Or as many observers fear, in a future crisis, will these two states through an amalgam of faulty intelligence, miscalculation, and misperception stumble across the precipice into the abyss of nuclear war? This is one of the central questions that this book will attempt to answer. To that end the book will carefully muster, examine, and assess the evidence from five recent crises in Indo-Pakistani relations. Two of these crises took place before the overt nuclearization of the region, in 1987 and 1990 respectively. The third crisis involved the 1998 nuclear tests. The final two crises took place in 1999 over Kargil and the last stemmed from a terrorist attack against India's parliament on 13 December 2001.

Notes

[1] The literature on this subject is vast and much of it is quite partisan. For some of the more useful pieces of literature, see Russell Brines, *The Indo-Pakistani Conflict* (New York: Pall Mall, 1968); also see Sumit Ganguly, *Conflict Unending: India-Pakistan Tensions Since 1947* (New York: Columbia University Press, 2002); for sophisticated Indian and Pakistani perspectives on the dispute, see Sisir Gupta, *Kashmir: A Study in India-Pakistan Relations* (Bombay: Asia Publishing House, 1966); and S.M. Burke, *Mainsprings of Indian and Pakistani Foreign Policies* (Minneapolis: University of Minnesota Press, 1974); and Ahmad Faruqui, *Rethinking National Security of Pakistan: The Price of Strategic Myopia* (Aldershot: Ashgate, 2003).

[2] For a discussion of the concept of 'opacity' in general, see Avner Cohen, *Israel and the Bomb* (New York: Columbia University Press, 1998).

[3] The literature on partition is simply voluminous. See for example, Penderel Moon, *Divide and Quit: An Eyewitness Account of the Partition of India, 1936–1947* (Delhi: Oxford University Press, 1998); Anita Inder Singh, *The Origins of the Partition of India* (Delhi: Oxford University Press, 1999); C.H. Phillips and Mary Doreen Wainwright (eds), *The Partition of India: Policy and Perspectives* (London: Allen and Unwin, 1970).

[4] For a discussion of the status of the princely states see Barbara Ramusack, *The Princes of India in the Twilight of Empire: Dissolution of a Patron-Client System, 1914–1939* (Columbus: Ohio State University Press, 1978).

[5] For a discussion of this problem, see Alan Campbell-Johnson, *Mission with Mountbatten* (London: Hale, 1972).

[6] Other problems also arose with such princely states as Junagadh and Hyderabad. For a discussion from the Indian standpoint, see V.P. Menon,

The Story of the Integration of the Indian States (Princeton: Princeton University Press, 1956), and for a Pakistani account, see Chaudhuri Mohammed Ali, *The Emergence of Pakistan* (New York: Columbia University Press, 1967).

[7] Alastair Lamb, a British historian, has questioned whether or not the state of Jammu and Kashmir abutted the emergent state of India. On this point, see Alastair Lamb, *Kashmir, 1947: Birth of a Tragedy* (Hertingfordbury: Roxford Books, 1992); for an Indian rejoinder to Lamb, see Prem Shankar Jha, *Kashmir, 1947: Rival Version of History* (New Delhi:Oxford University Press, 1996); also see Shereen Ilahi, 'The Radcliffe Boundary Commission and the Fate of Kashmir', *India Review*, vol. 2, no. 1 (January 2003).

[8] An early and thoughtful discussion of Indian secularism remains Donald Eugene Smith, *India as a Secular State* (Princeton: Princeton University Press, 1963).

[9] For a discussion of the concept of irredentism, see Naomi Chazan, *Irredentism and International Relations* (Boulder: Westview Press, 1991).

[10] For an assessment of Maharaja Hari Singh's rule, see Ian Copland, *The Princes of India in the Endgame of Empire, 1917–1947* (Cambridge: Cambridge University Press, 1997); also see Barbara N. Ramusack, *The Indian Princes and Their States* (Cambridge: Cambridge University Press, 2004).

[11] For evidence of Pakistani support to the rebels, see Major-General Akbar Khan, *Raiders in Kashmir* (Karachi: Pak Publishers, 1970); and also H.V. Hodson, *The Great Divide: Britain, India, Pakistan* (Karachi: Oxford University Press, 1997).

[12] On this point, see Richard Sisson and Leo Rose, *War and Secession: Pakistan, India, and the Creation of Bangladesh* (Berkeley: University of California Press, 1990).

[13] For a discussion of this military operation, see Lieutenant General Lionel Protip Sen, *Slender Was the Thread* (Orient Longman, 1988).

[14] For a discussion of the allegations of impropriety and counter-arguments, see Kuldip Nayar, *Distant Neighbours: A Tale of the Subcontinent* (Delhi: Vikas, 1972).

[15] For the best evidence on Pakistani complicity, see Major General Akbar Khan, *Raiders in Kashmir* (Karachi: Pak Publishers,1970).

[16] Sen, *Slender Was the Thread*.

[17] Sumit Ganguly's interview with the prominent Indian defence analyst, K. Subrahmanyam, December 1992, New Delhi.

[18] On the absorption of Junagadh and Hyderabad, see V.P. Menon, *The Story of the Integration of the Indian States* (Calcutta: Orient Longman, 1956).

[19] On this subject, see Chandrasekhar Dasgupta, *War and Diplomacy in Kashmir, 1947–48* (New Delhi: Sage Publications, 2002).

[20] For a discussion of the Kashmir question at the Security Council in its early years, see Joseph Korbel, *Danger in Kashmir* (Princeton: Princeton University Press, 1966).

[21] For a particularly thoughtful discussion of the delineation of these disputed borders, see Parshotam Mehra, *The McMahon Line and After: A Study of the Triangular Contest on India's Northeastern Frontier between Britain, China and Tibet, 1904–47* (New Delhi: Macmillan, 1974).

[22] The term, 'appeasement' is used in its pristine form. In its original form, prior to the meaning it acquired before Chamberlain's attempt to placate Hitler at Munich in 1938, the term meant making accommodations to the legitimate demands of a rival great power. For a discussion of this subject, see Paul Kennedy, *Diplomacy and Strategy, 1870–1945: Eight Studies* (London: Allen and Unwin, 1983).

[23] Sumit Ganguly, 'From the Defense of the Nation to Aid to the Civil: The Army in Contemporary India', in David Louscher and Charles H. Kennedy (eds), *Civil-Military Interaction in Asia and Africa* (The Hague: E.J. Brill, 1991).

[24] Sumit Ganguly's interview with a senior, retired Indian military officer, July 1988, New Delhi.

[25] For a discussion of the concept of 'compellence', see Thomas Schelling, *Arms and Influence* (New Haven: Yale University Press, 1966).

[26] The best account of the Indian military rout can be found in Major General D.K. Palit (retd) *War in the High Himalaya: The Indian Army in Crisis* (London: C. Hurst and Company, 1988).

[27] For a detailed discussion of these changes, see Raju G.C. Thomas, *Indian Defense Policy* (Princeton: Princeton University Press, 1986).

[28] Sumit Ganguly, 'Deterrence Failure Revisited: The Indo-Pakistani War of 1965', *Journal of Strategic Studies*, vol. 13, no. 4 (December 1999), pp. 77–93.

[29] Timothy Crawford, 'Kennedy and Kashmir, 1962–63: The Perils of Pivotal Peacemaking in South Asia', *India Review*, vol. 1, no. 3 (July 2002), pp. 1–38.

[30] For a discussion of these legislative directives, see Brines, *The Indo-Pakistani Conflict*.

[31] An extended discussion of the origins and course of this war can be found in Sisson and Rose, *War and Secession*.

[32] For a particularly vivid account, see Anthony Mascarhenas, *The Rape of Bangladesh* (Delhi: Vikas Publications, 1971).

[33] India's diplomatic efforts to resolve the crisis are discussed in J.N. Dixit, *India-Pakistan in War and Peace* (New York: Routledge, 2002).

[34] Robert Horn, *Soviet-Indian Relations: Issues and Influence* (New York: Praeger, 1982).

[35] Air Chief Marshal P.C. Lal (retd) *My Years with the I.A.F.* (New Delhi: Lancers International, 1986).

[36] For a discussion of the Indian naval operations, see S.N. Kohli, *We Dared* (New Delhi: Lancers International, 1989).

[37] Much of the evidence and description of the wars has been drawn from Ganguly, *Conflict Unending*.

[38] On this point, see Sumit Ganguly, 'Wars Without End: The Indo-Pakistani Conflict', *The Annals of the American Academy of Social and Political Science*, 541 (1995), pp. 167–78.

[39] It may be noted, en passant, that on occasion key leaders in both states did make hyperbolic public statements about either undoing partition or seizing New Delhi. These statements, however, cannot be taken as policy pronouncements. They were made to rally domestic audiences, to bolster the morale of troops on the eve of war, and to demonstrate resolve.

[40] One of the few reliable discussions of Pakistan's military-industrial base can be found in Stephen P. Cohen, *The Pakistan Army* (Berkeley: University of California Press, 1998); for a discussion of India's military-industrial capabilities, see Raju G.C. Thomas, *The Defence of India: A Budgetary Perspective on Strategy and Politics* (Delhi: Macmillan, 1978).

[41] Sumit Ganguly, 'Discord and Cooperation in India-Pakistan Relations', in Kanti P. Bajpai and Harish C. Shukul (eds), *Interpreting World Politics: Essays for A.P. Rana* (New Delhi: Sage Publications, 1995), pp. 401–12.

[42] On this point, see Air Marshall Asghar Khan (retd) *The First Round* (New Delhi: Vikas Publishing House,1979).

[43] For the initial discussion of the 'stability–instability' paradox see Glenn Snyder, 'The Balance of Power and the Balance of Terror', in Paul Seabury (ed.), *The Balance of Power* (San Francisco: Chandler Publishing Company, 1965); also see Robert Jervis, *The Meaning of the Nuclear Revolution: Statecraft and the Prospect of Armageddon* (Ithaca: Cornell University Press, 1989).

[44] For a discussion of the concept of a 'limited probe', see Alexander George and Richard Smoke, *Deterrence in American Foreign Policy: Theory and Practice* (New York: Columbia University Press, 1974).

[45] For one of the most thoughtful discussions of Pakistani plans and objectives in the Kargil operation, see Owen Bennett Jones, *Pakistan: Eye of the Storm* (New Haven: Yale University Press, 2002).

[46] P.R. Kumaraswamy, 'India and Israel: Emerging Partnership', in Sumit Ganguly (ed.), *India as an Emerging Power* (London: Frank Cass, 2003).

3

1984

India, Pakistan, and Preventive War Fears

Events in the 1970s and early 1980s injected a new issue into Indo-Pakistani relations: nuclear weapons. India had long been pursuing nuclear capabilities,[1] primarily through indigenous research and development, but with substantial infusions of foreign technology. New Delhi's fundamental grand strategic aim was to give itself the option of building nuclear weapons in short order should India's security predicament eventually warrant such a move. India's gradual nuclearization from the 1940s to the 1980s was motivated by a number of factors at different levels of analysis. Domestically, what one analyst has termed a 'strategic enclave' of 'research establishments and production facilities'[2] pushed Indian political leaders along the nuclear path, for both national security and prestige purposes. Scientists and engineers within this strategic enclave created the vital technological foundation for Indian nuclear prowess, providing India's nuclear programme with inexorable momentum, even as successive political leaders demonstrated a profound ambivalence about India's becoming a nuclear weapon state.[3]

Internationally, Indian leaders' main concern for most of this period was with China, India's chief competitor for power and prestige in Asia. As discussed in the previous chapter, China trounced India in a 1962 border war. Soon thereafter (1964), China tested its first nuclear explosive device, and thereby joined what would become the exclusive nuclear weapon club established by the Nuclear Non-Proliferation Treaty (NPT) (1970). Indian leaders also took close note of three developments in the eventful year of 1971: US President Richard Nixon's dramatic opening to China in July, the October seating of China in the United Nations General Assembly and Security Council, and the December movement of a US aircraft carrier task force towards the Bay of Bengal during the third Indo-Pakistani war. In 1972, Indian Prime Minister Indira Gandhi authorized the building of a nuclear explosive device that could be tested, and in 1974, she gave the final go-ahead for India's first nuclear explosion.[4]

Pakistan's nuclear programme dates back to the 1950s, when the country's leaders began to explore the idea of using nuclear energy for civilian purposes.[5] Within a decade, military priorities had supplanted civilian ones in the nuclear thinking of Pakistani leaders. The chief proponent of a Pakistani nuclear bomb was foreign minister Zulfiqar Ali Bhutto, who argued in the wake of the 1965 humiliation by India that Pakistan needed a nuclear equalizer. The 1965 war had revived serious concerns about Pakistan's long-term security, especially given the country's lack of strategic depth. Moreover, as Bhutto began to mount his own challenge to President Ayub Khan's rule, he perceived that nuclear nationalism would be an effective way to rally Pakistan's masses behind him. Pakistan's nuclear aspirations were further fuelled by the 1971 Bangladesh war, and the consequent loss of roughly half of Pakistan's territory and population. In 1972, given the huge asymmetry that had emerged in Indian and Pakistani military capabilities, now President Bhutto ordered Pakistan's own strategic enclave to begin developing nuclear arms. Pakistani leaders apparently believed that 'a small nuclear programme would enable the Pakistanis to do in nuclear terms what their ground and air forces could not do in conventional terms: threaten to punish any Indian attack so severely that consideration of such an attack would be deterred from the outset.'[6]

As India and Pakistan inched towards achieving nuclear weapon capabilities in the late 1970s, fears grew—both in South Asia and in Washington—that the two sides might be tempted to launch disabling preventive strikes against the adversary's nuclear infrastructure.[7] Because India's nuclear facilities were by the early 1980s vast and scattered, the likelihood of Pakistan's even attempting to carry out a preventive strike against India was considered slim.[8] Of much greater concern to analysts was that the country with the nuclear advantage—India—would order preventive attacks against Pakistan to prevent it from levelling the nuclear playing field.[9] Between 1979 and 1984, rumours abounded in Islamabad, New Delhi, and Washington that India might indeed be poised to launch such an attack against Pakistan's Kahuta uranium enrichment facility and perhaps other nuclear installations. These rumours and the alarm they generated snowballed into a minor crisis in 1984, when two squadrons of IAF Jaguar fighter-bombers seemed suddenly to disappear from view. A number of Pakistani and US officials grew alarmed, believing that the Indian Jaguars might have been moved in preparation for preventive air strikes against Pakistan. This first crisis of South Asia's nuclear era was ultimately resolved without resort to war, but it marked the definitive introduction of nuclear weapon dynamics into the India–Pakistan relationship—dynamics which have only grown more intense with the passage of time.

This chapter examines the crisis of 1984, the first in South Asia's nuclear era. We situate our case study of this crisis in the context of the three propositions developed in Chapter One. Our main argument in this chapter is that each of the three propositions by itself is exceedingly weak in explaining South Asia's non-war of 1984, and that a hybrid form of deterrence best explains why India and Pakistan did not fight. This hybrid, which we call 'boosted conventional deterrence', is a product of the grey area that characterizes countries' transitions to nuclear weapon status. It is not pure nuclear deterrence, because no actual nuclear weapons are deployed by the states involved; but it is not pure conventional deterrence either, because the deterrent effect on decisionmaking derives not from a balance of conventional forces, but from the prospect that conventional assets can be used to cause massive destruction when targeted against nuclear installations. The next section of this chapter describes the international and domestic political contexts that provide the backdrop for the 1984 crisis. The third section discusses the broad contours of the India–Pakistan nuclear arms competition in the early 1980s. Section four discusses in general terms the preventive war imperatives facing decision-makers before and during the crisis. Next, we recount the details of the 1984 crisis itself. In the final section, we first analyse how well the empirical evidence matches our theoretical propositions and then develop our argument concerning 'boosted conventional deterrence'.

Levels of Analysis: The International and Domestic Contexts

Bipolarity continued to define the international system of the early 1980s. The US–Soviet détente process of the 1970s ended abruptly in December 1979, when the Soviet Union invaded Afghanistan to prop up a faltering Marxist regime, and put down a rapidly spreading Islamist insurgency. For the first three decades of the Cold War, as during the 'Great Game' of the nineteenth and early twentieth centuries, Afghanistan had enjoyed the status of a buffer state between the Russian empire and Western interests in South Asia.[10] Moscow's 1979 military incursion sharply altered this delicate balance of power in the northwestern subcontinent, with staggeringly tragic consequences that continue to unfold today.[11] The Soviet occupation of Afghanistan quickly revived the Pakistani-US security partnership, which had formed in the 1950s, declined in the 1960s, and lay in ruins after the 1971 Bangladesh war.[12] As a former Carter administration official recalled, the president and his advisors viewed Moscow's southward thrust as 'a qualitative change in Soviet behaviour, calling for a global response. Pakistan, now a front-line state, became an essential line of defence and an indispensable element of any strategy that sought to punish the Soviets' for their aggression in Afghanistan.[13] Discussions soon began over the terms of renewed US aid for Pakistan. Although Pakistani President Mohammad Zia-ul-Haq rejected Carter's aid proposals as insufficient, the new Reagan administration formulated and implemented a six-year (1982–7), $3.2 billion military and economic assistance package for Islamabad. The flow of US aid to Pakistan significantly improved Pakistan's conventional defence capabilities. Islamabad received modern tanks, helicopters, howitzers, and anti-tank missiles, as well as forty F-16 fighter aircraft. A senior US official told Congress that Washington's support for Islamabad was intended to 'raise the cost of potential aggression' against Pakistan, and to 'demonstrate that a strong security relationship exists between the United States and Pakistan which the Soviet Union must take into account in its calculations'.[14] Thus began a new phase of US-Pakistani collaboration that lasted until 1990. The 'Reagan doctrine' of rolling back Soviet-supported communist regimes in the Third World brought Pakistan billions of dollars in US aid. Washington also funnelled through

Islamabad and Peshawar billions more dollars worth of weapons and supplies for the Islamist resistance in Afghanistan, in what would become the largest US covert operation since the Vietnam War.

Notwithstanding the reinvigorated security partnership between Washington and Islamabad, the early 1980s also brought faint signs that bipolarity was beginning to loosen, at least in its South Asian manifestations. The most significant of these was a gradual, almost imperceptible, warming of ties between the US and India. India's special relationship with the Soviet Union had begun with Josef Stalin's death in 1953 and culminated in the 1971 Indo-Soviet peace and friendship treaty. Moscow had played a substantial part in New Delhi's economic development strategy throughout the Cold War, both by providing direct economic assistance and by importing Indian goods, which were generally uncompetitive in world markets. Furthermore, as India undertook a large military build-up in the 1970s and 1980s, New Delhi bought most of its top-of-the-line weaponry from Moscow on concessionary terms. Still, the relationship was changing. Although India refused publicly to condemn Moscow's brutalization of Afghanistan, Indian leaders were privately and acutely distressed by their ally's behaviour. How could New Delhi sustain its position as a champion of Third World interests while its superpower patron was systematically devastating a small, neighbouring country?

Indian officials had also begun to understand that economic relations with the Soviet Union were of declining utility. As the information technology revolution gained momentum, India wanted to develop the electronic, digital, and telecommunications sectors of its economy. In these areas, the US could be a much more useful partner than the stagnating Soviet Union. New Delhi began to explore quietly new cooperation with Washington early in the 1980s, and momentum accelerated when Rajiv Gandhi succeeded his mother as Prime Minister in 1984.[15] Gandhi (the younger) was a former airline pilot, enamoured of the latest technologies, and responsive to the developmental potential of economic liberalization. A May 1985 agreement in science and technology removed India from the US list of 'diversion-risk' countries, paving the way for increased American investment and technology transfers. One important result of this gradual easing of Indo-US mistrust was that Washington had more influence in New Delhi than in previous decades, when US relations with India and Pakistan were often perceived in zero-sum terms.[16] The process of unipolarization was underway.

The 1970s had been a decade of relatively peaceful relations between New Delhi and Islamabad. After the Bangladesh war, India and Pakistan had signed the Simla Agreement, which committed the two sides to settling their political differences peacefully. The post-war settlement essentially froze the Kashmir dispute. Moreover, the asymmetry in power between India and Pakistan after 1971 was so great that Islamabad was in no position to challenge the regional status quo. Lastly, the Bangladesh humiliation had prompted a national identity crisis in Pakistan: if Islam was insufficient to maintain unity between the erstwhile eastern and western wings of Pakistan, would it suffice to keep the ethnically diverse rump Pakistan together? In order to shore up Pakistan's Islamic identity and attract some much-needed international support, President Bhutto turned to the Islamic oil-producing states of West Asia.[17] With Pakistan projecting itself as a Southwest Asian rather than a South Asian country, Indo-Pakistani relations eased in the decade after Simla.

This changed in the 1980s. The most crucial bone of contention was each side's insistent claim that the other was meddling in its internal ethnic disputes.[18] Particularly important early in the decade, was Pakistan's alleged support for the Sikh insurgency that was raging in the Indian border state of Punjab. In 1981, the Akali Dal—the main Sikh political party—had launched a sustained agitation against the Indian state. Sikh leaders hoped to resolve certain long-standing disputes, one of which concerned the status of Chandigarh, which had been the capital of both Punjab and the neighbouring state of Haryana since the old state of Punjab was linguistically reorganized in 1966. As negotiations between Sikh leaders and Indira Gandhi's government failed to bear fruit, the Sikh political movement descended into militancy. With the violence escalating, Sikh insurgents turned the Golden Temple in Amritsar—Sikhism's holiest shrine—into a sanctuary and base of operations. Some called for the creation of Khalistan, an independent Sikh state. In June 1984, the Indian Army launched Operation Bluestar, an assault on the Golden Temple and other Sikh temples where militant leaders had taken refuge. Perhaps a thousand people were killed in the bloody, three-day siege. The Indian Home Ministry claimed that the Sikh insurgency was a prelude to the creation of Khalistan, supported by 'neighbouring and foreign powers', which would have 'crippled the armed forces in any future confrontation across the borders'. In October 1984, Indira Gandhi was murdered by two Sikh members of her personal security detail. In the assassination's aftermath, some 2,700 Sikhs were slaughtered in Delhi's worst violence since partition. Mrs Gandhi was succeeded by her son, Rajiv, who, in December, won the prime ministership in his own right.[19]

In the meantime, Pakistan had its own concerns about Indian cross-border meddling. Islamabad accused New Delhi of fomenting violence in the southern Pakistani province of Sindh, which had seen a huge influx of migrants since independence. The first wave of settlers consisted of *muhajirs* (refugees) from India, who fuelled the commercial and industrial growth of Karachi, Pakistan's largest city. Later settlers included Punjabis and, especially during the Afghanistan war, Pakistani Pathans and Afghans of various ethnicities. Sindhi nationalism had grown in the 1970s, as a response to what ethnic Sindhis felt was their increasing subordination to outsiders. In 1983, an opposition coalition called the Movement for the Restoration of Democracy launched violent protests against the Zia regime. This agitation soon took on a sharp regionalist tone, with Sindhis demanding greater provincial autonomy, reduced disparities in economic development, a more equitable distribution of federal government funds, and increased representation in the military and civil services.[20] In the summer of 1983, thousands of Sindhis engaged in a 'rural mass movement', the first of its kind in the country's short history.[21] When the insurgents began to carry out armed attacks against property, infrastructure, and Pakistan Army forces, the Zia government deployed two army divisions and helicopter gunships to smash the rebellion.[22] Throughout the early 1980s, Islamabad vociferously accused Indian operatives of aiding and abetting the violence in Sindh.

Another element of Indo-Pakistani conflict emerged in April 1984, when Indian military forces were deployed on the Siachen Glacier in northern Kashmir, just south of China's Xinjiang province. Pakistani forces soon followed suit, and sporadic battles have been fought between the two sides from June 1984 to the present.[23] The glacier measures some 1,000 square miles of territory in the Karakoram mountain range, much of which lies at elevations above 20,000 feet. The question of which country is sovereign over the Siachen Glacier constitutes a dispute within a dispute. Because both India and Pakistan claim all of Kashmir as their own, each country also claims complete control over the glacier. Competing claims over the glacier itself have their roots in the vagueness of the 1949 Karachi Agreement, which demarcated the CFL between India and Pakistan after the first Kashmir war. That pact delineated the ostensibly 'temporary' boundary between the Indian state of Jammu and Kashmir, and Azad ('Free') Kashmir and the Northern Areas, both held by Pakistan. When the CFL was drawn, roughly forty miles of the boundary leading up to the Chinese border was left undelineated, because the area 'was considered an inaccessible no-man's land'. The issue remained unresolved by the Simla Agreement of 1972, which replaced the CFL with the new LoC without addressing the matter of the undrawn boundary. The Siachen Glacier fighting, in which more casualties have been inflicted by fierce weather conditions than by enemy fire, has become something of a metaphor for the larger Kashmir dispute, involving irreconcilable territorial claims, substantial loss of life, and the waste of scarce resources, all with no end in sight.[24]

The South Asian Nuclear Arms Competition in the Early 1980s

The early 1980s saw the steady maturation of Indian and Pakistani nuclear weapon capabilities, a process made mutually visible by conflicting US policy objectives in South Asia. The new Reagan administration wanted, of course, to head off a regional nuclear arms race; but it also wanted to provide whatever resources were necessary for the Afghan resistance to put up a good fight against the Soviet occupation. In order to achieve this latter goal, Washington had to beef up Pakistan's conventional military forces and funnel covert assistance to the Afghan fighters via Islamabad. US policy towards South Asia for much of the 1980s was driven by policy tensions between a staunchly anti-communist administration whose first priority was to punish the Soviets in Afghanistan, and a small group of powerful US legislators who worried more about the long-term consequences of permitting Pakistan to achieve a nuclear weapon capability. The rolling outcome of this domestic political competition was a series of implicit and explicit deals between Pakistan and the US, in which Islamabad agreed to keep its nuclear progress within the bounds of markers laid down by Washington. In the process, a great deal of light was shed on Pakistan's evolving nuclear weapon programme, giving it a measure of credibility that Islamabad could not have attained without actually testing a nuclear explosive device.

At the same time, Pakistani leaders were remarkably forthright about how they were acquiring their country's nuclear capabilities. President Zia said in February 1980, 'We are not making any bomb... It is a modest experiment that we are carrying on... We are only trying to acquire technology. It takes particularly long when you have to acquire this technology through backdoor, clandestine methods.'[25] In 1981, Congressional hearings on the Reagan administration's pending aid package for Pakistan, senior US officials tried to convince influential legislators that enhancing Islamabad's conventional military capabilities would actually serve the objective of nuclear non-proliferation in South Asia: a 'program of support which provides Pakistan with a continuing relationship with a significant security partner... may remove the principal underlying incentive for acquisition of the nuclear option.' Without such a commitment, the administration argued, Washington would 'forfeit the opportunity to influence future decisions.'[26] Congress was ultimately persuaded of the administration's logic. In December 1981, it passed a provision allowing the president to waive a section of US non-proliferation law for six years, if he determined that aid to Pakistan was in the national interest. At the same time, Congress modified another part of the law to cut off US aid to Pakistan if it actually exploded a nuclear device. As long as Islamabad refrained from testing nuclear weapons, it would remain eligible for US economic and security assistance.[27]

Meanwhile, India showed signs of revising its policy of not actually building nuclear weapons, established after its 1974 nuclear explosive test. Morarji Desai, India's Prime Minister from 1977 to 1979, was Gandhian in temperament and passionately opposed to nuclear weapons; however, when Indira Gandhi returned to power in 1980, she firmly signalled India's resolve to keep its nuclear options open. In September

1981, she 'claimed that India and "the rest of the world" knew that Pakistan was developing the capacity to build nuclear weapons and would soon explode a nuclear device. She said this might prompt India... to explode another nuclear device of its own.'[28] Although press reports throughout the early 1980s speculated that both countries were making preparations for a nuclear test, one prescient analyst raised the possibility that Pakistan had 'given up the idea of aping India by actually detonating an underground nuclear device and has instead opted for the Israeli strategy of reaching, or letting the world believe it has reached, a high level of nuclear technology without actually staging a nuclear test.'[29]

This analysis proved to be correct. A US State Department document said in March 1983, 'we do not expect Pakistan to attempt a test of a nuclear device in the near future.' According to this report, President Reagan had reiterated to President Zia in December 1982 that developing nuclear weapons would be 'inconsistent with the continuation of the US security and economic assistance program.' With US aid now flowing to Islamabad, Washington was assured by Zia personally 'that Pakistan has no intention of testing a nuclear device of any kind.' The State Department analysts argued hopefully that 'while this movement by the government of Pakistan is insufficient to meet our long-term non-proliferation objectives, it demonstrates that Pakistan may be influenced to move in the proper direction through appropriate US attention to Pakistan's legitimate security needs.' The US assistance programme, they wrote, 'is our most effective weapon in dissuading that nation from continuing its nuclear explosives program.'[30]

By 1984, it was clear that even if Pakistan did not test a nuclear explosive device, it would still hedge its bets by quietly developing all of the capabilities necessary to keep its options open. Another State Department analysis, written in June of that year, found 'unambiguous evidence that Pakistan is actively pursuing a nuclear weapons development programme. Pakistan's near-term goal is to have a nuclear test capability, enabling it to explode a nuclear device if Zia decides its [*sic*] appropriate for diplomatic and domestic political gains. Pakistan's long-term goal is to establish a nuclear deterrent to aggression by India, which remains Pakistan's greatest security concern.' In the judgment of the US intelligence community, Pakistan had 'already undertaken a substantial amount of the necessary design and high explosives testing of the explosive triggering package for a nuclear explosive device', and was 'now capable of producing a workable package of this kind'. Islamabad had not, however, 'produced the fissile material necessary for a nuclear explosive device or a nuclear weapon'.[31]

As always, Pakistan walked a fine line between demonstrating its nuclear muscle to India and raising the ire of the US Congress. Growing evidence that Islamabad was enriching uranium (though not yet to weapons-grade) sparked intense deliberations between non-proliferation-minded legislators and the Reagan administration throughout 1984. The compromise that emerged, subsequently known as the Pressler Amendment, made continued US assistance to Pakistan contingent upon the president's making an annual certification that Islamabad did not 'possess a nuclear explosive device'. In explaining the majority's position, the Senate Foreign Relations Committee concurred with the administration's view that the 'preservation of our existing program of security assistance to Pakistan is essential for our efforts to discourage that country from obtaining a nuclear capability.'[32] Meanwhile, President Reagan had sent a stern letter to President Zia in September 1984, warning of 'grave consequences' should Islamabad enrich uranium beyond a 5 per cent level (93 per cent is considered the minimum required to construct a usable nuclear bomb).[33]

Predictably, Pakistan's evident nuclear strides sparked a renewed Indian debate about how to respond. Just before her death in October 1984, Indira Gandhi called Islamabad's recent progress in developing nuclear weapons a 'qualitatively new phenomenon in our security environment', one which added a 'new dimension' to Indian defence planning.[34] By the middle of 1985, Mrs Gandhi's son and successor, Rajiv, admitted that in light of Pakistan's nuclear progress, India was reconsidering its own commitment not to build nuclear weapons.[35] In June 1985, Rajiv Gandhi was quoted as saying that Pakistan was 'very close' to building a bomb; as for India, he said: 'In principle we are opposed to the idea of becoming a nuclear power. We could have done so for the past 10 or 11 years, but we have not. If we decided to become a nuclear power, it would take a few weeks or a few months.'[36] Four months later, Rajiv Gandhi said that 'Pakistan has either already got the bomb or will get one in a matter of months and may not even need to test it.'[37] In October 1985, a high-level US delegation failed to convince the Indian government that Islamabad's nuclear programme was not as far along as New Delhi feared. As Rajiv said: 'The US seems to believe that Pakistan has not got the enriched uranium yet. We believe they have.'[38] The next month, the Indian foreign minister charged that Islamabad had enough weapons-grade uranium for three to five atomic bombs.[39]

Preventive War Pressures

Speculation grew at the end of the 1970s that Pakistan's growing nuclear infrastructure would be disabled by preventive attacks, either from the air or by saboteurs. In August 1979, Carter administration officials said that an inter-agency task force was debating various options for inhibiting Islamabad's acquisition of nuclear weapons, including a covert operation to sabotage the Kahuta uranium enrichment facility.[40] One American analyst reports that 'there was a great deal of anxiety in Islamabad in August 1979 that, having failed to influence Pakistani nuclear policy, Washington would shortly undertake covert military action' against Kahuta and other Pakistani nuclear installations. She continues: 'This move was expected either through direct US action or as a commando raid by either the Israelis or the Indians. These rumours were taken seriously enough for PAF [Pakistan Air Force] Mirages to overfly the facility and air defenses to be set up on an alert basis.'[41] Indeed, PAF interceptor aircraft were a common sight in the skies over Islamabad (near Kahuta) throughout the early 1980s, and US officials confirmed that the Zia government had ringed Kahuta with surface-to-air missiles to ward off Indian bombers.[42] Ultimately, the Carter administration abandoned the idea of disabling Kahuta, reportedly because it was 'too dangerous and politically provocative'.[43]

In 1982, US intelligence officials were quoted as saying that Indian military planners had in 1981 presented Indira Gandhi with a contingency plan to destroy Islamabad's nuclear facilities.[44] Indian scholar W.P.S. Sidhu and American scholar George Perkovich have closely examined this period in Indian decisionmaking, and Perkovich's analytical synthesis is worth quoting at length:

...Sidhu suggested indirect evidence that the Indian Air Force conducted a brief study in June 1981 on the feasibility of attacking Kahuta. This was part of an air force review of strategy following the induction of British-procured Jaguar strike aircraft in 1980... A quick study was immediately conducted, and according to Sidhu's interview with the former Indian Air Force director of operations, it concluded that India could 'attack and neutralise' Kahuta. Another Indian defence official recalled that the air force believed it could accomplish the mission but calculated that perhaps 50 percent of the attacking Jaguars would be lost, as they were slow-flying compared to the Pakistani F-16s that would defend the plant.[45]

Indira Gandhi apparently rejected the preventive war plan, but 'did not foreclose the option of striking if Pakistan appeared on the verge of acquiring a nuclear weapons capability'.[46] Again, Sidhu's and Perkovich's scholarship bears lengthy quotation:

... as the former director of operations reasoned, 'The question was what will happen next? In my estimate, Pakistan would go to war. The international community would condemn us for doing something in peacetime, which the Israelis could get away with but India would not be able to get away with. In the end it will result in a war.'

Interviews with former Indian military, political, and nuclear officials corroborate this negative conclusion regarding the efficacy of an attack on Pakistan's nuclear infrastructure. These former officials acknowledged that India had photographs of the Kahuta facility and knew that it was defended against air attack by surface-to-air Crotale missiles and balloon barrages. 'If we attack Kahuta,' a former air force official explained, 'the whole border would go up. It would be war.' He continued, '[T]he Israeli model [in attacking Iraq's Osiraq reactor] would not apply. A clean attack without escalation to a wider war could not be done in the Indo-Pak context.'[47]

Mrs Gandhi's main concern in vetoing the IAF's preventive war plan was reportedly that Islamabad would order reprisal raids against India's own nuclear facilities.[48] In this regard, Perkovich writes that 'India had as much or more to lose than Pakistan' in carrying out a preventive strike, because Pakistan could then 'attack India's nuclear reactors and reprocessing plants with a grave risk of causing radioactive contamination in India.' As a former Atomic Energy Commission official put it, '[I]f we blew up Kahuta, uranium might be dispersed in Pakistan, but uranium is not nearly as toxic as plutonium, and our plants, which Pakistan could have counterattacked, have plutonium and are located closer to large populations.' Indeed, in 1983, the chairman of Pakistan's Atomic Energy Commission, Munir Ahmad Khan, made this exact point to his Indian counterpart, Raja Ramanna. Khan told Ramanna that an Indian strike against Kahuta and other Pakistani nuclear facilities would 'release very little radioactivity', while a Pakistani counter-attack on India's sprawling Trombay nuclear facility—near Mumbai—'would be huge and could release massive amounts of radiation to a large populated area causing a disaster.'[49]

The 1984 Crisis

Preventive war pressures came to a climax in 1984, when Islamabad, New Delhi, and Washington were gripped by alarm about the possibility of India's moving to smother Pakistan's nuclear baby in its crib.[50] In September, leaks from a CIA briefing to the Senate Select Committee on Intelligence suggested that Indira Gandhi was again being urged by India's military leadership to order the destruction of Kahuta.[51] President Zia had already been warning Washington about Pakistan's concerns in this regard, and the US ambassador to Islamabad, Deane Hinton, assured Zia on 16 September that 'if the United States were to see signs of an imminent Indian attack, Pakistan would be notified immediately.'[52] Hinton also told a Pakistani public-lecture audience on 10 October that 'the United States would be "responsive" if India attacked Pakistan.' Other senior US officials repeated this assertion, 'which led to Indira Gandhi's seeking verbal reassurances from the Soviet Union, and the latter agreeing that American actions were a threat to India and the Soviet Union.'[53]

The main cause for US concern was the failure of US intelligence agencies to locate two squadrons of IAF Jaguars; some analysts feared that India's top-of-the-line attack aircraft had been moved in preparation for a raid across the border.[54] Perkovich writes that 'the intelligence focused on satellite photographs of the Ambala air base in Haryana (roughly three hundred miles from Kahuta),' which 'appeared to show the Jaguars missing.... In fact, according to a former high-ranking IAF officer, the planes had been hidden in woods adjacent to the airfield as part of a passive air defense drill.'[55] Senior Pakistani officials said that they regarded the possibility of attacks on their nuclear installations as a 'serious threat' and had taken 'appropriate defensive measures',[56] such as increasing fighter patrols in the skies around Kahuta.[57] One account suggests that Pakistani leaders also 'sent an explicit message to New Delhi through diplomatic channels': if India attacked Kahuta, the PAF would 'strike every nuclear installation in India, civilian as well as military', raising the possibility of massive radiation poisoning.[58] In press interviews, senior Pakistani officials drove home the point that Islamabad would view Indian preventive strikes as 'naked aggression', which would leave 'no alternative but to retaliate'.[59] Regarding the possibility of air raids on Kahuta, Indian leaders coyly conceded that 'in a purely theoretical sense, some people may be looking at such scenarios'; however, they also recognized that this course of action would 'legitimise an action to which India would itself be vulnerable'.[60] That Indian sense of vulnerability caused New Delhi to alert its air defences around Trombay. As a senior IAF officer recalled later, 'if they think you're going to attack Kahuta, they may pre-empt you.'[61]

Why No War?

Ultimately, of course, India and Pakistan did not go to war in 1984. As Perkovich argues, India actively considered the option of taking out Pakistan's nuclear facilities, but 'instead of taking any decisive and risky measure to redress militarily the Pakistani threat, India pursued cautious diplomacy and concentrated on challenges to internal order, particularly in Punjab.'[62] The question this chapter attempts to answer is, why? This puzzle is framed by the three propositions outlined in Chapter One of this book. As applied to the 1984 crisis, the first proposition argues that the Indian and Pakistani governments, despite compelling incentives to attack one another, were dissuaded from doing so by timely and forceful US intervention. This answer to the question would seem to be weakly supported by the case study presented above. Although the US played a small role in urging India and Pakistan away from the brink of war, its interventions were lukewarm at best. With bipolarity slightly waning, but continuing to structure the international system, Washington's top priority in South Asia was fighting the Soviet Union in Afghanistan. Although the US sincerely tried to get Pakistan to abandon its nuclear aspirations, the Afghanistan war made Washington unwilling to play its most valuable bargaining chip with Islamabad—a threat to cut off the $3.2 billion US economic and military assistance package. With each non-proliferation initiative towards Pakistan, the Reagan administration ensured that Islamabad had sufficient 'wiggle room' to meet its commitments to the US without giving up its nuclear ambitions. Even more to the point, Washington's actions during the 1984 crisis may have actually had a disturbing, rather than soothing, effect. Washington's Afghanistan-driven support for Pakistan caused India both to seek reassurances from the Soviet Union and to re-think its prior nuclear restraint. P.R. Chari's observation that US diplomacy was 'both helpful and unhelpful' is apt. While the US did try to nudge the two sides away from the brink, it also 'fanned the idea that India would attack Pakistan's nuclear installations and facilities on the basis of very tenuous evidence without making any serious efforts to verify their suspicions before going public'.[63]

Our second proposition suggests that the Indian and Pakistani governments, despite compelling incentives to attack one another during the 1984 crisis, were dissuaded from doing so by the fear that war might escalate to the nuclear level. This answer to our animating question seems quite weak. India did not desist from attacking Pakistan's nuclear weapons infrastructure due to a fear of Pakistani *nuclear* reprisals. The Indian government knew, based on its own intelligence and that which was leaking out of Washington, that Pakistan had not yet achieved the capability to assemble and deliver nuclear weapons.[64] The issue for New Delhi throughout the crisis was how to *prevent* Islamabad from becoming a nuclear weapon state and thus neutralizing India's strategic advantages. India resisted the preventive temptation owing to its fear that Pakistan would retaliate for an IAF raid on Kahuta by striking Indian nuclear targets—perhaps killing hundreds of thousands of Indians and smashing in one blow India's enormously expensive, decades-long pursuit of nuclear sophistication. In short, the Indian government realized that succumbing to preventive war imperatives would hurt India more than Pakistan.

Our third proposition argues that the Indian and Pakistani governments, despite compelling incentives to attack one another during the 1984 crisis, were dissuaded from doing so by their lack of sufficient conventional military superiority to pursue a successful blitzkrieg strategy. This explanation, too, appears weak. While Pakistan obviously could not have contemplated a successful blitzkrieg against India, New Delhi had the wherewithal in 1984 to deal Islamabad a decisive blow—even as the US aid package enhanced Pakistan's long-in-the-tooth conventional military capabilities. A comprehensive analysis of the subcontinental military balance written in 1985 suggests that India could have launched a successful blitzkrieg against Pakistan if the political leadership in New Delhi had deemed such a course desirable. According to this analysis, 'Islamabad's receipt of US military equipment has done little to alter the marked asymmetries in Indo-Pakistani strength levels. India continues to enjoy an overwhelming numerical and qualitative advantage in most weapon categories.' India's offensive strike capability, 'in concert with close air support and interdiction operations by the Indian Air Force, would permit rapid advances into Pakistan'. Pakistan's security problems were 'compounded by a lack of strategic depth and poor defensive terrain adjacent to Pakistan's economic and cultural heartland'.[65]

Employing Mearsheimer's theory of conventional deterrence, since India's chances of carrying out a successful blitzkrieg were so favourable in the early 1980s, conventional deterrence cannot explain New Delhi's decision not to pursue war against Pakistan. Although Chari maintains that a 'state of conventional deterrence was... obtaining' during the 1984 crisis,[66] he fails to recognize the linkages between conventional and nuclear assets. Absent nuclear capabilities—including toxic fissile material on both sides of the border—India would have had neither the incentive to attack Kahuta, nor the profound fear of Pakistan's responding in kind. Had New Delhi wanted to punish Islamabad for supporting Khalistani elements in Punjab, it could likely have done so with acceptable costs.

If none of our propositions has proved to be very helpful, what *does* explain the fact that India and Pakistan restrained themselves from fighting a war in 1984? We are left with a hybrid form of deterrence, best termed 'boosted conventional deterrence'. This hybrid is a product of the grey area that characterizes countries' transitions to nuclear weapon status. It is not pure nuclear deterrence, because no actual nuclear weapons have been deployed by the states involved; but it is not pure conventional deterrence either because the deterrent effect derives not from a balance of conventional forces, but from the prospect that conventional assets can be used to kill far beyond their basic potential when targeted against nuclear installations. Perkovich alludes to this hybrid when he observes that 'the alarms over possible conventional military attacks on nuclear facilities in Pakistan and India showed that even without nuclear bombs each state was already at risk. This may have created a rudimentary form of deterrence...,'[67] that is, what we refer to here as boosted conventional deterrence.

Whatever variant of deterrence spared South Asia a major war in 1984, India and Pakistan learned valuable lessons from the tensions of the early 1980s. In December 1985, the two sides agreed verbally not to attack each other's nuclear facilities, the first deal of its kind in the nuclear era. Rajiv Gandhi initiated the non-attack proposal in order to lay the preventive war issue to rest once and for all.[68] 'The agreement was not signed until December 31, 1988, and not ratified until 1991; it was implemented by exchanges of lists of each side's nuclear installations in 1992 and 1993. But in 1985, it signaled a very important awareness by both sides that conflict involving nuclear facilities, let alone nuclear weapons, should be avoided.'[69]

International political life in South Asia would soon become even more complex, as India and Pakistan strove harder to improve their nuclear weapon capabilities. As one authoritative source says, Pakistan's nuclear programme 'reached a key milestone in 1985, when, despite numerous pledges to the United States that it would not produce weapons-grade uranium, Pakistan crossed the threshold. By 1986, Pakistan had apparently produced enough material to make its first nuclear device.... Pakistani sources now say that the nation acquired its first nuclear explosives capability in 1987.'[70] This was the South Asian nuclear state of play when the next India–Pakistan crisis erupted in late 1986.

Notes

[1] We distinguish between 'nuclear capabilities' and 'nuclear weapon capabilities'. The former term refers to basic technologies which can then be applied to either civilian or military uses; the latter refers to the application of those capabilities in the design of nuclear weapons.

[2] Itty Abraham, 'India's "Strategic Enclave": Civilian Scientists and Military Technologies', *Armed Forces and Society*, vol. 18, no. 2 (Winter 1992), p. 233.

[3] We now have several detailed historical accounts of the Indian nuclear weapon and delivery programmes. See Raj Chengappa, *Weapons of Peace: The Secret Story of India's Quest to Be a Nuclear Power* (New Delhi: HarperCollins, 2000); George Perkovich, *India's Nuclear Bomb: The Impact on Global Proliferation* (Berkeley: University of California Press, 1999); Itty Abraham, *The Making of the Indian Atomic Bomb: Science, Secrecy and the Postcolonial State* (London: Zed Press, 1998).

[4] For details, see Perkovich, *India's Nuclear Bomb*, pp. 161–89.

[5] The history of Pakistan's nuclear programme is substantially less complete than that of India's. Accounts of the early years include: Ashok Kapur, *Pakistan's Nuclear Development* (London: Croom Helm, 1987); Neil Joeck, 'Pakistani Security and Nuclear Proliferation in South Asia', in Neil Joeck (ed.), *Strategic Consequences of Nuclear Proliferation in South Asia* (London: Frank Cass, 1986); Warren H. Donnelly, *Pakistan and Nuclear Weapons* (Washington, DC: Congressional Research Service, 1990); Ziba Moshaver, *Nuclear Weapons Proliferation in the Indian Subcontinent* (New York: St. Martin's Press, 1991).

[6] US Defense Intelligence Agency, 'Operational and Logistical Considerations in the Event of an India-Pakistan Conflict'. Report DDB–2660–104–84, December 1984, p. 2.

[7] A great deal of confusion surrounds the terms 'preventive' and 'pre-emptive' war. A preventive attack is one that is carried out for fear of the ongoing augmentation of the adversary's capabilities. Preventive military operations are intended to destroy those growing capabilities in order to prevent the adversary from gaining the military advantage over time. All three historical examples of preventive strikes against countries in the earliest stages of the nuclear proliferation process have involved Iraq: Israel's 1981 strike against the Osirak nuclear facility, the UN coalition's 1991 air war, and the US and British invasion of 2003. In contrast, a pre-emptive attack is one that is ordered to 'get in the first blow', for fear that the adversary is about to strike first.

[8] Don Oberdorfer, 'US Sees India-Pakistan Rifts Not as Signals of Imminent War', *Washington Post*, 15 September 1984.

[9] For a discussion of the theoretical and historical underpinnings of this concern, see Scott D. Sagan, 'More Will Be Worse', in Scott D. Sagan and Kenneth N. Waltz, *The Spread of Nuclear Weapons: A Debate Renewed* (New York: Norton, 2003), pp. 53–63. For a more optimistic analysis, see Devin T. Hagerty, *The Consequences of Nuclear Proliferation: Lessons from South Asia* (Cambridge, Massachusetts: MIT Press, 1998), pp. 33–6.

[10] For a concise, informative treatment, see Anthony Arnold, *Afghanistan: The Soviet Invasion in Perspective* (Palo Alto, California: Hoover Institution Press, 1985).

[11] These include the ten-year Soviet bludgeoning of Afghanistan, which resulted in over a million deaths and the flight of some five million Afghan refugees into Iran and Pakistan; the subsequent Afghan civil war (1989–1996), which essentially destroyed the capital city of Kabul; the emergence of Pakistan's so-called 'Kalashnikov culture'; the brutal reign of the Taliban in Kabul (1996–2001); the establishment of Al Qaeda's base of terrorist operations in Afghanistan; and the 2001 US war against the Taliban and Al Qaeda in Afghanistan.

[12] See Devin T. Hagerty, 'The United States-Pakistan Entente: Third Time's a Charm?', in Craig Baxter (ed.), *Pakistan on the Brink: Politics, Economics, and Society* (Lanham, Maryland: Rowman and Littlefield, 2004), pp. 1–20; Devin T. Hagerty, 'The Foreign Policy of Z.A. Bhutto', *Journal of South Asian and Middle Eastern Studies*, vol. 14, no. 4 (Summer 1991), pp. 55–70; Devin T. Hagerty, 'The Development of American Defense Policy Toward Pakistan', *Fletcher Forum*, vol. 10, no. 2 (Summer 1986), pp. 217–42.

[13] Thomas Perry Thornton, 'Between the Stools? US Policy Toward Pakistan During the Carter Administration', *Asian Survey*, vol. 22, no. 10 (October 1982), p. 969.

[14] US Senate Committee on Foreign Relations, *Aid and the Proposed Arms Sales of F-16s to Pakistan*, 97th Cong., 1st sess., 12 November 1981, p. 7.

[15] As will be discussed below, Indira Gandhi was assassinated in October 1984.

[16] On the thaw between the US and India, see Stephen Philip Cohen, 'The Reagan Administration and India', in Harold A. Gould and Sumit Ganguly (eds), *The Hope and the Reality: U.S.-Indian Relations from Roosevelt to Reagan* (Boulder, Colorado: Westview Press, 1992), pp. 139–53; Dennis Kux, *India and the United States: Estranged Democracies, 1941–1991* (Washington, DC: National Defense University Press, 1993), pp. 379–423.

[17] Hagerty, 'Pakistan's Foreign Policy Under Z.A. Bhutto'.

[18] Both the Punjab crisis and the subsequent Kashmir crisis had their roots in a structural transformation of Indian politics during Indira Gandhi's rule

(1966–77 and 1980–4). The most salient changes included the increasing centralization of power in New Delhi, the decline of political, judicial, and administrative institutions at every level of government, and the consequent evolution of an institutional vacuum increasingly filled by populist and religious demagoguery of a decidedly unsecular tone. For more detailed analysis, see Paul R. Brass, *The Politics of India since Independence* (Cambridge: Cambridge University Press, 1990); Atul Kohli, *Democracy and Discontent: India's Growing Crisis of Governability* (Princeton: Princeton University Press, 1990); W.H. Morris-Jones, 'India After Indira: A Tale of Two Legacies', *Third World Quarterly*, vol. 7, no. 2 (April 1985), pp. 242–55.

[19] Robert L. Hardgrave, Jr and Stanley Kochanek, *India: Government and Politics in a Developing Nation*, 5th edn (Fort Worth, Texas: Harcourt Brace Jovanovich, 1993), pp. 152–60; Paul R. Brass, 'The Punjab Crisis and the Unity of India', in Atul Kohli (ed.), *India's Democracy: An Analysis of Changing State-Society Relations* (Princeton: Princeton University Press, 1988), pp. 169–213; Salamat Ali, 'The "Hidden Hand"', *Far Eastern Economic Review*, 28 June 1984, p. 14.

[20] Craig Baxter, Yogendra Malik, Charles Kennedy, and Robert Oberst, *Government and Politics in South Asia*, 2nd edn (Boulder, Colorado: Westview Press, 1991), pp. 182–4.

[21] Mary Anne Weaver, *Pakistan: In the Shadow of Jihad and Afghanistan* (New York: Farrar, Straus and Giroux, 2002), pp. 71–3.

[22] Owen Bennett Jones, *Pakistan: Eye of the Storm* (New Haven: Yale University Press, 2002), pp. 113–20; Samina Ahmed, 'The Military and Ethnic Politics', in Charles H. Kennedy and Rasul Baksh Rais (eds), *Pakistan: 1995* (Boulder, Colorado: Westview Press, 1995), pp. 108–12; Shahid Javed Burki, *Pakistan: The Continuing Search for Nationhood*, 2nd edn (Boulder, Colorado: Westview Press, 1991), pp. 73–4.

[23] The Siachen fighting is much more relevant to the Kargil conflict of 1999, covered in Chapter Seven. Here, only the barest details of the conflict are presented for contextual purposes.

[24] This paragraph draws heavily on Robert G. Wirsing, *Pakistan's Security Under Zia: The Policy Imperatives of a Peripheral Asian State* (New York: St Martin's Press, 1991), pp. 143–94.

[25] 'Learn a Lesson from History', *India Today*, 16 February 1980, p. 86.

[26] US House Committee on Foreign Affairs, *Security and Economic Assistance to Pakistan*, 97th Cong., 1st sess., 16 September 1981, pp. 23–4, and 17 November 1981, p. 297.

[27] Richard P. Cronin, *The United States, Pakistan and the Soviet Threat to Southern Asia: Options for Congress* (Washington, DC: Congressional Research Service, 1985), pp. 29–30.

[28] Michael Richardson, 'Arms and the Woman', *Far Eastern Economic Review*, 25 September 1981, p. 20.

[29] Dilip Bobb, 'Sinister Nuclear Strategy', *India Today*, 15 November 1981, p. 119.

[30] US Department of State, Bureau of Oceans, and International Environmental and Scientific Affairs, 'Pakistan's Nuclear Program,' secret report, 14 March 1983.

[31] US Department of State, 'The Pakistani Nuclear Program,' secret briefing paper, 23 June 1984.

[32] US Senate Committee on Foreign Relations, *International Security and Development Cooperation Act of 1984*, 98th Cong., 2nd sess., 1984, S. Rept. 98–400, pp. 7, 19, 58–9, 114. This legislation was signed into law in 1985.

[33] Leonard S. Spector, *The Undeclared Bomb* (Cambridge, Massachusetts: Ballinger, 1988), p. 127.

[34] Leonard S. Spector, *Going Nuclear* (Cambridge, Massachusetts: Ballinger, 1987), p. 78.

[35] Cronin, *Options for Congress*, p. 28.

[36] Maynard Parker, 'Rajiv Gandhi's Bipolar World', *Newsweek*, 3 June 1985; and Spector, *Going Nuclear*, p. 78.

[37] Spector, *Going Nuclear*, p. 270, n. 21. Gandhi's remark about testing was a reference to credible reports that China had given Pakistan vital nuclear weapon design information.

[38] Patricia J. Sethi and John Walcott, 'The South Asia Two-Step', *Newsweek*, 4 November 1985, p. 42; William Stewart and Ross H. Munro, 'An Interview With Rajiv Gandhi', *Time*, 21 October 1985, p. 50.

[39] 'Foreign Minister Speaks in Parliament on Pak Nuclear Bomb', confidential cable from the US Embassy in New Delhi to the Secretary of State, No. 28599, November 1985.

[40] Richard Burt, 'US Will Press Pakistan to Halt A-Arms Project', the *New York Times*, 12 August 1979.

[41] Shirin Tahir-Kheli, *The United States and Pakistan: Evolution of an Influence Relationship* (New York: Praeger, 1982), p. 136.

[42] Milton R. Benjamin, 'India Said to Eye Raid on Pakistan's A-Plants', *Washington Post*, 20 December 1982.

[43] Richard Burt, 'US Aides Say Pakistan Is Reported to Be Building an A-Bomb Site', the *New York Times*, 17 August 1979.

[44] Benjamin, 'India Said to Eye Raid on Pakistan's A-Plants'.

[45] Perkovich, *India's Nuclear Bomb*, p. 240. Perkovich cites W.P.S. Sidhu, 'The Development of an Indian Nuclear Doctrine since 1980' (PhD dissertation, Emmanuel College, University of Cambridge, 1997), p. 331. It is probably not coincidental that Indian air force planners were looking closely at this issue during the very same period when the US Congress was debating the Pakistan aid package with its forty F-16 fighters; preventive war would have been extremely tempting prior to the delivery of the first F-16s to Pakistan in 1982.

[46] Benjamin, 'India Said to Eye Raid on Pakistan's A-Plants'.

[47] Perkovich, *India's Nuclear Bomb*, pp. 240–1. Perkovich quotes Sidhu, 'Indian Nuclear Doctrine', p. 331.

[48] Benjamin, 'India Said to Eye Raid on Pakistan's A-Plants'.

[49] Perkovich, *India's Nuclear Bomb*, p. 241.

[50] Kanti P. Bajpai, P.R. Chari, Stephen P. Cohn, Pervaiz Iqbal Cheema, and Sumit Ganguly, *Brasstacks and Beyond: Perception and Management of Crisis in South Asia* (New Delhi: Manohar, 1995) claim that 'senior American intelligence officials concluded in mid-1984 that a war between India and Pakistan was imminent—or at least that an Indian attack on Kahuta was likely.' Because they don't source this statement, it is impossible to evaluate their claim.

[51] Oberdorfer, 'India-Pakistan Rifts.'

[52] Bajpai *et al.*, *Brasstacks and Beyond*, p. 74.

[53] Ibid., pp. 9–10.

[54] Oberdorfer, 'India-Pakistan Rifts.'

[55] Perkovich, *India's Nuclear Bomb*, p. 258.

[56] Don Oberdorfer, 'Pakistan Concerned About Attack on Atomic Plants', *Washington Post*, 12 October 1984.

[57] Perkovich, *India's Nuclear Bomb*, p. 258.

[58] William E. Burrows and Robert Windrem, *Critical Mass: The Dangerous Race for Superweapons in a Fragmenting World* (New York: Simon and Schuster, 1994), pp. 349–50.

[59] Oberdorfer, 'Pakistan Concerned'.

[60] Robert Manning, 'Talking Up the Tension', *Far Eastern Economic Review*, 4 October 1984, p. 27.

[61] Perkovich, *India's Nuclear Bomb*, p. 258.

[62] Ibid., pp. 226–7.

[63] P.R. Chari, 'Nuclear Crisis, Escalation Control, and Deterrence in South Asia', Working Paper, The Henry L. Stimson Center, Washington, DC, August 2003, p. 14.

[64] See Hagerty, *Consequences of Nuclear Proliferation*, pp. 81–5.

[65] Jerrold F. Elkin and W. Andrew Ritezel, 'The Indo-Pakistani Military Balance', *Asian Survey*, vol. 26, no. 5 (May 1986), pp. 518–9, 522, 529.

[66] Chari, 'Nuclear Crisis', p. 14.

[67] Perkovich, *India's Nuclear Bomb*, p. 259.

[68] Spector, *Going Nuclear*, p. 81; Perkovich, *India's Nuclear Bomb*, pp. 276–7.

[69] Perkovich, *India's Nuclear Bomb*, p. 277.

[70] Joseph Cirincione, *Deadly Arsenals: Tracking Weapons of Mass Destruction* (Washington, DC: Carnegie Endowment for International Peace, 2002), p. 211.

4

Threat Perceptions,
Military Modernization, and a Crisis

In this chapter, we will explore the reasons why the crisis that ensued from India's largest peacetime military exercise, Brasstacks, did not culminate in war. Once again three critical and possible explanations will be explored. First, we will examine if India lacked the requisite conventional capabilities to carry out a full-scale invasion of Pakistan. Second, we will test the proposition that both India and Pakistan were inhibited from proceeding towards war, thanks to timely American intervention. Third, we will examine the argument that both sides refrained from full-scale conflict owing to the incipient nuclearization of the region. The third explanation suggests that despite considerable provocation from Pakistan that contributed to the dissuasive military exercise, the fear of escalation to the nuclear level inhibited Indian decision-makers from actually embarking on a preventive war.

Background to the Crisis

As mentioned in the preceding chapter, on 30 October 1984 two of Prime Minister Indira Gandhi's Sikh bodyguards, who were distressed with the Indian Army's attack on their sacred shrine, the Golden Temple, assassinated her. In the aftermath of her assassination, the Congress Party found itself in considerable disarray. During her last decade in office, she had contributed significantly to the decline of the party's organizational and institutional structures.[1] In a bid for the sympathy of much of India's populace, the party chose to appoint Rajiv Gandhi, her son, for the post of Prime Minister. Until the death of his brother in a plane crash two years earlier, Rajiv Gandhi, a pilot with India's state-owned domestic airline, had shown scant interest in politics. Thus he entered political office with neither substantial political experience nor acumen. Nevertheless, the Congress stalwarts who put him in office had made an astute calculation: in the national elections that followed Congress won handsomely.

The new regime seemed eager to expand the scope of incipient economic reforms that had been undertaken in the last days of Indira Gandhi. However, it did not immediately seek to chart a fundamentally new course in the conduct of India's foreign and security policies. India's foreign policy elite continued to adhere to the long-held verities of non-alignment, the significance of the North–South dialogue, and the maintenance of a robust arms transfer relationship with the Soviet Union. Pakistan and China remained India's two principal security concerns. Rajiv Gandhi did, however, seek to bring about some incremental reforms in India's political economy, moving the country away from its hidebound, state-led developmental strategy to a more market-oriented economy.

Apart from the changes in that arena, the only other area that saw an important departure from the past was that of military modernization. Several factors explain this renewed emphasis on military modernization. At one level, there was an increased perception of threat from Pakistan. Thanks to Pakistan's growing military ties with the US, the conventional military balance between the two countries had started to change. The Soviet invasion and occupation of Afghanistan had led to a fundamental transformation of the US–Pakistan relationship.[2] The military regime of General Zia-ul-Haq had been ostracized during much of the Carter administration due to its poor human rights record, its pursuit of nuclear weapons, and its toppling of an elected government. However, in the aftermath of the Soviet invasion, the Carter administration had set aside these reservations and had courted Pakistan in order to prosecute a covert war against the Soviets in Afghanistan. The Reagan administration had embarked on a far more expansive effort and as early as 1981 had granted Pakistan a five-year arms and economic assistance package totalling

$3.2 billion. Included in this package was the much-coveted F-16 aircraft which would give the PAF a qualitative edge over India's Soviet-supplied MiGs. In 1986, as this package came to a close, the US renewed its assistance to Pakistan over India's objections and granted it another $4.02 billion over the next six years.

Given Pakistan's significant military modernization, the Indian security policy community perceived an increased threat from Pakistan. Apart from this structural change in the region's security architecture, other more contingent factors also contributed to India's move towards military modernization. The Soviet Union, keen on ensuring India's public quiescence on its occupation of Afghanistan, was eager to provide India with substantial amounts of military hardware.[3]

Finally, Prime Minister Rajiv Gandhi and his Minister of State for Defence, Arun Singh, were both personally interested in military modernization. Gandhi's interest in military modernization stemmed in large part from his own experience as an airline pilot, which had instilled in him a fascination for modern technology. Consequently, his interest in military modernization was closely related to his overall interest in technological progress. In his quest, he found support from his public school friend, Arun Singh. Singh, like Rajiv, was a recent entrant into the hurly-burly world of Indian politics. He had spent his early career as an advertising executive and had joined the government only at the behest of his high-school friend.

Gandhi and Singh, in turn, found an ideal counterpart in their quest for military modernization in General Krishnaswami Sundarji, the bright, charismatic and brash Chief of Staff of the Indian Army. Sundarji, who had studied at the US Army Command and Staff College at Fort Leavenworth, was also interested in introducing greater mobility and manoeuvrability into the Indian Army's armoured formations. Additionally, he wanted to upgrade the army's command, control, communications, and intelligence capabilities. Harnessing India's incipient but growing capabilities in software and electronics would enable the military to accomplish the latter goal.

Apart from his interest in and fascination with military transformation, Sundarji had also devoted some thought and attention to questions of the interaction of conventional and nuclear forces in battlefield conditions.[4] Finally, he had internalized the essential components of deterrence, a strategy that he had dubbed as one of 'dissuasion'. This strategy, pared to the bone, replicated the standard expectations of Western deterrence theory. Sundarji contended that a strategy of 'dissuasion' required clear communication of a threat, making the threat credible, and possessing the requisite military capabilities to carry out the threat.[5]

It was also during this period that the Sikh insurgency in Punjab was reaching its apogee. The origins of the insurgency can be traced to a series of factors including the transformation of the socio-economic landscape of Punjab as a consequence of the dramatic 'Green Revolution' in agriculture, the rise of a Sikh revivalist movement, and the exigencies and shortcomings of Indian federalism especially under the previous Prime Minister, Indira Gandhi.[6] While the origins of the insurgency were indigenous, material assistance from Pakistan as well as the provision of sanctuaries within Pakistan provided the insurgents with considerable sustenance. Pakistan, of course, formally denied any involvement whatsoever in supporting the insurgents.

In attempts to suppress the insurgency, India's internal security community had resorted to its tried-and-true counter-insurgency strategy. This involved the dramatic use of force against the insurgents while simultaneously holding out the promise of elections as long as the insurgents expressed a willingness to eschew violence, and to uphold India's territorial integrity. Despite faith in the long-term success of this strategy, India's internal security personnel had a heightened sense of concern about the Punjab insurgency. Unlike the insurgencies in the northeast, the insurgency in the Punjab was a festering sore in the heartland of the Indian body politic. More to the point, the state of Punjab abutted India's most intransigent, near-term adversary: Pakistan.

Getting Down to Brasstacks

There is little question that the military dimension of the Brasstacks exercise was the brainchild of General Sundarji.[7] The precise political goals of this exercise still remain somewhat murky and controversial. Some observers argue that Sundarji was not only interested in testing the robustness of his general proposition about India's 'dissuassive' capabilities and the newly raised army formations, but was also keen on provoking a war with Pakistan designed to demolish its incipient nuclear capabilities.[8] This claim must necessarily be viewed as highly controversial. Sundarji's virtual counterpart in Pakistan, General Khalid Mohammed Arif, makes no mention in his memoirs of a perceived conventional threat to Pakistan's nuclear capabilities from India in 1987. More to the point, there is no discussion of the Brasstacks Exercise in the entire volume. He does, however, discuss at some length the putative Indian plans to attack the Kahuta reactor in 1984.[9]

There is little question, however, that one of the principal goals of the exercise was to send an unequivocal political and strategic message to Pakistani decision-makers about India's robust military capabilities and its willingness to use them as the occasion demanded. Though no clear-cut evidence exists in the public domain, it can be inferred that the exercise was designed to send a message to General Zia that, despite India's troubles in the insurgency-wracked state of Punjab, it still possessed sufficient military capabilities and the requisite political resolve to impose significant military costs on Pakistan. Conveying this message was extremely important from the standpoint of India's decision-makers given Pakistan's feckless support of the Sikh insurgents.[10] Indeed, the political scenario that Sundarji had envisaged for this exercise involved the Indian Army's ability to cope with an insurgency in Kashmir and a Pakistani thrust into Indian territory in the Punjab to aid the Sikh insurgents. Though Sundarji's strategy was one of dissuasion the Brasstacks exercise had elements of compellence. It was in considerable measure designed to make Pakistan desist from what it been doing—supporting the Sikh insurgents in the Punjab.[11]

The controversy surrounding the precise political and strategic goals of the exercise cannot be fully settled here. Recently, for example, some insinuations have been made that General Sundarji sought to precipitate a war with Pakistan without the full knowledge of either Rajiv Gandhi or Arun Singh.[12] These allegations cannot be corroborated.

From a strictly military standpoint, the Brasstacks exercise had four key components.[13] The first was simply a map exercise held in May–June 1986. A sand model and computer simulation followed up this exercise and was held in November 1986. The third segment envisaged a set of complex exercises in November–December 1986 involving at least two of the three armed services. The fourth and final segment was scheduled for February–March 1987. The size of the exercise was ambitious. It drew on two armoured divisions, one mechanized division, and six infantry divisions. Two of these infantry divisions had been converted into the Reorganized Army Plains Infantry Division (RAPID) for the purposes of this exercise. These units were configured to hold areas defensively while simultaneously possessing sufficient capabilities to carry out counter-offensive operations.[14]

The military goals of this exercise were equally substantial. It was designed to test the viability of the RAPID forces; to evaluate the working of Plan AREN, an indigenously designed communications grid; to test a new command, control, communications, and intelligence system; and to assess the quality of officers and men in simulated battlefield conditions. Finally, the IAF was also expected to play an air support role in this exercise.[15]

Considerable secrecy surrounded the exercise. The Pakistanis, based upon their own intelligence assessments, had some sense of the size, scope, and dimensions of the exercise. The sheer scale of the exercise and its east–west axis caused some alarm in Islamabad. Accordingly, the newly appointed Pakistani Prime Minister, Mohammed Khan Junejo, sought to ascertain some details about the exercise from Rajiv Gandhi in November 1986 at the South Asian Association for Regional Cooperation (SAARC) meeting in Bangalore, India. Rajiv Gandhi, without providing any significant details, suggested to his counterpart that the exercise had been scaled down. Gandhi's parsimonious answers obviously did little to assuage Pakistani misgivings. Not surprisingly, they took appropriate steps to address what they perceived was a potential military threat from India.

The Crisis Unfolds

As the field elements of the military exercise got underway in late November and early December 1986, Pakistani forces were in the midst of holding their annual military manoeuvres in the Bawahalpur–Marot area near the Indian border states of Rajasthan and Punjab. The Pakistani military exercises had two distinct components. The first, code-named Saf-e-Shikan, was confined to the Bawahalpur area. This involved the First Armoured Division and the 37th Infantry Division of Pakistan's Army Reserve South. The second was Exercise Flying Horse, which took place in the Jhelum–Chenab River corridor involving the 6th and 17th Divisions of Army Reserve North.[16]

Indian misgivings about Pakistani intentions were aroused when Army Reserve South finished its winter exercises but remained in combat-ready mode in the Bawahalpur area. Additionally, Saf-e-Shikan was renamed Sledgehammer and Army Reserve North was moved to the Gujranwala region in the Ravi–Chenab corridor. Matters worsened in late December when Army Reserve South moved from its Bawahalpur exercise area north across the Sutlej River to the Okara area near Fazlika in India. Shortly thereafter, Army Reserve South crossed the Lodhran bridge across the Sutlej before moving closer to the Punjab border across from Bhatinda and Firozpur. The two military formations in concert were now in a position to carry out a pincer movement that could cut off Amritsar and Firozpur, thereby denying India access to the state of Jammu and Kashmir. Additionally, the PAF kept its satellite bases on a state of high alert even after their own military exercise, Highmark, had been completed.[17]

These moves coincided with some Indian intelligence reports that suggested that Pakistani authorities were considering a military manoeuvre in concert with Sikh secessionists. The secessionists, it was reported, would declare an independent state of Khalistan; Pakistan would recognize this state and simultaneously launch a thrust into the Punjab relying on Army Reserve North and South.[18] The Indian intelligence apparatus had suspected that these moves were underway, but could not provide clear-cut evidence thereof. This uncertainty about the precise location of the deployments of key Pakistani armoured and infantry formations caused much alarm in New Delhi, and even led Prime Minister Rajiv Gandhi to lose a degree of faith in both General Sundarji and the Minister of State for Defence, his long-standing friend, Arun Singh. It was also at about this time that Rajiv Gandhi, in a pique, insulted the popular and able Foreign Secretary, A.P. Venkateshwaran, at a press conference. Even before he could be removed from office, Venkateshwaran resigned. Rajiv's decision to fire Venkateshwaran in the midst of a crisis was typical of his idiosyncratic decision-making style and evinced his political naivete.

At any event, the location of the seemingly missing formations was eventually confirmed in mid-January in 1987. At this point, General Sundarji sought and received permission from Gandhi to bolster Indian forward military deployments to counter a potential Pakistani thrust into the Punjab. Pakistani decision-makers, however, construed these Indian military moves as a possible prelude to an attack on Pakistan.[19]

At this stage, both sides started to fear the onset of a spiral of hostility that could easily culminate in war. In an attempt to convey its growing concerns about an escalatory spiral, senior officials in the Indian Ministry of External Affairs summoned the Pakistani High Commissioner, Humayun Khan, and expressed their misgivings about the recent Pakistani troop and armour deployments. Simultaneously, they alerted the diplomatic representatives of the US and the Soviet Union about their reservations about the Pakistani military deployments across the border from the Punjab. The American ambassador in New Delhi, John Gunther Dean, suggested to his Indian interlocutors that there was a real danger of misperception, and that both sides should resume discussions using the existing hotline. No available evidence exists that the US shared intelligence with either side on troop deployments or movements during this crisis.

On 23 January, the Pakistanis via the Indian high commissioner in Islamabad and through the director-general of military operations proposed talks with India. On 24 January, India agreed to hold talks with Pakistan and conveyed a message that it was not interested in attacking its neighbour.

The de-escalation of the crisis took place fairly quickly. On 27 January, Pakistan Prime Minister Junejo called up Rajiv Gandhi and expressed an interest in reducing the ongoing border tensions. Gandhi promptly extended an invitation to his Pakistani counterpart for the onset of high-level talks. Accordingly, Abdus Sattar, the Pakistani Foreign Secretary, arrived in New Delhi on 30 January and held discussions with the Ministry of External Affairs over the next five days. Early in the next month, between 11 and 19 February, the first phase of the withdrawal was complete. Despite some difficulties in the second round of talks, held between 27 February and 7 March, the two sides did agree to a series of confidence-building measures (CBMs) designed to limit the possibilities of renewed conflict through processes of miscalculation and inadvertence. Most importantly, they pledged not to attack each other, to exercise the greatest restraint, and to avoid any actions along the border that could be deemed to be provocative. [20]

A Possible Nuclear Dimension?

Was there a nuclear dimension to this crisis? Some analysts have argued that there is little question that this crisis had a distinct nuclear dimension.[21] This assertion stems from an interview that Abdul Qadir Khan, one of the principal figures associated with the development of the Pakistani nuclear weapons programme, gave to Kuldip Nayar, a veteran Indian journalist, on 28 January. In this interview, Khan reportedly asserted that Pakistan had enriched uranium to weapons grade and possessed the requisite technical capabilities to test a nuclear weapon with laboratory simulations.

It is far from clear that the Pakistani politico-military elite intended Khan's interview with Nayar to be a form of nuclear signalling. It needs to be underscored that even if this was the intended goal of the interview (which was not published until 1 March in London), it was poorly timed. The crisis was mostly over when the interview took place, and key Indian and Pakistani decision-makers were already engaged in discussions pertaining to the logistical intricacies of troop disengagement. Consequently, while the Indian security establishment would have to take cognizance of Pakistan's growing nuclear capabilities in all future crises, it is hard to see how Khan's assertions affected the outcome of this one.[22] It is, nevertheless, reasonable to infer that Khan's interview was designed to send a warning to India that Pakistan was on the way to acquiring a nuclear option, and that the flexing of India's conventional military capabilities would not so easily cow it in the future.[23]

Seeking Explanations

A confluence of factors, stemming from regional politics, institutional decay, and the presence of particular personalities generated this crisis. At one level, any regime in India would have been compelled to respond militarily to Pakistan's ongoing support to the Sikh insurgents. However, the extraordinary leeway that General Sundarji possessed in planning and executing Brasstacks suggests that there was inadequate civilian oversight of the military. A naïve, inexperienced prime minister easily allowed an ambitious general to pursue a politico-military strategy fraught with considerable risk. More to the point, institutional mechanisms, such as the Cabinet Committee on Security, failed to function as an oversight body to carefully assess and evaluate the risks inherent in Sundarji's military manoeuvre. In the absence of careful, routinized institutional oversight, Sundarji with Arun Singh proceeded with impunity on a military exercise of mammoth proportions and with significant strategic risks. It is also clear from our analysis that they failed to adequately anticipate the possible escalatory potential inherent in this extremely fraught enterprise. When Pakistani military planners responded with alacrity to the Indian military exercise and resorted to dramatic troop movements, their Indian counterparts rapidly came to the realization that the calibrated application of military pressure short of war was highly risky even in a proto-nuclear milieu.

Why did war not ensue from this crisis? India certainly had political grounds to precipitate a war because of Pakistan's obvious involvement in the Sikh insurgency. If India did not lack the motivation to start a war, what then inhibited India from carrying through on possible war plans? One possible argument is that it lacked adequate conventional capabilities to inflict significant costs on Pakistan in the event of a war. Was this indeed the case? The evidence suggests that India may not have had the conventional capability to carry out significant military operations with impunity against Pakistan. It is true that the overall military balance was in India's favour. India had an eight-brigade manoeuvre advantage and had six regular divisions in reserve, while Pakistan had none. The forces along the border were almost evenly matched.[24] These crude force comparisons, however, are not entirely meaningful. Pakistan at this time was a major recipient of American military assistance, thanks to its support of American strategic goals in Afghanistan. Consequently, Pakistan possessed some qualitative advantages in terms of newly acquired aircraft, military communications and radar equipment.[25] Moreover, at any given time, India deploys as many as ten divisions along its Himalayan border with China. Given that it had had some border skirmishes with China in 1986, it could hardly afford to draw down its forces from the Himalayan frontier.[26] Consequently, India would have been hard pressed to muster the requisite conventional forces to launch a major military operation against Pakistan.

It is, nevertheless, important to underscore that it might have had the necessary capabilities to carry out a 'limited aims' strategy.[27] Such a strategy would have involved seizing some portions of Pakistani territory in a short, sharp war and then bargaining for concessions elsewhere, possibly in Kashmir. Pakistan, of course, had little incentive to start a war with India at a time when it faced a significant Soviet threat on its western border with Afghanistan.

Did the US, through its good offices, successfully stave off war? The evidence does not suggest that the US played a very significant role in this crisis. Its primary role seems to have been providing reassurance to both parties to dampen the development of a conflict spiral based upon incomplete information, misperception, and mutual distrust.[28] In marked contrast to the past, when Indian policy-makers routinely distrusted American assessments of Pakistani motivations, on this occasion the Indian policy-making establishment did accept American statements about Pakistani intentions as reliable and trustworthy. At best, the American role was salutary and it certainly did no harm. In the wake of the crisis, the US also managed to persuade India and Pakistan to adopt a set of confidence- and security-building measures. These, however, would soon fray in the aftermath of the indigenous Kashmir uprising of 1989.[29] Pakistan, sensing an opportunity to exploit India's self-inflicted wound, swiftly moved to exploit the outbreak of the insurgency. Pakistan's extensive involvement in the Kashmir insurgency directly contributed to the next crisis in Indo-Pakistani relations in 1990.

One of the central goals of Exercise Brasstacks, an end to Pakistani support to the Sikh insurgents, however, remained unfulfilled. The compellent element of Brasstacks failed as Indian decision-makers developed deep misgivings about the dangers of escalation to a wider and more protracted conflict. In the end, the insurgency was brought to a close through India's ruthless suppression of the insurgents and the promise of electoral rewards to Sikh moderates. As the insurgency in Punjab waned, Pakistan turned its attention to Kashmir where disaffection with Indian misrule was steadily growing.

Finally, what role, if any, did nuclear weapons play in the resolution of this crisis? As argued earlier, a number of analysts have asserted that there was a nuclear dimension to this crisis. Our evidence and analysis suggests otherwise. The crisis, as we have shown, was mostly over when the much-heralded interview and its implicit nuclear threat came to light. The only case that can be made for the role that nuclear weapons may have played in limiting the resort to war is purely inferential. Indian policy-makers, civilian and military alike, may simply have assumed that Pakistan possessed some incipient nuclear capabilities and that it was perhaps unwise to militarily threaten Pakistan beyond a point. Such an argument may not be entirely chimerical. At least one thoughtful analyst had previously argued that India and Pakistan were already nuclear-armed rivals in South Asia.[30] On the other hand, it is entirely likely that the crisis precipitated a Pakistani move to hasten its nuclear weapons programme and to start overt nuclear signalling in future crises. We will discuss the emergence and evolution of this process in considerable detail in the following chapter on the 1990 crisis.

Notes

[1] For an account of her contribution to the decline of the Congress Party and other political institutions in India, see Paul Brass, *The Politics of India Since Independence* (Cambridge: Cambridge University Press, 1994).

[2] For a discussion, see Dennis Kux, *The United States and Pakistan, 1947–2000, Disenchanted Allies* (Washington, DC: Woodrow Wilson Center Press, 2002).

[3] On this point, see Robert Horn, *Soviet-Indian Relations: Issues and Influence* (New York: Praeger, 1982).

[4] See Lieutenant General Krishnaswami Sundarji (ed.), 'Effects of Nuclear Asymmetry on Conventional Deterrence', *Combat Papers* no. 1(May 1981), College of Combat, Mhow, India.

[5] Sumit Ganguly, 'Getting Down to Brass Tacks,' *The World and I,* May 1987, pp. 100–4.

[6] For a popular but accurate account of the Sikh insurgency, see Mark Tully and Satish Jacob, *Amritsar: Indira Gandhi's Last Battle* (London: Jonathan Cape, 1985); for more scholarly accounts see Hamish Telford, 'The Political Economy of Punjab: Creating Space for the Sikh Insurgency', *Asian Survey,* vol. 32, no. 11 (November 1992), pp. 969–87; also see Paul Wallace in Martha Crenshaw (ed.), *Terrorism in Context* (College Park: Pennsylvania State University Press,1995); and Sarabjit Singh, *Operation Black Thunder: An Eyewitness Account of Terrorism in Punjab* (New Delhi: Sage Publications, 2002).

[7] For an extended discussion of the origins of Exercise Brasstacks, see Kanti Bajpai, P.R. Chari, Pervaiz Iqbal Cheema, Stephen P. Cohen and Sumit Ganguly *Brasstacks and Beyond: Perception and the Management of Crisis in South Asia* (New Delhi: Manohar, 1995).

[8] On this matter, see Raj Chengappa, *Weapons of Peace: The Secret Story of India's Quest to be a Nuclear Power* (New Delhi: Harper Collins, 2000).

[9] General Khaled Mohammed Arif, *Working With Zia: Pakistan's Power Politics, 1977–1988* (Karachi: Oxford University Press, 1999).

[10] On Indian concerns, see J.N. Dixit, *Anatomy of a Flawed Inheritance: Indo-Pak Relations 1970–1994* (New Delhi: Konark, 1995).

[11] For the distinction between the concepts of 'deterrence' and 'compellence', see Thomas Schelling, *Arms and Influence* (New Haven: Yale University Press, 1966); also see Robert J. Art and Patrick M. Cronin (eds), *The United States and Coercive Diplomacy* (Washington, DC: United States Institute of Peace, 2003).

[12] The principal source of these allegations comes from the memoirs of Lieutenant-General P.N. Hoon. See P.N. Hoon, *Unmasking Secrets of Turbulence: Midnight Freedom to a Nuclear Dawn* (New Delhi: Manas Publications, 2000). Hoon had been Deputy Chief of Staff under General Sundarji.

[13] Bajpai *et al.*, *Brasstacks and Beyond*, p. 28.

[14] Devin T. Hagerty, *The Consequences of Nuclear Proliferation: Lessons from South Asia* (Cambridge: MIT Press, 1998), p. 97.

[15] P.R. Chari, *Indo-Pak Nuclear Standoff: The Role of the United States* (New Delhi: Manohar Books, 1995), p. 129.

[16] Hagerty, *Consequences of Nuclear Proliferation*, p. 99.

[17] Bajpai *et al.*, *Brasstacks and Beyond*, p. 58.

[18] Much of the following paragraphs have been derived from Hagerty, *Consequences of Nuclear Proliferation*.

[19] Bajpai *et al.*, *Brasstacks and Beyond.*

[20] Sumit Ganguly and Ted Greenwood (eds), *Mending Fences: Confidence and Security-Building Measures in South Asia* (Boulder: Westview Press, 1996).

[21] See the seminal article on the subject, Seymour Hersh, 'On the Nuclear Edge', the *New Yorker*, 29 March 1993. Also see William E. Burrows and Robert Windrem, *Critical Mass: The Dangerous Race for Superweapons in a Fragmenting World* (New York: Simon and Schuster, 1994).

[22] On this subject, see Ashley J. Tellis, *India's Emerging Nuclear Posture: Between Recessed Deterrent and Ready Arsenal* (Santa Monica: RAND, 2001).

[23] Apart from Khan's interview, there are some claims that Pakistan may have delivered a nuclear threat to India during the midst of the crisis. The evidence on this is tenuous. The only assertion of this can be found in the Government of India's Kargil Committee Report. In an otherwise excellent analysis of Pakistani contemporary Pakistani politics and Pakistan's relations with India, a prominent British journalist argues that this threat, in all likelihood, limited the prospects of conventional conflict in 1987. See Owen Bennett Jones, *Pakistan: Eye of the Storm* (New Haven: Yale University Press, 2002), p. 214.

[24] Bajpai *et al.*, *Brasstacks and Beyond*, p. 80.

[25] For a thoughtful comparison of Indian and Pakistani capabilities, see Jerrold F. Elkin and W. Andrew Ritezel, 'The Indo-Pakistani Military Balance', *Asian Survey*, vol. 26, no. 5 (May 1986), pp. 518–38. The authors argue that despite Pakistani military modernization, India still had a substantial *conventional military* advantage over Pakistan in 1986.

[26] On the border skirmishes with China, see John Garver, *Protracted Contest: Sino-Indiana Rivalry in the Twentieth Century* (Seattle: University of Washington Press, 2000).

[27] For a succinct discussion of the 'limited aims' strategy, see John Mearsheimer, *Conventional Deterrence* (Ithaca: Cornell University Press, 1983).

[28] On the role of reassurance in international relations, see Sir Michael Howard, 'Deterrence and Reassurance: Western Defense in the 1980s', *Foreign Affairs*, vol. 61, no. 2 (Winter, 1982–83).

[29] On the origins of the Kashmir insurgency, see Sumit Ganguly, *The Crisis in Kashmir: Portents of War, Hopes of Peace* (Cambridge: Cambridge University Press, and Washington, DC: Woodrow Wilson Center Press, 1997).

[30] On this matter, see Onkar Marwah, 'India and Pakistan: Nuclear Rivals in South Asia', in George Quester (ed.), *Proliferation: Breaking the Chain* (Madison: University of Wisconsin Press, 1981).

5

The 1990 Kashmir Crisis[1]

In the winter and spring of 1990, India and Pakistan became embroiled in the third crisis of South Asia's nuclear era—and the first to grow directly out of the long-standing Kashmir dispute. The 1990 Kashmir imbroglio was a 'bridging' crisis in two senses. Viewed chronologically, during the crises of 1984 and 1986–7, India and Pakistan were essentially pre-nuclear weapon states and perceived each other that way; during subsequent crises—in 1998, 1999, and 2001–2—the two sides were established nuclear weapon states and perceived each other that way. The 1990 crisis was thus the bridge between these pre-nuclear and nuclear eras in South Asian history. Substantively, 1990 marked the moment in time when the region's two most troublesome security issues—Kashmir and nuclear weapons—were inextricably and irretrievably bound together. As the 1990 crisis unfolded, some decision-makers in India, Pakistan, and the US considered the two South Asian adversaries to be capable of deploying and using nuclear weapons on very short notice. Others discounted that possibility, believing that while both countries were capable of assembling nuclear weapons, neither had the ability to deliver them with any precision or reliability.[2] The 1990 crisis was not a nuclear crisis *per se*; rather, it was a political crisis between two hostile neighbours who had already fought three wars and who were secretly developing nuclear weapons.

Analysts continue to disagree over several fundamental issues: the nature and seriousness of the 1990 Kashmir crisis; whether New Delhi and Islamabad came close to a conventional war; why the crisis ended peacefully; what the role of the US was; and the influence of nascent nuclear weapon capabilities on Indian and Pakistani behaviour. These issues will be analysed below, but it will suffice at the outset to say that there was a significant possibility of war between India and Pakistan in 1990, and that no decision-maker in New Delhi, Islamabad, or Washington could entirely rule out the possibility that such a war might escalate to a nuclear exchange.

The remainder of this chapter unfolds in the following way. The second section is an overview of the global, regional, and domestic political context for the 1990 crisis. Section three describes the re-emergence of political violence in Kashmir during the late 1980s, which provided the immediate spark for the crisis. The fourth section covers the evolution of the uprising in Kashmir from a primarily domestic insurgency to an international crisis between India and Pakistan. Section five traces the contours of the crisis itself, focusing in particular on Indian and Pakistani military movements and the war of words between the two countries' leaderships. The sixth section is a snapshot of the conventional military equation at the height of the crisis in April 1990. Section seven describes the rising level of concern in Washington and the May mission to South Asia by Deputy National Security Advisor Robert M. Gates. The eighth section analyses the nuclear dimensions of the 1990 crisis. Section nine evaluates why the crisis ended peacefully and concludes that, while the Gates mission was a secondary factor in the outcome, the nascent Indian and Pakistani nuclear weapon capabilities were the main deterrent to war.

The Global, Regional, and Domestic Context

At the global level, the rapidly ending Cold War had serious repercussions for India and Pakistan as the 1990s began. The Soviet withdrawal from Afghanistan had taken away the rationale for the US-Pakistani strategic partnership, allowing submerged policy differences to resurface. The most important of these was Islamabad's continued development of nuclear weapons, which replaced the Afghanistan war effort as the foremost issue for US policy-makers concerned with Pakistan. India's relationship with the Soviet Union also suffered. As bipolarity faded and Moscow's attention turned inward, New Delhi lost its value as a bulwark of pro-Soviet sentiment in the Third World. Moreover, after Gorbachev's reforms plunged the Soviet economy into depression, the Kremlin was forced to alter the generous terms under which it had pursued its economic and military ties with allies. India's trade with the Soviet Union, previously conducted in rupees, was put on a more conventional commercial footing, and the terms of Soviet military sales also grew less attractive. In sum, as the new decade began, both New Delhi and Islamabad were losing their moorings in the international system.

Regionally, the turn of the decade saw the re-emergence of discontent in Kashmir, which quickly sent Indo-Pakistani relations into a another tailspin. In the late 1980s, agitation against the central government in New Delhi had grown among Kashmiri Muslims. By 1989, militants in the Vale of Kashmir were in rebellion, heralding a secessionist insurgency that continues today. The escalating sub-conventional war between Indian security forces and the Kashmiri insurgents, who were increasingly supported by Pakistan, radically and indefinitely worsened Indo-Pakistani relations. Adding to these global and regional instabilities, Indian and Pakistani domestic politics were equally volatile. After the restoration of democracy in Pakistan and Benazir Bhutto's election as prime minister in 1988, Pakistan was effectively ruled by a troika of leaders: President Ghulam Ishaq Khan, Army Chief General Mirza Aslam Beg, and the inexperienced Bhutto. While Ghulam Ishaq and Beg allowed the charismatic prime minister to represent Pakistan on the world stage, they dominated her when it came to vital national security issues like Kashmir and nuclear weapons. In India, although Prime Minister V.P. Singh's victory over Rajiv Gandhi in 1989 marked only the second time since independence that the Congress Party had been ousted from national office, Singh's position was equally tenuous. His government was a fragile coalition, forced to depend on the newly powerful, rightist Bharatiya Janata Party (the 'Indian People's Party', known as the BJP) for its survival.[3]

The interaction of these global, regional, and domestic developments made the subcontinent extremely unstable in early 1990. The Kashmir conflict re-ignited just as India and Pakistan were losing the support of their erstwhile Cold War patrons. The two countries' prime ministers were weak leaders, as evidenced by the fact that both were out of office by the end of the year. Taken together, this combustible mix had long-lasting effects on South Asia's domestic and international politics. Prior to the 1990 crisis, Indo-Pakistani relations were tense but manageable; after the crisis, New Delhi and Islamabad found themselves in a seemingly endless state of mutual hostility.

The Re-Emergence of Political Violence in Kashmir[4]

After the Simla Agreement, discussed in Chapter Two, the Indo-Pakistani dispute over Kashmir was dormant, although both sides continued to press their claims to the territory. New Delhi maintained that Kashmir was an integral part of the Indian union, its status as such legitimized both by its incorporation into the Indian constitution and decades of democratic Kashmiri political activity within the Indian federation. Islamabad disagreed: sovereignty over Kashmir remained contested, its status unresolved according to either the operative UN formula or the more direct Indo-Pakistani talks envisioned by the Simla signatories. Indeed, divergent interpretations of the Simla Agreement itself had become one more area of discord. For New Delhi, Simla had fundamentally supplanted the UN resolutions as a means of resolving the Kashmir dispute. After all, Indian leaders reasoned, the two parties had pledged to negotiate directly with one another, implicitly abandoning extra-regional diplomacy. Islamabad countered that Simla supplemented, but did not replace, the UN formulation. From this perspective, while Simla pledged Pakistan not to alter the territorial status quo unilaterally, it did not rule out the possibility of external mediation should India and Pakistan agree to seek it.[5]

In the 1980s, the decline of India's 'Congress Party system' had disastrous consequences for Kashmir.[6] State assembly elections were held in 1983, prior to which Indian Prime Minister Indira Gandhi offered to form an electoral alliance with Farooq Abdullah and his National Conference party. He refused, and the ensuing campaign was marked by violence. The National Conference won a convincing victory by sweeping the heavily Muslim Vale of Kashmir, while the Congress fared well in predominantly Hindu Jammu. After the election, the Congress worked furiously to destabilize the National Conference government, going as far as to brand Farooq pro-Pakistani and anti-Indian. In July 1984, Congress succeeded in ousting Farooq as Kashmir's chief minister by inducing the defection of a bloc of his loyalists in the state assembly. This bloodless coup ignited a cycle of political degeneration that would increasingly alienate young Kashmiri Muslims from the Indian state.

In anticipation of new state elections in 1987, Indian Prime Minister Rajiv Gandhi insisted that the National Conference join the Congress in an electoral alliance and subsequent governing coalition. Farooq accepted this time and was elected chief minister once again. The 1987 elections were demonstrably rigged,[7] and the new government proved to be corrupt and inefficient. Adding to the disgruntlement caused by the venality of 1984 and 1987, many well-educated Muslim youths who had been denied their voice in Kashmiri politics were also unable to find decent jobs.[8] By 1988, political estrangement blended with economic angst to produce a critical mass of alienated Kashmiri Muslims. Anti-government agitation erupted in the form of sporadic violence and organized strikes. Militants set off bombs in Srinagar, and security forces, judges, and other government officials became murder targets. As *India Today* editorialized in September 1989: 'Today, thanks to rampant nepotism, corruption and notorious maladministration Farooq's compact with his people seems to have broken. He has lost his trust with them. Some of them have turned to guns and others, who initially blamed only Farooq's government for their woes, now increasingly blame New Delhi.'[9]

From Domestic Insurgency to International Crisis

Robert Oakley, the US ambassador to Pakistan during the crisis, remembers that prior to 1990, Kashmir was not a major irritant in India–Pakistan relations: 'Kashmir was so calm it was not discussed... there was a series of meetings during 1989 between the two prime ministers and the defense ministers and the foreign ministers and the foreign secretaries—no one raised Kashmir. Punjab always; but Kashmir, no.'[10] This situation changed dramatically in early 1990, when the Vale of

Kashmir descended into virtual anarchy. New Delhi accused Pakistan of waging a sub-conventional war against India by financing, arming, and training Kashmiri Muslim 'terrorists'. Islamabad responded that it provided only diplomatic and moral support to the Kashmiri 'freedom fighters', but eschewed military or other material assistance. Pakistani leaders further charged that the insurgency was produced by decades of Indian abuses in Kashmir, not by Pakistani meddling. Most contemporaneous commentators agreed that the deepest roots of the insurgency could be found in India's domestic affairs; Pakistani support for the militants was typically viewed as an important, but secondary factor.[11]

V.P. Singh was elected as Prime Minister in December 1989, after pledging in his campaign against the Congress to solve the myriad ethnic disputes that had scarred the Indian body politic in the 1980s. His message was one of national healing in the wake of Hindu–Muslim communalism, caste conflicts, and sustained political–military competition between New Delhi and disaffected elements in practically every corner of India. Anxious to turn his words into deeds, Singh appointed, as his home minister, a Kashmiri Muslim, Mufti Mohammed Sayeed. Soon thereafter, Sayeed's daughter was kidnapped by Kashmiri militants and held hostage until the government released five imprisoned insurgents. Political kidnappings were hardly unusual, but this particular abduction seemed to illustrate dramatically the advanced state of political decay in Kashmir.

From that point until the present, Kashmir has been in a state of civil war. In January 1990, the militants undertook larger operations like ambushes of military convoys and open engagements with Indian security forces. In turn, the government resolved to fight fire with fire: New Delhi sent to Kashmir a former governor of the state, Jagmohan, known for his no-nonsense approach to militancy. Jagmohan's appointment signalled New Delhi's unambiguous resolve to pacify Kashmir with sticks rather than carrots; as he put it, 'the best way of solving the crisis is to assert the authority of the State and create an impression that, no matter what the cost, the subversionists and their collaborators will be firmly dealt with and eliminated.'[12] Farooq Abdullah resigned as chief minister, New Delhi imposed presidential rule in

Kashmir, and Jagmohan began a sustained crackdown of curfews and house-to-house searches in an attempt to imprison or kill as many insurgent leaders as possible.

By this time, the secessionist movement had begun to affect every aspect of life in the state. Local businesses had already suffered severe losses owing to the dwindling flow of tourists; now, insurgent-imposed shutdowns and government curfews brought economic activity to a virtual standstill. New Delhi flew in thousands of paramilitary soldiers to implement Jagmohan's policies.[13] On 20 January, tension between the militants and security forces exploded into what would be the first of many spasms of mass violence, with Srinagar police spraying bullets into a crowd of demonstrators. An estimated thirty-two people were killed, among a total of roughly 100 killed in the two weeks after New Delhi's imposition of direct rule over Kashmir.[14]

The events of January 1990 transformed the Kashmiri insurgency from a mainly Indian affair into renewed Indo-Pakistani conflict. Oakley remembers that the initial uprising in Kashmir was 'primarily spontaneous'. He adds, however, that 'Pakistan, willy-nilly, began to play a much more active role. Unofficially, groups such as Jamaat-i-Islami [an Islamic political party] as well as ISI [the Inter-Services Intelligence Directorate, Pakistan's main espionage organization] and the Pakistan Army began to take a more active role in support of the Kashmiri protests. Training camps of various kinds multiplied... There was much more activity. There were more people and more material going across the border from Pakistan into Kashmir.'[15] Initially, Prime Minister Bhutto tried in vain to maintain a temperate stand on the deteriorating situation. In early January, she sent a senior Pakistani diplomat, Abdus Sattar, to New Delhi for talks. According to Sattar, Kashmir was raised only briefly in his meetings with Prime Minister Singh, who told him that New Delhi was concerned about reports of Pakistani support for the insurgents in Kashmir. Sattar also recalls that he was 'taken aback' by the rising concern over Kashmir in the Indian media, which initially were more strident than the new government in their accusations of Pakistani complicity in the uprising.[16]

As the conflict intensified, Pakistan's opposition parties beseeched Bhutto to take a stronger stand in support of the militants. On 20 January, the day of the Srinagar massacre, Pakistan's ruling troika met to discuss the Kashmir situation. Bhutto later parried charges of Pakistani complicity in the insurgency by declaring that Kashmiri discontent was indigenous. Unable any longer to resist pressure from conservative elements urging a more aggressive posture, she proclaimed the Kashmiris' right to self-determination.[17] The next day, Pakistani Foreign Minister Sahibzada Yakub Khan travelled to New Delhi for talks with Indian leaders. According to India's the then ambassador to Pakistan, J.N. Dixit, one of Yakub Khan's motivations 'seemed to be to pressurise, perhaps even intimidate, India on the Jammu and Kashmir issue... He was stern and admonitory in his pronouncements... He cautioned [Indian foreign minister Inder K.] Gujral that war clouds would hover over the subcontinent if timely action was not taken.'[18] According to George Perkovich, who interviewed Gujral in 1999, India's foreign minister 'comprehended the nuclear connotations of Yakub's warning and reported immediately to Prime Minister Singh'. That night, under instructions from the Prime Minister, Gujral told Yakub not to 'mistake our kind words for weakness'.[19] Dixit, who was with the two foreign ministers during this second meeting, writes that Gujral told Yakub Khan that his 'warnings and accusatory remarks... during the course of the day were unacceptable and they had caused concern and resentment in the Government of India. Gujral said that such an attitude... would only evoke a firm and decisive response from India.'[20] Perkovich writes, 'according to Gujral, Yakub put up his hands as if to say that his bellicose threat earlier had been misinterpreted.'[21]

In early February, during deliberations in Pakistan's national assembly, opposition politicians demanded that Bhutto pursue a *jihad* (in this context, 'holy war') in Kashmir. The Jamaat-i-Islami leader urged the government to build nuclear weapons in order to meet the Indian threat.[22] Meanwhile, Indian behaviour led some observers to speculate that New Delhi was raising its nuclear profile, perhaps to send a deterrent message to Pakistan. For one newsweekly, the appointment of Raja Ramanna— a former chairman of India's Atomic Energy Commission—as minister of state for defence 'can only mean that India has decided to give higher priority to its nuclear weapons and missile-development programs'. In February, Prime Minister Singh 'said India would have to review its peaceful nuclear policy if Pakistan employed its nuclear power for military purposes'. Singh also 'told newsmen that Pakistan's going nuclear would bring about a radical change in the security environment in the region. If this were to happen, "we will have to take stock of the situation and act accordingly".' An influential nuclear trade publication interpreted Singh's actions to mean that India was quietly increasing its nuclear preparedness.[23]

Military Movements and a War of Words

By this time, conventional military preparations had begun on both sides of the border. For purposes of clarity, these activities can be grouped into three regions: Kashmir, Punjab, and the border between Rajasthan and the Pakistani provinces of Punjab and Sindh. Early in the insurgency, India supplemented its security forces in Kashmir and Punjab with reinforcements, primarily infantry, from the Indian Army. According to the then Army Chief V.N. Sharma, New Delhi's main concern in these areas was to stem the infiltration of Pakistan-backed Sikh and Kashmiri terrorists into India. As Sharma told an interviewer in 1993: 'Terrorist groups backed by agencies in Pakistan were able to attack railway stations and vital installations which could affect any military movement on our side.' The Indian Army needed to 'go in there to take care of the communication lines and other bottlenecks so that if there was a military flare-up, we could conveniently move our fighting forces from locations deep in the country to border areas.'[24]

According to Sharma, tank units of Pakistan's 2nd Corps had moved into the desert region of Bahawalpur and Bhawalnagar, astride the Indian states of Punjab and Rajasthan. In addition, he claims, parts of Pakistan's 1st Corps, including a tank division, had moved into the Shakargarh salient, just across the border from the vital road linking Jammu to Punjab. Indian military planners were concerned, too, about residual deployments of Pakistan Army forces after a late-1989 integrated air-land exercise; *Zarb-i-Momin*, the largest military exercise in Pakistan's history, had begun on 9 December in Punjab. General Beg, the Pakistan army chief, said at the time that the exercise would test a new strategy: 'In the past we were pursuing a defensive policy; now there is a big change since we are shifting to a policy of offensive defence. Should there be a war, the Pakistan Army plans to take the war into India, launching a sizeable offensive on Indian territory.'[25] *Zarb-i-Momin* was Beg's response to India's Brasstacks exercises of 1986–7, as discussed in Chapter Four. It included seven infantry divisions and one armoured division in an attempt to demonstrate Pakistan's conventional military prowess and send a firm dissuasive message to the Indian Army.[26] After the exercise was over, says Sharma, 'we found that these troops were not going back to their peace stations, but they were staying on in the exercise area, which is quite close to the international border and the cease-fire line in Jammu and Kashmir.' The Indian assessment of these movements 'was that Pakistan was keeping troops ready as a back-up support to the increased terrorist activities, in Indian territory, across the border and could take full advantage of terrorist successes to support military intervention'.[27]

Further south, according to Sharma, the Indian Army in February sent two new tank units for training at its field firing range at Mahajan, in Rajasthan. With Brasstacks fresh in their minds, Pakistani planners grew alarmed that the Indian armoured units at Mahajan were 'beginning up another large exercise of that nature, or, indeed, preparing to launch an attack from the training range'.[28] US officials relayed these concerns to the Indian defence ministry; its representatives explained their version of events and invited US officials to take a closer look at the situation on the ground. US defence attaches in New Delhi concluded that the Mahajan training activity was normal for that time of year, when the cool weather makes it comfortable to conduct manoeuvres in the desert. Moreover, Sharma told US Ambassador William Clark that the Indian Army could not launch an effective offensive from Mahajan, and Clark's embassy staff concurred.[29]

The then US air attache in New Delhi, Colonel John Sandrock, remembers that 'what was unusual from our perspective was the deployment of additional troops in Kashmir as a result of the reported crossborder infiltration from Pakistan into Kashmir and then along the border, south through the rest of Jammu and Kashmir and into [the Indian state of] Punjab.' These forces consisted of both regular Indian Army soldiers—from the 8th Mountain Division[30]—and troops from the paramilitary Border Security Force (BSF). The BSF had the 'primary responsibility for border security', while the army's role was to 'act as a back-up' in the event of 'real hostilities'. According to Sandrock, there was no evidence that the army's activities included the movement of tanks and artillery, which appeared to corroborate the Indian claim that the 'buildup of forces on the border was to prevent cross-border infiltration and did not constitute a buildup of forces preparing for any hostile action against Pakistan'. US military attaches in New Delhi took the first of several reconnaissance trips in February, confirming their impression that Indian forces were not preparing for an offensive military thrust. US attaches in Pakistan undertook similar missions on their side of the border, also finding little unusual military activity. Of special importance, one of the attaches noted later, was that the two Pakistani strike corps were not on the move, and that the Pakistan Air Force's forward operating bases had not been opened.[31]

Meanwhile, the war of words between New Delhi and Islamabad escalated another notch. On 13 March, with massive demonstrations ongoing in Srinagar, Bhutto travelled to the Pakistani side of the LoC, where she promised a 'thousand-year war' in support of the militants.[32] V.P. Singh quickly responded that India would react decisively against Pakistani intervention in Kashmir: 'I do not wish to sound hawkish,' he told the Indian parliament, 'but there should be no confusion. Such a misadventure would not be without cost.'[33] Opposition leaders exhorted the Singh government to impose that cost on Pakistan immediately. In early April, the BJP's national executive committee passed a resolution urging the Indian government to 'knock out the training camps and transit routes of the terrorists'. The BJP contended that 'Pakistan's many provocations amount to so many acts of war today. It is literally carrying on a war against India on Indian territory.' The party further argued that the doctrine of 'hot pursuit is a recognized defensive measure'.[34] Congress party leader Rajiv Gandhi went even further, practically goading the government to take 'some very strong steps on Kashmir'. The former prime minister added: 'I know what steps are possible. I also know what is in the pipeline and what the capabilities are. The question is, does the government have the guts to take strong steps?'[35]

Over the next week, V.P. Singh made a series of forthright public statements, intended both to deter any adventurism Islamabad might be contemplating and to neutralize his opposition within India. On 10 April, he warned Indians to be 'psychologically prepared' for war. 'Our message to Pakistan,' he said, 'is that you cannot get away with taking Kashmir without a war. They will have to pay a very heavy price and we have the capability to inflict heavy losses.' Pakistan's strategy, Singh charged, was to avoid direct confrontation while continuing to destabilize India by fanning the flames of violence in Kashmir. If this were successful, a limited Pakistani intervention might follow, to consolidate the insurgents' gains. Finally, as if to dispel any notion that Pakistan's nuclear weapon capabilities would give Islamabad a deterrent umbrella under which to carry out attacks against India, Singh said that if Pakistan were to deploy nuclear weapons, India would follow suit.[36]

Pakistan's leading English-language newspaper called the Indian prime minister's warning 'one of the most serious ever hurled at this country in recent years'.[37] On 11 April, General Beg convened a meeting of his corps commanders to carry out a 'detailed threat assessment'. Beg told his subordinates that India had deployed a strike force of up to 100,000 men within fifty miles of the border in Rajasthan. He was referring to the Indian Army units that had been on winter exercises in the Mahajan area, which Pakistani officials now stated had been extended. Pakistan Army sources estimated that the Indian units were deployed in such a way as to 'halve India's normal mobilisation time to one week'. In addition, Islamabad noted that New Delhi continued to move paramilitary forces into Kashmir. One reporter wrote: 'The concern in Islamabad is that India might be preparing an attack on Pakistani Kashmir on the pretext of destroying Kashmiri "freedom fighter" training camps. There is also concern that a simultaneous attack might be launched into Sindh province, where the only road and rail link between north and south Pakistan is located about 40 km from the Indian border.' On 14 April, a senior Pakistani official told a parliamentary committee that the country's military forces were on a 'high state of preparedness and vigilance to meet any external threat'. He continued: 'If, out of sheer frustration, India dragged Pakistan into military confrontation, it would find that Pakistan has the full capability of meeting the Indian invasion by mobilising all its national resources.'[38]

Indian intelligence officials confirmed that New Delhi was putting more military forces into Kashmir, but claimed that these reinforcements were a response to Pakistan's build-up on its side of the LoC. Diplomats in New Delhi said 'forces on both sides of the border were on a higher than normal state of alert, but several levels lower than would indicate imminent hostilities.'[39] Indian officials denied Beg's claim regarding the formation of an Indian strike force in Rajasthan, saying that their units had retreated to 'normal positions' after the winter exercise.[40] Western military analysts reported no major troop mobilization near the international frontier, but speculated that by extending their exercises, Indian planners may have positioned tanks and heavy artillery near the border. In the words of one such analyst, 'everything the Indians have been doing fits under the category of defensive preparedness, but some of it is ambiguous.'[41] On 14 April, the Indian prime minister explained the logic of these preparations in a discussion with journalists. According to one account, 'Singh said... that Pakistan is preparing to launch an attack across India's western border, where he asserted that Pakistan has deployed new armored regiments and sophisticated radar. Singh added that Pakistan's army and air force were on "red alert" along' the LoC, and that Pakistani artillery had been moved to forward positions across from Kashmir and Punjab. The prime minister 'said his intention was to avert war: "Many wars have been prevented by a timely warning. It is indecision and confused signals that have usually triggered a conflict".' Claiming that political jockeying among Pakistan's ruling troika made it difficult to know exactly who was in charge, Singh said: 'Had anyone been in control, it would not have been necessary for me to issue a public warning.' Still, sentiment was growing among influential Indians for strikes against Pakistan. Home Minister Sayeed, for example, argued that war 'would be fully justified if the objective of freeing Kashmir from the stranglehold of the secessionists was achieved.' BJP leader L.K. Advani took an even stronger line, warning that Pakistan would 'cease to exist' if it attacked India.[42]

The Conventional Military Equation

By mid-April 1990, the disposition of military forces near the Indo-Pakistani border and the LoC in Kashmir was as follows. In Kashmir,

India had deployed up to 200,000 troops, drawn from both the Indian Army and paramilitary soldiers. Pakistan had deployed a smaller force of at least 100,000 soldiers in the part of Kashmir under its control. The Indian and Pakistani forces were reported to be 'eyeball to eyeball' across the LoC, in some cases as close as 200 metres apart. Demonstrating the heightened tension in the disputed territory, the UN Military Observer Group in India and Pakistan reported a quadrupling of LoC violations in the January–March period of 1990, as compared to the same period in 1989.[43]

In Punjab, Indian and Pakistani infantry were reported to be in frontline bunkers, but the bulk of both countries' armour and artillery were held back in their cantonments. Across from Pakistan's Lahore sector, India had moved towards the border two infantry divisions, which were spread out into small unit formations, lending credence to New Delhi's claim that its forces in Punjab were charged with a defensive, counter-infiltration mission.[44] Complicating military planning in Punjab was a 375-mile-long wall erected by India along the border, stretching from the Chenab River, north of Jammu city in Kashmir to Fort Abbas, adjacent to the Indian state of Rajasthan. The wall consisted of two twelve-foot-high fences of barbed wire, set about twenty feet apart. Intermingled with the barbed wire in the fence nearest to Pakistan was electrified wire. The space between the fences was filled with concertina wire. Powerful searchlights, watch towers, and machine-gun nests lined the wall at intervals of 100–200 yards. According to Lieutenant General Alam Jan Mahsud, commander of the Pakistan Army's 4th Corps, the Indians had sealed the border so tightly that 'not even a rabbit can slip through it'.[45]

In Rajasthan, across from southern Punjab province in Pakistan, was a three-division Indian Army strike force, which included one armoured division. These forces were opposed by a Pakistani corps based in Multan, whose armoured division remained in its cantonment. In all three regions, only one of the four armoured divisions fielded by the two armies (two Indian and two Pakistani) was in an unusual position. This was the Indian division that had been left behind in Mahajan after its February exercises. The other Indian and Pakistani armoured divisions remained in their cantonments. Only the Indian division in Rajasthan was near the border, and none of the four divisions was moving, intact, towards the frontier. At the time, diplomats in New Delhi and Islamabad said they had detected 'no troop movements that could be construed as anything more than logical precautions given the war of words between the two capitals'.[46] The Stimson Center's account of the crisis observes that 'the Indian military leadership deliberately refrained from moving armour associated with its strike forces out of peacetime cantonments,' and Pakistan 'deliberately refrained from moving its two strike corps to the front.'[47]

Decision-makers in both India and Pakistan were most concerned about the possibility of invasion at traditionally weak points.[48] For India, this vulnerability is the road connecting Jammu city in Kashmir with Pathankot in Punjab, which is a section of the only major ground link between the Vale of Kashmir and India proper. Pakistan had attempted to sever this link during the 1965 war. At a lower level of concern, but a higher level of probability, analysts in New Delhi expected that Islamabad would continue its efforts to foment violence on the Indian side of the LoC in Kashmir. Pakistan could, at low cost, keep Indian blood spilling and Indian rupees haemorrhaging from the exchequer; it was also thought possible, though highly unlikely, that the Kashmiri insurgents would succeed in their efforts to overturn Indian control of the state, which would allow Pakistan some role in the ultimate settlement of Kashmir's status.

Pakistan's perceived weak point was the area directly across from Rajasthan, particularly the Sukkur Barrage in Sindh. Islamabad's nightmare was a massive Indian armoured thrust that would have severed the vital road, rail, and communications links connecting the northern and southern parts of Pakistan. Anti-government militancy had raged in Sindh since 1983, and the possibility of a Sindhi insurgency developing into a quest for statehood if Indian forces 'liberated' the province was not unthinkable to Pakistani leaders. The Bangladesh war provided a compelling precedent, and the 1986–7 Brasstacks exercises offered seeming evidence as to Indian intentions: why would the Indian Army focus so intently on desert exercises if it were not thinking in terms of a conventional thrust into Pakistan from Rajasthan? Islamabad's secondary fear was that India would carry out more limited raids against militant strongholds in the Pakistani part of Kashmir.

US Concern and the Gates Mission to South Asia

In April 1990, the US began to exhibit public alarm over developments on the subcontinent. On 18 April, Washington made its first senior-level statement regarding the Indo-Pakistani troop build-up. Robert M. Kimmitt, the third-ranking official in the State Department, warned of a 'growing risk of miscalculation which could lead events to spin dangerously out of control'. Kimmitt urged the two sides to 'take immediate steps to reduce the level of tension by lowering rhetoric and avoiding provocative troop deployments'.[49] US concern about events in South Asia crystallized in mid-May with a visit to the region by Deputy National Security Advisor Robert Gates. According to a then senior Bush administration official, the Gates mission was intended to avert the immediate possibility of war, rather than to address the longer-term political problems besetting the India–Pakistan relationship: 'There was a considerable chance of war... the analogy I used at that time was that the environment reminded me of something out of August 1914... people were not acting with sufficient sobriety. There was a little bit of recklessness in the air.'[50] US intelligence estimated at the time that there was a fifty–fifty chance of war.[51]

In Islamabad, Gates met with the President, Ghulam Ishaq Khan, and the Army Chief, Mirza Aslam Beg. According to several accounts of the meeting, the main points made by the Americans were that: (1) Washington had thoroughly war-gamed a potential Indo-Pakistani war, and Pakistan was the loser in every scenario; (2) in the event of a war, Islamabad could expect no assistance from Washington; and (3) Pakistan should refrain from supporting terrorism in Indian Kashmir, avoid military deployments that New Delhi could interpret as threatening, and tone down the war rhetoric. The Pakistani leadership responded defensively, claiming that *India* was using terrorist tactics in Kashmir, that Pakistani public statements had been moderate, and that Pakistani military movements had been less menacing than India's. In India, Gates met with the Prime Minister, V.P. Singh, and senior defence and foreign policy officials. His message was similar to that given to the Pakistanis: avoid provocation that could spiral out of control. In sum, the gist of the Gates message was that it would be to neither side's advantage to go to war. India would win, but even if it did, the long-term costs would exceed any short-term benefits.[52] One potential cost, Gates told the Indians, was 'that it might go nuclear.'[53]

Within two weeks of the Gates mission to South Asia, the crisis had passed. In early June, India announced that the armour it had sent to the Mahajan range in February would return to its normal station. Pakistan responded cautiously at first, but grew more enthusiastic as it became clear that the Indians were, in fact, pulling back their forces. Analysts speculated that the withdrawal may have stemmed more from the searing summer heat in the Rajasthan desert than from Indian magnanimity, but all agreed that moving armour away from the area where Pakistan considered itself most vulnerable was an important step in the right direction. New Delhi also put forward a package of confidence-building measures, which became a topic of discussion for the two countries' diplomats and military officers, and thereby contributed to the easing of tension.

The Nuclear Shadow

The most controversial aspect of the 1990 crisis involves nuclear weapons.[54] In the years immediately after 1990, several journalistic accounts argued that India and Pakistan had been on the brink of war, that Pakistan had readied its nuclear weapons for use in the event of an Indian invasion, that Islamabad had clearly signalled these intentions to New Delhi, and that the main reason for the Gates mission to South Asia had been US alarm about the possibility of nuclear war on the subcontinent.[55] However, as Hagerty wrote in 1998, 'these accounts of the crisis are subject to considerable doubt. Most damaging to their credibility have been the categorical denials by US diplomats and military attaches posted in Islamabad and New Delhi in the spring of 1990. In particular, the US ambassadors involved in the crisis decision-making, Robert Oakley in Islamabad and William Clark in New Delhi, directly contradict the central claims' of the early accounts. 'Senior officials—US, Indian, and Pakistani—concur that, at a minimum', these stories 'exaggerated the nuclear dimension of the crisis'.[56] Referring to the author of the most alarmist account of the crisis, Oakley says: 'Let me make this very clear. I tried to make it clear to Mr [Seymour] Hersh, and he diddled with it. But at least from Islamabad, we never believed, in part because of what we did see and in part because of the very good information which Bill [Clark] was getting from the Indian Army, that there was going to be an explosion in the spring of 1990.' Rather, Oakley recounts, 'we feared that if the momentum of this ratcheting up were not stopped by the fall, the prime fighting season, the two armies might be face-to-face again, as they had been at the time of Brasstacks, and the momentum would be so strong that it couldn't be stopped. So we wanted intervention in the spring in order to pre-empt something we feared might happen in the fall.' Oakley continues: 'Despite what Hersh says—at least in Islamabad, we were not worried about a conflict becoming nuclear. There's always that potential, but there was nothing at that time to indicate that this was the case.' Clark agrees, adding that 'my views were not as apocalyptic' as Hersh's. 'My comments really didn't fit his thesis, and so you will not find me in the article anywhere... he chose not to use what I said'.[57] In the words of a then-senior Bush administration official:

I think for most of us who were involved, nuclear weapons formed the backdrop for the crisis... the concern was not that a nuclear exchange was imminent; the concern was that this thing was beginning to spin out of control and that would lead to clashes, potentially conventional warfare. Most of our analysis suggested that India would fare better than Pakistan, and that very early on, as a result, Pakistan might want to consider threatening... a nuclear action. Or, that India, thinking about that, would escalate conventionally very early on, to eradicate it.

According to this official, the Hersh article 'exaggerated considerably the sense that there was kind of a situation where the nuclear trigger was cocked or something'.[58]

Important questions remain: What were India's and Pakistan's actual nuclear capabilities as the crisis unfolded? What was the adversary's perception of these capabilities? Did New Delhi and Islamabad manipulate their nuclear capabilities for political purposes? What role did nuclear weapons play in resolving the crisis? This section will attempt to answer the first question; the others will be dealt with in the next section, which analyses various explanations for South Asia's non-war of 1990.

In the continuing disagreement over the influence of the nuclear shadow on the 1990 crisis, much rests on varying assessments of Indian and Pakistani nuclear weapon capabilities at the time of the crisis.[59] India, of course, had conducted a nuclear explosive test at Pokhran in 1974. While New Delhi's 'peaceful nuclear explosion' may have had a limited strategic impact, it at least demonstrated India's basic capability to build nuclear weapons. As Perkovich writes: 'for twenty-four years following the Pokhran PNE, India managed to maintain a rudimentary nuclear deterrent without further nuclear explosive tests.'[60] From 1974 to 1990, Indian scientists and engineers had worked fitfully, but inexorably, to refine their nuclear capabilities—as well as to develop reliable delivery options.[61] Perkovich summarizes India's nuclear weapon posture in the years leading up to 1990:

India's ballistic missile program progressed to the point where it began flight-testing the Prithvi and Agni missiles in 1988 and 1989, respectively. The strategic enclave continued to enhance its nuclear weapon capabilities in laboratories and on missile test ranges. Between 1988 and 1990, according to one source, it readied at least two dozen nuclear weapons for quick assembly and potential dispersal to airbases for delivery by aircraft for retaliatory attacks against Pakistan.[62]

At a minimum, Perkovich concludes, 'devices were made that could be turned into weapons if India was attacked.'[63] An official close to the Indian prime minister said in the spring of 1989 that, if need be, India could produce a bomb 'overnight'.[64]

Although Pakistan had not yet tested a nuclear explosive device, the virtually unanimous view of concerned states and the private non-proliferation community by late 1989 was that Pakistan was a *de facto* nuclear weapon state.[65] In 1986, a US Special National Intelligence Estimate concluded that Pakistan could produce weapons-grade fissile material.[66] During the Brasstacks crisis of 1986–7, Pakistan's nuclear weapon capabilities had not yet 'flowered'; they were 'nascent', but 'not yet actual'.[67] In March 1987, despite strong nonproliferation pressures, Pakistani President Zia-ul-Haq admitted that 'Pakistan can build a [nuclear] bomb whenever it wishes. Once you have acquired the technology, which Pakistan has, you can do whatever you like.'[68] One year later, a detailed and well-sourced article on Pakistan's nuclear programme said that the prevailing US government view was 'that it would take Pakistan at most a few weeks or months to assemble a bomb', although some officials believed it to be more 'a matter of hours or days'. According to this account, the 'different estimates largely depend on officials' uncertainty over whether the Pakistanis have yet taken one of the final steps—precision machining the uranium metal core.' The article quoted US Representative Stephen Solarz as saying that Islamabad had 'the nuclear equivalent of a Saturday night special. It may not be technically elegant, but it's capable of doing the job'.[69] Later in 1988, US officials confirmed that Pakistan had obtained a nuclear weapon design from China.[70] Soon after taking office as prime minister in December 1988, Benazir Bhutto made two secret promises to Washington: first, that Pakistan would stop enriching uranium to weapons-grade; and, second, that it would not convert its existing stock of weapons-grade uranium from gas to metal, which could then be machined into bomb cores.[71] By 1989, all of the components were in place for an as-yet unassembled Pakistani nuclear weapon. In addition, Pakistan tested its first ballistic missiles in February 1989.[72] Mirza Aslam Beg, Pakistan's army chief in 1990, later revealed that, by 1989, Pakistan 'had acquired a meaningful low-level deterrence capability and... this capability was good enough to deter India, which had a larger capability.'[73] According to Perkovich, Islamabad 'retained at least one unassembled [nuclear] weapon' just prior to the 1990 crisis.[74]

Clear evidence supports the conclusion that the nuclear shadow played an important role in the crisis. During the early spring of 1990, prior to the Gates mission, Islamabad reneged on its nuclear-restraint promises of the previous year. Oakley recalls: 'We had ascertained beyond a shadow of a doubt that the promises that Mrs Bhutto had made and kept during 1989... had been broken and the nuclear program had been reactivated.'[75] As Indo-Pakistani tension grew, Islamabad resumed enriching uranium[76] and apparently 'fabricated cores for several nuclear weapons from pre-existing stocks of weapons-grade uranium'.[77] However, accounts differ as to whether Pakistan fully weaponized its nuclear capability during the 1990 crisis. Mitchell Reiss quotes then the undersecretary of defence Paul Wolfowitz as saying: 'We knew that Pakistan assembled a nuclear weapon. That is why we cut off assistance... later that year.' Reiss also writes that the 'accumulation of discrete data' led Richard Haass, then the National Security Council's senior director for the Near East and South Asia, 'to believe in early May that Pakistan had probably assembled "one or even more nuclear weapons".'[78] But Oakley remembers that the autumn 1990 suspension of US aid to Pakistan 'had nothing to do... at least, so far as we knew, with the preparation or deployment of nuclear weapons. It had to do with other factors, which were required for certification.'[79] Even at the height of the crisis, US analysts were deeply divided over the precise nature of Pakistan's nuclear capabilities. As one said: 'The intelligence community is divided as to whether this is a real threat or just bluff. Some people in the CIA believe that Pakistan has nuclear weapons already, others believe they could put a bomb together in two weeks. A third faction thinks they may be as much as six months away from going nuclear.'[80]

Perkovich argues that, on the Indian side, new Prime Minister V.P. Singh was told by scientific advisor V.S. Arunachalam at the beginning of 1990 'that if Pakistan waged a nuclear attack against India, the means existed to deliver a nuclear response'.[81] Raj Chengappa contradicts this account, writing about Singh: 'he does recall Arunachalam briefing him on the [nuclear] status and says, "India could then only assemble nuclear weapons but not deliver them. We could laboratory test everything to nano seconds but the bomb delivery was still in process."'[82] When Singh asked Air Chief Marshall S.K. Mehra whether India was vulnerable to a Pakistani nuclear attack, Mehra responded that 'India could not prevent a treetop attack by Pakistani aircraft but that India could retaliate in kind.' Singh then 'instructed Mehra to increase the air force's preparations to carry out such missions', and Mehra reportedly 'raised the air force's alert level'.[83] Even though Pakistan then possessed 'ready-to-assemble nuclear weapons', Singh seems to have believed in 1990 that 'Pakistan had not quite acquired the bomb'. Soon thereafter, Singh asked a former senior Indian defence official, Arun Singh, to 'perform a detailed modeling and analysis of the Indo-Pak nuclear relationship to anticipate possible circumstances under which Pakistan might use nuclear weapons and assess how India could or should prevent such use or respond to it'.[84]

After the Kashmir crisis intensified considerably in April 1990, the Gates mission travelled to South Asia in May. 'Importantly,' writes Perkovich:

the American team did not find the Indians worrying explicitly about a nuclear threat from Pakistan. The Indians did not know of the activity detected by

American intelligence and Gates did not tell them about it. Interviews with Indian officials who would have been alerted had New Delhi perceived this as a nuclear crisis corroborate the view that India perceived the situation in terms of domestic politics, instability in Kashmir, and Pakistani subversion, not a nuclear threat. They worried about Pakistan's nuclear capability, but not as an acute threat at this moment.[85]

Chengappa reports that at least some Indian military leaders were less sanguine about the nuclear equation than Perkovich's account suggests:

India did take the threat of a nuclear strike seriously. The armed forces, who were not briefed either about India or Pakistan's nuclear capability, were worried... Mehra recalls: 'We really didn't know if Pakistan's F-16s were capable of delivering such weapons or not. Nor were we absolutely sure of what we had. The feeling was that we were sitting ducks. It was a worrying situation for us to be in.'[86]

Chengappa adds that V.P. Singh 'asked Arunachalam to keep everything ready for a nuclear counterattack'. Although Arunachalam advised the prime minister that Pakistan would not resort to using nuclear weapons, 'India did review its ability to strike back'. In fact, argues Chengappa, 'India's "option" was still not ready. Said a senior official involved in the crisis: "We could have tightened the bolts (of the bomb) but admittedly we were far from ready (to deliver it)." Fortunately, Pakistan did not suspect that sixteen years after India exploded a nuclear device its arch enemy still did not possess a fail-safe delivery system.'[87] Summing up the nuclear dimension of the crisis, Clark recalls that 'there was a little bit of nuclear tension: "don't threaten me with yours because I've got mine." I don't think it went beyond that. Nobody was loading weapons, and I'm not convinced they have weapons they can load.'[88]

Why Peace?

The most convincing explanation for why India and Pakistan did not fight a war in 1990 is that Islamabad and New Delhi were deterred from war by their recognition of each other's nuclear weapon capabilities, and by the possibility that any direct military hostilities between them might have escalated to a nuclear exchange. In other words, 'existential deterrence'[89] was the primary cause of peace on the subcontinent in 1990. Marc Trachtenberg defines existential deterrence as a strategic interaction in which 'the mere existence of nuclear forces means that, whatever we say or do, there is a certain irreducible risk that an armed conflict might escalate into a nuclear war. The fear of escalation is thus factored into political calculations: faced with this risk, states are more cautious and more prudent than they otherwise would be.'[90] Bundy argued that the threat of losing even one city to an opponent's nuclear strike is a disaster any political leader would do his utmost to avoid; in other words, nuclear weapons deter war not through the classical modalities identified by deterrence theorists—relative capabilities, demonstrated resolve, nuclear doctrines, escalation dominance, and pointed threats—but through the fact of their existence and the accompanying possibility that they might be used at all.[91] In sum, Bundy writes, 'the uncertainties which make existential deterrence so powerful have the... consequence that what either government says it might do, or even believes it might do, in the event of open conflict cannot be relied on either by friends or by opponents as a certain predicter of what it would actually do.'[92] When it comes to existential deterrence, uncertainty deters.

A strong case can be made that India and Pakistan were deterred from war in 1990 by the existence of nuclear weapon capabilities on both sides and by the chance that, no matter what Indian and Pakistani decision-makers said or did, any direct military clash could have escalated to the nuclear level.[93] India and Pakistan were objectively judged to be nuclear weapon-capable by 1990. After the Brasstacks crisis, both India and Pakistan increased their nuclear preparedness. By warning of Indian and Pakistani nuclear strides and exhorting New Delhi and Islamabad to forgo nuclear weapons, concerned states and private non-proliferation analysts inadvertently gave credibility to the condition of mutual existential deterrence. Increasing evidence of India's and Pakistan's growing nuclear prowess raised mutual concerns that a fourth Indo-Pakistani war would be fought in the shadow of nuclear weapons. In their military planning at the turn of the decade, both sides assumed that the other could quickly deploy nuclear weapons early in a war. Public statements by leaders in each country fuelled profound concern in the other. While the evidence suggested that both sides were nuclear weapon-capable, mutual mistrust meant that the opponent's capabilities loomed even larger than objective circumstances would warrant.

There is also ample evidence that nuclear signals were both sent and received during the crisis. Yakub Khan's bellicosity during his February visit to New Delhi was interpreted by his hosts as having nuclear overtones. At the height of the war of words in April, India's prime minister warned Pakistan not to underestimate India's nuclear capabilities. His message was reiterated by India's former Army Chief, K. Sundarji, a man whose public utterances were taken very seriously in Pakistan. Sundarji said in a widely circulated interview: 'Any sensible planner sitting on this side of the border is going to assume Pakistan does indeed have nuclear weapons capability. And by the same token, I rather suspect the view from the other side is going to look very similar.' Sundarji acknowledged that 'on the other side, there may be the odd person who has kidded himself into believing that they have the nuclear weapon capability and we don't', but called this view 'stupid. The sooner they wake up to this reality, the better'.[94] Clark recalls that the Pakistanis, too, made 'slightly veiled threats' to the effect that 'we have something that will make you very sorry.' The Indians replied that 'if something happens, we will respond in the appropriate manner.' Clark says, 'I know how to read that: "we've got one too".'[95]

Another way to assess the existential deterrence thesis is to look at the crisis from a counterfactual perspective: would India have refrained from attacking across the LoC or the international border, in the absence of the small but not negligible chance that such a course might escalate to the use of nuclear weapons? The 1990 crisis was driven by a serious political dispute that had already thrust India and Pakistan into two wars. The Kashmiri insurgency was widely viewed in India as a fundamental challenge to the integrity of the Indian state. India's human rights record was taking a severe beating, and the carnage in Kashmir threatened to pin down hundreds of thousands of Indian soldiers indefinitely. New Delhi had a number of promising offensive options, ranging from air strikes against militant training camps on the Pakistani side of the LoC to a more decisive ground thrust across the border into Sindh. In a non-nuclear South Asia, India would have been much more likely to punish Pakistan for its transgressions in Kashmir. The contrast with 1965 was stark:

The awareness on both sides of a nuclear capability that can enable either country to assemble nuclear weapons at short notice induces mutual caution. This caution is already evident on the part of India. In 1965 when Pakistan carried out its 'Operation Gibraltar' and sent in infiltrators, India sent its army across the cease-fire line to destroy the assembly points of the infiltrators. That escalated into a full-scale war. In 1990 when Pakistan once again carried out a massive infiltration of terrorists trained in Pakistan, India tried to deal with the problem on Indian territory and did not send its army into Pakistan-occupied Kashmir.[96]

Critiques of the existential deterrence thesis suffer from two main weaknesses. The first is their underlying assumption that existential deterrence in 1990 depended on both sides possessing operationally ready nuclear weapons. For example, Robert Wirsing writes: 'Were it to turn out that the Pakistan side, at least, was actually in no condition in 1990 to launch a nuclear strike on India and, moreover, that its nuclear saber-rattling, as in 1987, was mere bluff, then Hagerty's confident assertion of linkage between subcontinental peace and the region's nuclear weaponization would have to be reappraised.'[97] Wirsing's critique misses the fundamental point that *existential deterrence thrives on uncertainty.* With the entire world pronouncing India and Pakistan to be nuclear weapon-capable, the two sides' leaders hardly required a precise and accurate depiction of each other's nuclear capabilities, deployment postures, or doctrines in order to be existentially deterred. As Bundy observes, nuclear weapons deter aggression by virtue of the simple fact that they exist, and not because of 'strategic theories or declaratory policies or even international commitments'. Existential deterrence 'rests on uncertainty about what *could happen*, not in what has been asserted'.[98]

A second and more critical weakness is the failure of critics to offer plausible alternative explanations for South Asia's non-war of 1990. The one advanced most often is that the Gates mission succeeded in defusing the crisis.[99] Although few informed observers would characterize the US intervention as a failure, no serious analysis has demonstrated that it was the main cause of crisis de-escalation. The prevailing view on all sides has been that New Delhi and Islamabad used the Gates mission as a face-saving mechanism to pull back from a brink over which they had already decided not to go. As Clark says: 'At the end of the day, I think you could say that both Delhi and Islamabad used Bob Gates and his mission as an excuse, if you will, to back off positions they had been taking.' Abdus Sattar characterizes the Gates mission as an 'illustration of good, useful preventive diplomacy.' Clark reports that Indian officials, too, appreciated the chance to ease the tension: 'I did have several senior people, including the Prime Minister, tell me afterwards that it had been a useful visit, it had allowed a way to back off for both sides, without one having to back down to the other.'[100] Few knowledgeable people would likely quibble with the conclusion of a former senior Bush administration official: 'At worst, you could say that what we did was unnecessary... I think that at the risk of sounding self-serving, it was a success... my instincts are we slowed it down, we forced people to face up to the consequences... we certainly didn't make the situation worse, and my guess is we made it better.'[101] While the Gates mission was a secondary 'cause of peace' in 1990, its lesser impact is evidenced by the fact that, in the absence of Indian and Pakistani nuclear weapon capabilities, the US diplomatic initiative would not have been undertaken in the first place. As one US official put it, 'when you have nuclear capabilities that can be brought into play, it leads you to err on the side of caution, or in this case, greater diplomatic activism rather than less. If there was a situation where there were two countries and the worst that could happen if they went to war was there'd be a few bloody noses, O.K., well then, that we can live with.'[102]

Notes

[1] This chapter is a substantially revised and updated version of a book chapter published by Hagerty in 1998. It reflects five additional years of scholarly research by others and him, as well as considerable new analysis based on that research. For the earlier version, see Devin T. Hagerty, *The Consequences of Nuclear Proliferation: Lessons from South Asia* (Cambridge, Massachusetts: MIT Press, 1998), pp. 133–70. Accounts of the 1990 crisis written since 1998 include: Sumit Ganguly, *Conflict Unending: India-Pakistan Tensions since 1947* (New York: Columbia University Press and Washington, DC: Woodrow Wilson Center Press, 2001), pp. 91–5; George Perkovich, *India's Nuclear Bomb: The Impact on Global Proliferation* (Berkeley: University of California Press, 1999), pp. 306–13; P.R. Chari, Pervaiz Iqbal Cheema, and Stephen Philip Cohen, *Perception, Politics, and Security in South Asia: The Compound Crisis of 1990* (New York: RoutledgeCurzon, 2003); and J.N. Dixit, *India and Pakistan in War and Peace* (New York: Routledge, 2002), pp. 271–6.

[2] For a variety of perspectives, see Perkovich, *India's Nuclear Bomb*, pp. 306–13; Chari *et al.*, *Perception, Politics, and Security*, pp. 118–21. Immediately prior to the 1990 crisis, a prominent American nuclear proliferation expert wrote that: 'India and Pakistan are currently capable of deploying small nuclear forces comprised of atomic bombs that could be delivered by advanced fighter-bombers, with India's capabilities being considerably greater than Pakistan's. Neither country is believed to have integrated nuclear weapons into its military forces, however, and it is possible that neither has manufactured complete nuclear devices.' Leonard S. Spector with Jacqueline R. Smith, *Nuclear Ambitions: The Spread of Nuclear Weapons, 1989–1990* (Boulder, Colorado: Westview Press, 1990), p. 59. Three months before the 1990 crisis erupted, the *Washington Post* opined that South Asia was the 'likeliest place in the world for a nuclear war'. 'The Next Nuclear War', *Washington Post*, 13 October 1989.

[3] The BJP won 86 seats in the 1989 parliamentary elections, a vast improvement over the two seats it won in 1984. For a concise account of the BJP's quick ascension, see Devin T. Hagerty, *The Rise of the Bharatiya Janata Party*, unpublished manuscript, University of Pennsylvania, April 1991.

[4] For background on the Indo-Pakistani conflict over Kashmir, see Chapter Two of this book; Sumit Ganguly, *The Crisis in Kashmir: Portents of War, Hopes of Peace* (Washington, DC: Woodrow Wilson Center Press and Cambridge: Cambridge University Press, 1997); Victoria Schofield, *Kashmir in Conflict: India, Pakistan, and the Unending War* (London: I.B. Taurus, 2003); Devin T. Hagerty, 'Kashmir and the Nuclear Question', in Charles H. Kennedy and Rasul Baksh Rais (eds), *Pakistan: 1995* (Boulder, Colorado: Westview Press, 1995), pp. 159–92; and Devin T. Hagerty, 'Kashmir and the Nuclear Question Revisited', in Charles H. Kennedy and Craig Baxter (eds), *Pakistan 2000* (Lanham, Maryland: Lexington Books, 2000), pp. 81–106.

[5] In point of fact, many Pakistanis question the very legitimacy of the Simla agreement. An extremely senior Pakistani official, then out of government, told one of the authors in 1998 that Simla had, for all practical purposes, been dictated to Pakistan at gunpoint and was therefore irrelevant to resolution of the Kashmir conflict.

[6] On renewed conflict in Kashmir in the 1980s, see Ganguly, *Crisis in Kashmir*, pp. 80–109; and Chari *et al.*, *Perception, Politics, and Security*, pp. 41–64.

[7] Inderjit Badhwar, 'A Tarnished Triumph', *India Today*, 15 April 1987, pp. 76–8; Inderjit Badhwar, 'Farooq Under Fire', *India Today*, 15 September 1987, pp. 42–7.

[8] Sumit Ganguly, 'Avoiding War in Kashmir', *Foreign Affairs*, vol. 74, no. 1 (Winter 1990/91), p. 61.

[9] 'Indianise Kashmir', *India Today*, 30 September 1989, p. 11.

[10] Michael Krepon and Mishi Faruqee (eds), *Conflict Prevention and Confidence Building Measures in South Asia: The 1990 Crisis*, Occasional Paper No. 17 (Washington, DC: The Henry L. Stimson Center, 1994), p. 5. This is a transcript of a meeting convened by the Stimson Center to discuss the 1990 crisis. Participants included the 1990 US ambassadors to India and Pakistan, as well as senior South Asian diplomats and military officers.

[11] See, for example, 'The Enemy Within', *India Today* (editorial), 31 March 1990, p. 11; Ganguly, 'Avoiding War in Kashmir', pp. 63, 65; M.J. Akbar, *Kashmir: Behind the Vale* (New Delhi: Viking, 1991), p. 215; 'Crossfire: Kashmir', *India Today*, 31 August 1991, pp. 77–87; George Fernandes, 'India's Policies in Kashmir: An Assessment and Discourse', and Jagat Mehta, 'Resolving Kashmir in the International Context of the 1990s', both in Raju G.C. Thomas (ed.), *Perspectives on Kashmir: The Roots of Conflict in South Asia* (Boulder, Colorado: Westview Press, 1992), pp. 286, 394–5.

[12] Inderjit Badhwar, 'Asserting Authority', *India Today*, 28 February 1990, p. 31.

[13] Pankaj Pachauri and Zafar Meraj, 'Drifting Dangerously', *India Today*, 15 January 1990, pp. 8–13; Shekhar Gupta, 'Militant Siege', *India Today*, 31 January 1990, pp. 22–32.

[14] 'Kashmir: Echoes of War', *The Economist*, 27 January 1990, p. 33; 'Kashmir: Fighting Words', *The Economist*, 3 February 1990, p. 32.

[15] Krepon and Faruqee, *1990 Crisis*, p. 6.

[16] Hagerty interview with Abdus Sattar, 5 August 1994.

[17] S. Viswam and Salamat Ali, 'Vale of Tears', *Far Eastern Economic Review*, 8 February 1990, pp. 19–21.

[18] Dixit, *India and Pakistan in War and Peace*, p. 273.

[19] Perkovich, *India's Nuclear Bomb*, p. 307.

[20] Dixit, *India and Pakistan in War and Peace*, p. 274.

[21] Perkovich, *India's Nuclear Bomb*, p. 307.

[22] Malcolm Davidson, 'Bhutto Says Pakistan Does Not Want War With India Over Kashmir', *Reuter Library Report*, 10 February 1990.

[23] 'Echoes of War'; 'Indian Prime Minister on His Country's Nuclear Policy', *Xinhua General Overseas News Service*, 21 February 1990; and 'Iyengar, Ramanna Appointments Open Bomb Speculation in India', *Nucleonics Week*, 22 February, 1990.

[24] 'It's All Bluff and Bluster', *Economic Times* (Bombay), 18 May 1993.

[25] Mushahid Hussain, 'Pakistan "Responding to Change"', *Jane's Defence Weekly*, 14 October 1989, p. 779; Malcolm Davidson, 'Pakistan Army Chief Vows to Stay Out of Politics', *Reuter Library Report*, 10 December 1989.

[26] Salamat Ali, 'The Counter-Punch', *Far Eastern Economic Review*, 26 October 1989, p. 25.

[27] 'Bluff and Bluster'; What Chari *et al.*, call 'authoritative Pakistani sources' dispute this interpretation of Pakistani military movements. For a discussion of these conflicting claims, see p. 81 of *Perception, Politics, and Security in South Asia*.

[28] Comments of the US ambassador to New Delhi, William Clark, in Krepon and Faruqee, *1990 Crisis*, p. 3.

[29] Hagerty interview with William Clark, 27 March 1995.

[30] Chari *et al.*, *Perception, Politics and Security in South Asia*, pp. 77, 107.

[31] Krepon and Faruqee, *1990 Crisis*, pp. 13–19.

[32] Raja Asghar, 'Bhutto Predicts Victory for Kashmir Independence Campaign', *Reuter Library Report*, 13 March 1990.

[33] Moses Manoharan, 'Indian Leader Tells Pakistan to Stay Out of Kashmir Uprising', *Reuter Library Report*, 13 March 1990.

[34] 'Crush Pak Camps: BJP', *Times of India*, 8 April 1990.

[35] David Housego, 'India Urged to Attack Camps in Pakistan Over Strife in Kashmir', *Financial Times*, 9 April 1990.

[36] David Housego and Zafar Meraj, 'Indian Premier Warns of Danger of Kashmir War', *Financial Times*, 11 April 1990; Coomi Kapoor, 'Indian Threat of Armed Reprisals', *The Times* (London), 11 April 1990; Tony Allen-Mills, 'India Ready for War After Hostages Are Executed', the *Independent* (London), 12 April 1990; Mark Fineman, 'India's Leader Warns of an Expected Attack by Pakistan', *Los Angeles Times*, 15 April 1990; 'VP Urges Nation to Be Ready as Pak Troops Move to Border', *The Times of India*, 11 April 1990.

[37] 'Unwarranted Bellicosity', *Dawn* (Karachi), 12 April 1990.

[38] 'Indian Threats Demand Vigilance', *Dawn* (Karachi), 12 April 1990; James Clad and Salamat Ali, 'Will Words Lead to War?', *Far Eastern Economic Review*, 26 April 1990, pp. 10–11; Malcolm Davidson, 'Pakistan Condemns Indian Premier's Talk of War Over Kashmir,' *Reuter Library Report*, 11 April 1990; Malcolm Davidson, 'Kashmir Row Sparks Dangerous Period for India and Pakistan', *Reuter Library Report*, 13 April 1990; 'Pakistan Ready to Meet Indian Invasion, Minister Says', *Reuter Library Report*, 14 April 1990.

[39] 'Indian Troops Reinforced Near Kashmir Border With Pakistan', *Reuter Library Report*, 12 April 1990.

[40] Davidson, 'Dangerous Period for India and Pakistan'.

[41] Steve Coll, 'Indian Troops, Separatist Violence Aggravate Kashmir Crisis', *Washington Post*, 13 April 1990.

[42] Fineman, 'India's Leader Warns of an Expected Attack by Pakistan'; 'The Makings of a Bloody, Old-Fashioned War', *The Economist*, 21 April 1990, p. 35; Steve Coll, 'Assault on Pakistan Gains Favor in India', *Washington Post*, 15 April 1990; 'Indian Forces Battle Moslems in Kashmir', *Chicago Tribune*, 16 April 1990.

[43] Subhash Chakravarti and Amit Roy, 'Militants Fan War Fever Over Kashmir', *Sunday Times* (London), 15 April 1990; Clad and Ali, 'Will Words Lead to War?'; James Clad, 'Valley of Violence', *Far Eastern Economic Review*, 24 May 1990, p. 22; Zahid Hussain, 'Protest Flag Becomes Focus of Kashmir Border Strife', *The Times* (London), 24 April 1990; Ahmed Rashid, 'Kashmir Talks Too Far Off to Ease Rising Tensions', the *Independent* (London), 16 April 1990; Jose Katigbak, 'Indo-Pakistan Border Violations on the Rise, Says UN', *Reuter Library Report*, 23 April 1990.

[44] Rashid, 'Rising Tensions'; Christopher Lockwood, *Daily Telegraph* (London), 20 April 1990; Salamat Ali, 'Avoiding Action', *Far Eastern Economic Review*, 3 May 1990, p. 26.

[45] Lockwood, *Daily Telegraph*; Mark Fineman, 'Nervous Pakistanis Watch "the Wall" and Indian Troops', *Los Angeles Times*, 20 April 1990; Ali, 'Avoiding Action', p. 26.

[46] Malcolm Davidson, 'Pakistani General Says More Indian Troops Deployed Near Border', *Reuter Library Report*, 19 April 1990.

[47] Krepon and Faruqee, *1990 Crisis*, p. v.

[48] The remainder of this section is based on Hagerty's numerous anonymous interviews with senior Indian, Pakistani, and US officials.

[49] Al Kamen, 'US Voices Concern Over Kashmir', *Washington Post*, 19 April 1990.

[50] Hagerty interview with former senior Bush administration official, 24 November 1993.

[51] Hagerty interview with senior US intelligence analyst, 4 August 1994.

[52] Hagerty interview with former senior Bush administration official, 24 November 1993; Krepon and Faruqee, *1990 Crisis*, pp. 4, 8–9; John F. Burns, 'US Urges Pakistan to Settle Feud With India Over Kashmir', the *New York Times*, 21 May 1990; 'The Killing of Hopes for Peace in Kashmir', *The Economist*,

26 May 1990; Seymour M. Hersh, 'On the Nuclear Edge', *New Yorker*, 29 March 1993, pp. 67–8.

[53] Robert M. Gates, 'Preventive Diplomacy: Concept and Reality', excerpts from a speech to a Conference on Preventive Diplomacy, Taipei, Taiwan, 29 August 1996, Center for Strategic and International Studies Pacific Forum, PacNet No. 39, 27 September 1996. Quoted in Chari *et al.*, *Perception, Politics, and Security in South Asia*, p. 110.

[54] Hagerty, *Consequences of Nuclear Proliferation*, pp. 152–70.

[55] William E. Burrows and Robert Windrem, *Critical Mass: The Dangerous Race for Superweapons in a Fragmenting World* (New York: Simon and Schuster, 1994), pp. 61–2, 82; Hamish McDonald, 'Destroyer of Worlds', *Far Eastern Economic Review*, 30 April 1992, p. 24; Hersh, 'Nuclear Edge'; James Adams, 'Pakistan "Nuclear War Threat"', *Sunday Times* (London), 27 May 1990; Charles Smith, 'Atomic Absurdity', *Far Eastern Economic Review*, 30 April 1992, p. 25.

[56] Hagerty, *Consequences of Nuclear Proliferation*, p. 156. In turn, a senior US intelligence analyst told Hagerty that those who subsequently denied the early journalistic accounts are guilty of 'historical revisionism'. Interview, 4 August 1994.

[57] Krepon and Faruqee, *1990 Crisis*, pp. 2, 4, 8, 39.

[58] Interview with former senior Bush administration official, 24 November 1993.

[59] However, as I shall argue below, the actual physical state of each side's capabilities may have been less important than the adversary's perception of those capabilities.

[60] Perkovich, *India's Nuclear Bomb*, p. 183.

[61] Hagerty, *Consequences of Nuclear Proliferation*, pp. 78–89, 117–31.

[62] Perkovich, *India's Nuclear Bomb*, p. 293. Perkovich's source was the dean of Indian nuclear analysts, K. Subrahmanyam. For additional details on India's nuclear weapon and delivery preparations in the lead-up to the 1990 crisis, see Perkovich, pp. 293–306.

[63] Perkovich, *India's Nuclear Bomb*, p. 295.

[64] Ross Munro, 'Superpower Rising', *Time*, 3 April 1989, p. 16.

[65] As Perkovich writes: 'By now [1988–90] Pakistan, too, had acquired the capability to assemble nuclear weapons.' *India's Nuclear Bomb*, p. 293. For a detailed account of Pakistan's nuclear strides in the 1980s, see Hagerty, *Consequences of Nuclear Proliferation*, pp. 78–89, 117–31.

[66] Leonard S. Spector, *The Undeclared Bomb* (Cambridge, Massachusetts: Ballinger, 1988), pp. 129–30.

⁶⁷ Hagerty interview with Abdus Sattar, 5 August 1994.

⁶⁸ William R. Doerner, 'Knocking at the Nuclear Door', *Time*, 30 March 1987, p. 42.

⁶⁹ Hedrick Smith, 'A Bomb Ticks in Pakistan', the *New York Times Magazine*, 6 March 1988, p. 77.

⁷⁰ Nayan Chanda, 'See No Evil', *Far Eastern Economic Review*, 5 January 1989, p. 12.

⁷¹ McDonald, 'Destroyer of Worlds', p. 23; 'Pakistan Missile Flap Ongoing', *Associated Press*, 13 May 1994.

⁷² Hagerty, *Consequences of Nuclear Proliferation*, p. 130.

⁷³ 'Pakistan Missile Flap Ongoing'.

⁷⁴ Perkovich, *India's Nuclear Bomb*, p. 303.

⁷⁵ Krepon and Faruqee, *1990 Crisis*, p. 40.

⁷⁶ R. Jeffrey Smith, 'US Stiffens Policy on Nuclear Arms, Pakistan Aid', *Washington Post*, 20 November 1990.

⁷⁷ Joseph Cirincione, Jon B. Wolfsthal, and Miriam Rajkumar, *Deadly Arsenals: Tracking Weapons of Mass Destruction* (Washington, DC: Carnegie Endowment for International Peace, 2002), p. 211.

⁷⁸ Mitchell Reiss, *Bridled Ambition: Why Countries Constrain Their Nuclear Capabilities* (Washington, DC: Woodrow Wilson Center Press, 1995), p. 188.

⁷⁹ Krepon and Faruqee, *1990 Crisis*, p. 45.

⁸⁰ Adams, 'Pakistan 'Nuclear War Threat'.

⁸¹ Perkovich, *India's Nuclear Bomb*, pp. 304–5.

⁸² Raj Chengappa, *Weapons of Peace: The Secret Story of India's Quest to Be a Nuclear Power* (New Delhi: Harper Collins, 2000), p. 354.

⁸³ Perkovich, *India's Nuclear Bomb*, p. 305.

⁸⁴ Ibid., pp. 305–6.

⁸⁵ Ibid., p. 310.

⁸⁶ Chengappa, *Weapons of Peace*, p. 357.

⁸⁷ Ibid.

⁸⁸ Hagerty interview with William Clark, 27 March 1995.

⁸⁹ The concept of existential deterrence was invented by McGeorge Bundy. See his 'Existential Deterrence and Its Consequences', in Douglas MacLean (ed.), *The Security Gamble: Deterrence Dilemmas in the Nuclear Age* (Totowa, NJ: Rowman and Allanheld, 1984), pp. 3–13. For a lengthy discussion of the concept, see Hagerty, *Consequences of Nuclear Proliferation*, pp. 39–62.

[90] Marc Trachtenberg, 'The Influence of Nuclear Weapons in the Cuban Missile Crisis', *International Security*, vol. 10, no. 1 (Summer 1985), p. 139.

[91] For additional examples of Bundy's thinking, see his 'To Cap the Volcano', *Foreign Affairs*, vol. 48, no. 1 (October 1969), pp. 9–12; 'The Bishops and the Bomb', *New York Review of Books*, 16 June 1983, p. 4; and *Danger and Survival: Choices About the Bomb in the First Fifty Years* (New York: Random House, 1988), pp. 391–462.

[92] Bundy, 'Existential Deterrence', p. 9. Of course, there are significant differences between the thermonuclear stand-off that shaped Bundy's perspective and the much more limited nuclear competition between India and Pakistan in 1990. Hagerty addresses these differences, at length, in *Consequences of Nuclear Proliferation*, pp. 45–56. In a letter dated 30 December 1993, Bundy expressed his agreement with the substance of Hagerty's argument: 'I generally agree with your view of the nuclear stand-off in the subcontinent... most political leaders at the hour of choice will be on guard against most clever briefers. Moreover, as I listen to officials from nuclear-weapon states, I find an implicit acceptance of existential deterrence. I don't think it guarantees against all smaller conflict, but it does afford a thickening deterrent to acts of escalation. I find this line of thought consistent with my own assessments of existential deterrence between the superpowers.'

[93] The case for existential deterrence is admittedly circumstantial; as with all deterrence theory, tracing the causality of non-events is practically impossible. Perkovich writes that in a 1995–6 article Hagerty undermines the case for existential deterrence as an explanation for the peaceful resolution of the 1990 crisis: 'For the role of nuclear deterrence to explain India's and Pakistan's restraint, he wrote, authoritative officials would have [to] "admit that they were planning to go to war, but were dissuaded from doing so by the possibility that conventional conflict might escalate to a nuclear exchange."' (Perkovich, *India's Nuclear Bomb*, p. 311.) But Perkovich takes Hagerty's words out of context. The remainder of the paragraph quoted by Perkovich makes it clear that Hagerty acknowledges the impossibility of *proving* the existential deterrence thesis, not the impossibility of demonstrating that it is the most *plausible* of the available explanations. (Devin T. Hagerty, 'Nuclear Deterrence in South Asia: The 1990 Indo-Pakistani Crisis', *International Security*, vol. 20, no. 3 (Winter 1995/96), p. 108). Further along, Perkovich demonstrates a misunderstanding of the concept of existential deterrence, while unwittingly recognizing its power. He writes that 'if nuclear threats—and therefore nuclear deterrence—did not play a clear and direct role in the outcome of the 1990 crisis, both sides since the early 1980s had recognized that nuclear disaster could result if they pushed each other too hard militarily.' (p. 312) The words 'nuclear threats' and 'clear and direct role' are the vocabulary

of classical, not existential, nuclear deterrence theory. The words after the comma—'nuclear disaster could result if they pushed each other too hard militarily'—are pure existential deterrence theory, as is Perkovich's argument that 'both sides recognized the now inherent possibility that war could escalate to the nuclear level.' Perkovich writes that 'this reality merely added to, and did not create, the mutual interest in turning away from conflict. The result would have been similar if neither possessed nuclear capabilities' (p. 311). Perkovich fails to support this claim with convincing evidence and proffers no compelling alternative to the existential deterrence thesis, other than to say that 'there is no evidence to date, especially on the Indian side, that leaders wanted anything but to avoid a war. Rather than leaning forward towards conflict, both leaderships were being backed into it' (p. 311). But this is exactly what existential deterrence would suggest: harried decision-makers being pressured toward brinks they would rather not topple over for fear of the uncertain and potentially catastrophic consequences that might ensue—and ultimately avoiding war.

[94] 'If Pushed Beyond a Point By Pakistan, We Will Retaliate', *India Today*, 30 April 1990, p. 76.

[95] Hagerty interview with William Clark, 27 March 1995.

[96] K. Subrahmanyam, 'Capping, Managing, or Eliminating Nuclear Weapons?', in Kanti P. Bajpai and Stephen P. Cohen (eds), *South Asia After the Cold War* (Boulder, Colorado: Westview Press, 1993), p. 184.

[97] Robert G. Wirsing, *Kashmir in the Shadow of Nuclear War: Regional Rivalries in a Nuclear Age* (Armonk, New York: M.E. Sharpe, 2003), p. 53.

[98] Bundy, 'Existential Deterrence', pp. 8–9.

[99] Cirincione, *Deadly Arsenals*, p. 208.

[100] Krepon and Faruqee, *1990 Crisis*, p. 4.

[101] Hagerty interview, 24 November 1993.

[102] Hagerty interview with former senior Bush administration official, 24 November 1993.

6

Out of the Closet

The 1998 Nuclear Tests Crisis¹

New Delhi stunned the world by conducting a series of nuclear explosive tests on 11 and 13 May 1998. A few weeks later, after considerable external pressure and internal debate, Islamabad followed suit. Long after they had become *de facto* nuclear weapon states, India and Pakistan came out of the closet and declared themselves to be full-fledged, *de jure* nuclear weapon states. In one important sense, however, not much had changed, at least in terms of the Indo-Pakistani relationship itself. For all practical purposes, India and Pakistan had considered each other to be functioning nuclear weapon states since the late 1980s. New Delhi, of course, had conducted a nuclear explosive test in 1974 and since then had refined its nuclear weapon and delivery capabilities in fits and starts. Pakistan was no less convinced of India's nuclear weapon status in April 1998 than it was on 13 May of that year. For its part, Islamabad had not conducted nuclear explosive tests prior to 1998, but it had repeatedly informed the international community in no uncertain terms that it was, in fact, nuclear-weapon capable. Leaked US intelligence estimates and the assessments of the global nuclear non-proliferation community had affirmed Pakistani leaders' pronouncements in this regard. Before May 1998, most of India's strategic elites viewed Pakistan as an established, albeit opaque, nuclear weapon state; after Islamabad's tests, the number of Indian doubters dropped to zero.²

The tit-for-tat South Asian nuclear tests sparked yet another crisis in Indo-Pakistani relations. The 1998 crisis was different from the ones in 1984, 1986–7, and 1990, in that it was precipitated not by an underlying, international political-military 'event', but rather by India's nuclear aspirations and domestic political compulsions. As will be discussed below, the timing of India's decision to carry out nuclear tests in May 1998 was attributable largely to factors within Indian politics, especially as they concerned the recently ascendant Bharatiya Janata Party—the 'Indian Peoples' Party', known by its acronym, the BJP. In turn, Pakistani decisionmaking from 11 May to 28 May was influenced both by Islamabad's dramatically changing international security environment and by intense domestic political pressures—pressures which forced a weak civilian regime to see no alternative but to match its adversary's new flexing of nuclear muscle. What made the period from early May until the beginning of June a crisis was that the two sides' nuclear tests were accompanied by exceedingly bellicose rhetoric, significant movements of military forces in preparation for the possibility of war, and severe pre-emptive war pressures.[3]

As with the previous crises under study here, the 1998 crisis was ultimately resolved short of war. This chapter examines why India and Pakistan did not fight a military conflict in 1998, despite the severe political and military pressures that will be described in detail below. The next section sets the stage by describing the global and regional political contexts that structured Indian and Pakistani decisionmaking in May 1998. The third section builds on the early parts of Chapter Three by discussing why India and Pakistan made their fateful decisions that month. The chapter's fourth and fifth sections, respectively, look at what was known in 1998 about the magnitude of each country's nuclear tests, and what each government must have assumed in 1998 about the other side's nuclear weapon and delivery capabilities. Section six details the crisis itself, tracing India–Pakistan nuclear-political dynamics in the late spring and early summer of 1998. The concluding section uses the prism of our three introductory propositions to analyse why New Delhi and Islamabad chose peace rather than war in 1998. We argue that the main cause of peace was nuclear deterrence. Our propositions concerning conventional deterrence and the US role turn out to have much less explanatory power.

Levels of Analysis[4]

The main structural difference between 1998 and previous Indo-Pakistani crises was that the international system had become fully unipolar, at least for a time. The Soviet Union, which played a small role in the drama of 1990, had completely passed from the scene. In 1998, the US was, far and away, the most powerful external actor in South Asian affairs. As noted in Chapter Five, with the Cold War having ended, Washington's main concern in the region became nuclear proliferation, in particular, the prospect that India and Pakistan would engage in a destabilizing and potentially catastrophic arms race. After taking office in 1993, the Clinton administration pursued a variety of means to try and convince Islamabad and New Delhi to observe restraints on their nuclear competition; its overarching goal was 'first to cap, then over time reduce, and finally eliminate the possession of weapons of mass destruction and their means of delivery'.[5] This approach reflected, in Washington, an 'emerging genuine acceptance among key government officials and non-governmental experts that nuclear weapon capabilities would remain part of South Asian reality for the foreseeable future. The challenge now was to encourage India and Pakistan to capitalize on the basic deterrence they had achieved and to stop short of an overt weaponization process that could become destabilizing...'[6] For most of the 1990s, both New Delhi and Islamabad avoided crossing any nuclear Rubicons, preferring instead to quietly refine their nuclear weapon and delivery capabilities. The prevailing perception in both capitals was that these non-weaponized capabilities conferred deterrence benefits, even without actual deployments.[7]

However, India was less content than Pakistan with this adolescent nuclear stand-off. While Islamabad's nuclear weapon programme was purely the product of strategic concerns about India, New Delhi—as always—played on a larger field. As one of the authors wrote in 1999, bipolarity's end 'resulted in the loss of a critical counterweight to the Chinese threat: the security guarantee implied in the 1971 treaty with the Soviet Union disintegrated with the Soviet collapse.'[8] Moreover, as Ashley Tellis argues, this structural 'shift from bipolarity to unipolarity has only been complemented by a second external reality: discomforting changes in the regional environment centered on, among other things, the rise of a new great power, China.' Tellis captures India's strategic predicament in the late 1990s:

...the growth of China's economic power, its continued nuclear and conventional military modernization, and its increasing influence in various areas of strategic relevance to South Asia, all combine to forebode serious Indo-Chinese military-strategic competition down the line... It places increased pressure on India to revitalize its economy and modernize its defense capability in order to avoid becoming disadvantaged in an age when external superpower assistance is no longer automatically available—as it notionally was during the bipolar era.[9]

Just as India's strategic predicament was growing more challenging, Washington was pushing hard to institutionalize the perceived 'peace dividend' by enshrining a variety of nuclear proliferation-related arms control agreements. In quick succession, the Nuclear Non-Proliferation Treaty was extended indefinitely (1995) and the Comprehensive Test Ban Treaty was adopted (1996). New Delhi chafed against these nuclear straightjackets, and sentiment grew in the mid-1990s that India must test its nuclear weapons again before it was 'too late'. National security imperatives[10] and the strategic enclave's lobbying[11] ultimately bore fruit.

Regionally, India and Pakistan continued their inconclusive struggle over Kashmir.[12] Unlike in 1990, however, Kashmir played little role in the 1998 crisis. Indeed, by the late 1990s, it had appeared as if the Kashmiri insurgency against the Indian state was waning. Newspaper accounts in 1998 suggested that normalcy was returning to the Vale of Kashmir. The tourist industry had picked up, after collapsing in the early 1990s. Indian officials estimated that roughly 2,500 separatist militants continued their guerrilla war in the state of Jammu and Kashmir, down from some 5,000 to 10,000 a few years earlier. India's army commander in the Vale, Lieutenant General Krishan Pal, guessed that probably fewer than 1,000 of these insurgents were 'active gun-toting militants'.[13] Representative were the impressions of one reporter, who wrote in the summer of 1998 that 'Srinagar is a town risen from the dead.'[14]

The Causes of South Asian
Nuclear Proliferation in 1998

Scholars over the years have advanced a variety of arguments as to why states acquire nuclear weapons.[15] The most common argument is that states acquire nuclear weapons strictly to enhance their national security. From this perspective, a government's decision to develop nuclear weapons rests primarily on perceived external threats to its security. A second prominent argument is that states acquire nuclear weapons as a means of earning respect from other states. In this view, the main incentive for a government to acquire nuclear weapon status is the political power it hopes to gain, not the military power associated with the national security argument. A third, less widespread, argument is that states acquire nuclear weapons for a variety of domestic political reasons. From this standpoint, powerful domestic constituencies—politicians, civil servants, military officers, scientists, and the bureaucratic collectivities into which they are organized—are the main driving force behind a government's decision.[16]

The Indian and Pakistani decisions of 1998 exhibit elements of all three arguments. In terms of national security, India's acquisition of nuclear weapons has been driven primarily by concerns about China and secondarily by concerns about Pakistan. India and China have been natural competitors in Asia since they emerged as modern, post-colonial states in the late 1940s. Both are ancient civilizations with extraordinarily rich cultures. Both were compelled to submit to colonial masters during the age of imperialism. Both were reborn in the first half of the twentieth century via nationalist movements that inspired millions of people around the world. After regaining their independence, India and China pursued contrasting development paths, which in turn provided competing models for scores of other newly independent Third World states. When assessing their country's status in the hierarchy of nations, post-independence Indian decision-makers have reflexively cast their gaze at China for purposes of comparison. What they see often displeases them. After early expressions of neighbourly solidarity, Sino-Indian relations soured in the late 1950s. As discussed in Chapter Two, China trounced India in a 1962 border war whose underlying territorial disputes are unresolved even today. The national security roots of India's nuclear weapon programme lie in the 1962 defeat, and in China's 1964 nuclear explosive test. The programme's fundamental *raison d'être* is to deter another attack by China, which, while considered highly unlikely even in New Delhi, cannot be entirely ruled out by any Indian leader.

Closely related to this national security dimension of Indian nuclear planning is the issue of international respect. Between the first Chinese nuclear test of 1964 and the first Indian test of 1974, the NPT entered into force in 1970. The NPT created a club of 'legitimate' nuclear-weapon states whose membership was frozen at five: the US, the Soviet Union (subsequently Russia), the UK, France, and China. When the door to the club slammed shut, India found itself on the outside, consigned to being either a nuclear 'have-not' or an 'illegitimate' nuclear-weapon state. Soon thereafter, several events further enhanced China's international stature. In July 1971, US President Richard Nixon announced that he would travel to Beijing to begin the process of normalizing US relations with China. Next, in October of that year, a seat at the UN—and a permanent seat on the Security Council—were given to Beijing. Indian leaders noted both the symbolic bestowal of great power status on China, as well as the fact that the membership lists of the Security Council and the nuclear club were now identical. In December 1971, Washington intervened in the third Indo-Pakistani war by sending an aircraft carrier task force into the Bay of Bengal, apparently as a means of signalling to India that it should not compound its impending liberation of East Pakistan by also overrunning West Pakistan. India's 1974 nuclear blast followed in short order.

India strives for the same degree of international respect enjoyed by China. It wants to be treated as one of, say, ten potential great powers in the world today. This quest for international respect can scarcely be disentangled from the national security dimension of India's nuclear posture. No reasonable Indian analyst believes that China has any serious interest in attacking India; however, most Indian analysts *do* believe that in any jockeying for international position vis-à-vis China, a non-nuclear India will always come out second best. In that sense, Indian leaders view the military and political characteristics of nuclear weapons as inseparable. As India's foreign minister phrased this thinking in

1998: 'Nuclear weapons remain a key indicator of state power. Since this currency is operational in large parts of the globe, India was left with no choice but to update and validate the capability that had been demonstrated 24 years ago in the nuclear test of 1974.'[17]

But why did this occur in 1998, following 24 years of restraint? This is where domestic politics dominates the equation. Leaders in New Delhi had considered additional nuclear tests at several points from 1974 to 1998.[18] Each time, the relevant decision-makers decided that the costs of such a course would outweigh the benefits. But no previous government had ever staked its political life on restoring the Indian people to national greatness, at least not to the extent that the BJP had in its 1998 campaign rhetoric. As party president (and soon-to-be home minister) L.K. Advani said during the campaign, 'the BJP rejects the notion of nuclear apartheid and will actively oppose attempts to impose a hegemonistic nuclear regime. We will not be dictated to by anybody in matters of security and in the exercise of the nuclear option.'[19] The BJP's manifesto includes this statement: if elected, it would 'reevaluate the country's nuclear policy and exercise the option to induct nuclear weapons'.[20] If the newly elected, BJP-led government had decided *against* testing nuclear weapons in 1998, Indian voters would have perceived it to be more of the same: yet another in a succession of weak, vacillating coalition governments that had come to characterize the national political scene in the 1990s. In democratic India, there are few votes to be found in a posture of nuclear dovishness.

Relative to India, the incentives for Pakistan to test its nuclear weapons were more strictly national security oriented. Under different geographical circumstances, Pakistan would be a large and powerful country in its own right; but Pakistan had the misfortune to be born in the shadow of a much-larger India, which is the transcendent fact of Pakistani geopolitical life. Pakistan has fought three major wars with India, and while occasionally acquitting itself well on the battlefield, never achieved the underlying political objectives it sought. The 1971 war was a particularly devastating defeat, with India intervening in Pakistan's civil war to create the new state of Bangladesh. If the 1962 China war provided Indian leaders with their seminal national security lesson, Pakistan's 1971 humiliation was even more traumatic—despite the fact that, over the long-term, the rump Pakistan has been a more cohesive and robust country than the united Pakistan had ever been.

The core aim of Pakistan's nuclear weapon programme is to prevent a repetition of 1971. By declaring its nuclear status, Pakistan's leaders are trying to deter an Indian attack that might reduce Pakistan's size even further, or perhaps even put the country out of existence entirely. These fears may seem paranoid to non-Pakistanis, but the Bangladesh debacle provides Pakistanis with a hint of the possibilities they face. Islamabad's security challenges are exacerbated by Pakistan's limited strategic depth and its inherent inferiority to India in conventional forces. It does not take a fervent imagination to picture an Indian Army strike corps moving rapidly across the border dividing Rajasthan and southern Pakistani Punjab, slicing Pakistan's main north–south infrastructural links and effectively decapitating Sindh. Add to this scenario the seething discontent among Karachi's muhajir (migrants from India) community, and the Punjabi-dominated Pakistan Army's threat perceptions begin to take on a pronounced worst-case quality. In a world where Latvia, Georgia, and Slovakia have become sovereign states, why not Sindh?

A quest for international respect also plays a role in Pakistan's nuclear ambitions, but much less so than is suggested by the term 'Islamic bomb'. This chimerical characterization has more to do with the preconceptions of ill-informed non-proliferation analysts than with any objective reality. There will always be Westerners who see the Islamic world conspiring to revolt against the West, but they tend to overstate the degree of intra-Islamic unity today. Pakistan's bomb is a Pakistani bomb, not an Islamic bomb. Of course, Pakistanis take great pride in the fact that theirs was the first Islamic country to master nuclear-weapon technology, all the more so considering how resource-constrained Pakistan is relative to the oil-producing states of West Asia. But that in itself would not be sufficient incentive to undertake and sustain a nuclear weapon programme; the *sine qua non* of Pakistan's bomb is the perceived security threat from a more powerful India whose military forces could overrun Pakistan in a matter of weeks, if there were a compelling enough political objective to do so.

As with India, Pakistan's domestic politics had an enormous influence on the timing of the decision to test nuclear weapons. In the aftermath of the 1998 Indian tests, Pakistani Prime Minister Nawaz Sharif was visibly discomfited by the choices before him. Contrary to the perceptions of many analysts, his ultimate decision to proceed with the 28 and 30 May nuclear tests was not inevitable. After fifty years of being portrayed by New Delhi as a praetorian, war-mongering, terrorist-supporting state, Pakistan had a rare window of opportunity to look good relative to India. If it could somehow manage to refrain from following India's lead, it would bask in international acclaim. New US and multilateral aid might have been forthcoming, with donors looking kindly on Pakistan's courageous restraint in the face of India's provocation. But this was not to be. Despite his comfortable parliamentary majority, Nawaz Sharif was not a strong leader. He loosely governed what is, in essence, a national-security state with pronounced fissiparous tendencies. From 13 to 28 May, Sharif was buffeted by an unrelenting barrage of voices urging him to match India's nuclear tests. As a weak prime minister faced with a tidal wave of nationalistic sentiment from every quarter of Pakistani society, Sharif ultimately chose to order Islamabad's own series of nuclear tests on 28 and 30 May. 'Today', he said before a national television audience on 28 May, 'we have settled a score'.[21]

The May 1998 Nuclear Tests

The precise number and yield of the May 1998 Indian and Pakistani nuclear tests remain uncertain. What does seem certain is that both New Delhi and Islamabad exaggerated the magnitude of their respective nuclear explosions. Subsequent seismological findings strongly suggest that 'both governments misled each other—and the international community—about the nuclear tests' conducted in 1998.[22] New Delhi claimed to have 'successfully conducted three underground nuclear tests' on 11 May, 1998. The devices said to have been tested were a 'fission device, a low-yield device, and a thermonuclear device.'[23] On 13 May, New Delhi reported that it had tested another two low-yield nuclear devices.[24] In a joint statement released four days later, India's Atomic Energy Commission and Defence Research and Development Organization announced that the thermonuclear device tested on 11 May had produced a yield of 43 kilotons, the fission device tested on 11 May had yielded 12 kilotons, and the three low-yield devices tested on 11 and 13 May had yields of 0.2, 0.5, and 0.3 kilotons.[25] According to Brajesh Mishra, a senior aide to Indian Prime Minister Atal Behari Vajpayee, the tests 'established that India has a proven capability for a weaponised nuclear program. They also provide a valuable database which is useful in the design of nuclear weapons of different yields for different applications and for different delivery systems.'[26] P.K. Iyengar, a former chairman of India's Atomic Energy Commission, characterized the size of each 11 May explosion in more concrete terms. The largest device was 'not a full hydrogen bomb... the device contained only a token amount of the hydrogen variant tritium. It showed that India's thermonuclear technology worked, but did not produce the megaton explosion typical of a full H-bomb.' The 'standard fission device' was of a 'size that might be dropped from a bomber plane'. The low-yield device was 'the size that might be fired as an artillery shell or dropped from a combat support airplane'.[27] On 17 May 1998, Dr Abdul Kalam, the main driving force behind India's ballistic missile programme, announced that 'weaponisation was now complete'. Lest anyone doubt India's nuclear-weapon capabilities, Kalam added that India's Prithvi and Agni missiles were now capable of delivering 'any type of warhead'.[28] Kalam subsequently claimed that, in total, the Indian nuclear tests yielded 58 kilotons, 'plus or minus 5 kilotons'.[29]

These official Indian claims have been consistently rebutted by non-Indian assessments, official and non-official. Immediately after India's 11 May tests, US officials estimated the total yield of the three explosions at 10 to 20 kilotons.[30] Two other early estimates put the combined size of the Indian tests at 20 kilotons and 9–16 kilotons, respectively.[31] In what appears to a non-geologist to be the most systematic early analysis, Terry C. Wallace of the Southern Arizona Seismic Observatory determined that 'the May 11 event had a yield of 10–15 kilotons.'[32]

Islamabad claimed to have carried out five nuclear explosive tests on 28 May. Three were said to be sub-kiloton devices, and the other two were reported to measure 25 and 12 kilotons.[33] Subsequent Pakistani reports put the total yield of the 28 May tests at 40–45 kilotons.[34] Islamabad conducted another nuclear test on 30 May, reporting that it yielded 15–18 kilotons.[35] In the immediate aftermath of the Pakistani tests, US officials cast severe doubt on Islamabad's claims, saying that they had 'detected only a single, relatively weak seismic signal from the test site' on 28 May.[36] Preliminary US analysis estimated the resultant yield at 6 kilotons. Pakistan's 30 May test was reported to be slightly less powerful.[37] Later analysis suggested that Pakistan's total yields were 6–13 kilotons on 28 May and 2–8 kilotons on 30 May.[38] Wallace's estimates for 28 May and 30 May were 9–12 kilotons and 4–6 kilotons, respectively.[39]

Nuclear Weapon and Delivery Capabilities in 1998

As with the magnitude of their nuclear testing, there was a good deal of uncertainty about India and Pakistan's precise nuclear weapon and delivery capabilities in the late spring of 1998. Very few people knew how many nuclear warheads each country had, if any; which delivery systems those warheads could be effectively mated with; whether or not the two sides actually deployed operational nuclear weapon systems; and, if so, in what modes. Estimating from open sources, the number of Indian and Pakistani nuclear weapons is sheer conjecture. The only reasonable way to have done this would have been to calculate how much fissile material the two sides could *potentially* generate, given what was known about their respective nuclear infrastructures.[40] But this tells us very little about how much fissile material India and Pakistan had *actually* generated by May 1998, not to mention how much of that material they had actually used to fabricate nuclear warheads. Guesses abounded at the time,[41] but their endless repetition served only to construct a 'truth' that may, in fact, have been untrue.[42] A more productive avenue of analysis is to ask what each side must have assumed about the other's nuclear weapon capabilities in 1998; after all, these assumptions— not guesses about overall capabilities—underpinned their mutual decision-making during the crisis. With regard to aircraft, at a minimum, New Delhi and Islamabad would have assumed that the other country had sufficient fissile material to deploy a small number of atomic bombs on aircraft capable of delivering them across the border: the Mirage 2000, MiG-27, MiG-29, Su-30, and Jaguar for India, and the A-5, F-16, and Mirage 3 for Pakistan. The most likely nuclear delivery aircraft would have been India's MiG-27s and Jaguars, and Pakistan's F-16s, which would have given both countries a crude counter-city nuclear weapon capability in 1998.[43]

Less certain at the time were India and Pakistan's ballistic missile capabilities. Both sides deployed operational ballistic missiles that may have been able to deliver nuclear warheads up to 250–300 kilometres: India's Prithvi series and Pakistan's early-version Hatf series (including the renamed M-11 missile acquired from China). New Delhi and Islamabad had also tested longer-range missiles, but these were not yet operational. India's most advanced missile-in-development was the Agni-II, a mobile, solid-fuelled delivery platform that could reportedly have carried a 1,000-kilogram warhead up to 2,000 kilometres. According to then-Indian missile tsar Abdul Kalam, '*Agni*-II is designed to carry a nuclear warhead if required... we tested an *Agni*-class payload' in 1998.[44] Pakistan's most-advanced missile-in-development was the *Ghauri*-II, a liquid-fuelled ballistic missile that could, at least on paper, carry a 700-kilogram warhead up to 1,500 kilometres. Pakistani officials claimed at the time that their missiles, too, were nuclear-weapon capable;[45] indeed, owing to the fact that China had reportedly transferred to Pakistan a tested missile-warhead design,[46] Pakistan may have had more reliable nuclear missiles than India in 1998. Although neither the *Agni*-II nor the *Ghauri*-II was yet operational, Indian and Pakistani officials steadfastly claimed that all of their ballistic missiles could deliver nuclear weapons well into the other side's territory. In sum, while it was uncertain whether India and Pakistan had yet deployed nuclear warheads on ballistic missiles by 1998, prudent leaders in Islamabad and New Delhi must have assumed that military forces across the border *could have been* equipped with nuclear-armed ballistic missiles capable of reaching virtually any important target on the subcontinent.[47]

The Crisis Itself: May–June 1998

The 1998 crisis erupted when India surprised the world with its second, third, and fourth nuclear tests. George Perkovich describes the event:

At 3:45 p.m. on May 11, almost twenty-four years to the day since India conducted its first nuclear test, the desert ground near Pokhran shook again.

India's strategic enclave simultaneously detonated three nuclear devices. Shock waves rippled through the test area, cracking walls in a nearby village and shaking the edifice of the international nonproliferation regime. The scientists exulted. Minutes later the phone rang at Prime Minister Vajpayee's official residence. Principal Secretary Brajesh Mishra received the message that the deed was done. He went to an adjoining room and notified Vajpayee, Home Minister L.K. Advani, Finance Minister Yashwant Sinha, Planning Commission Deputy Chairman Jaswant Singh, and [Defence Minister] George Fernandes. According to *India Today*, Advani, the firebrand leader of the BJP was seen wiping away tears.[48]

Two days later, India announced that it had conducted its fifth and sixth nuclear tests. In the week following 11 May, senior Indian officials unleashed a torrent of truculent, ambiguous, and downright confusing messages to the world in general, and to Pakistan, in particular. On 12 May, the Minister of State for Science and Technology, Murli Manohar Joshi, 'announced that India's missiles would be armed and deployed with the country's new nuclear weapons'.[49] New Delhi's clumsy efforts to convince the existing nuclear weapon states of its enhanced nuclear status had the effect—perhaps intended—of unnerving Islamabad, where senior officials would have been justified in thinking that Joshi's declaration was being implemented immediately. Unfortunately, India's head of government clarified matters not one bit:

Prime Minister Vajpayee further alarmed the international community when he gave his first interview since the tests. 'We have a big bomb now,' he declared to *India Today*, suggesting an ominous triumphalism. Speaking to party workers the same day, Vajpayee said his government 'will not hesitate to use these weapons in self-defence'. Other officials moved to correct the impression left by the prime minister. The government retracted the 'big bomb' statement, and *India Today* deleted it from the published version of the Vajpayee interview, although transcripts with the offending phrase already had been distributed by the prime minister's office. Then, on May 18, the prime minister's office 'modified' Vajpayee's statement about not hesitating to use nuclear weapons in self-defense. The government wanted to remove the impression that Vajpayee meant to contemplate defending India through *first use* of nuclear weapons. 'India will not be the first to use nuclear weapons against anyone,' the prime minister's office now insisted. Observers could be forgiven for wondering if the Indian government knew what it was doing.[50]

As would be expected, Pakistani leaders immediately tried to trump Indian officials' bellicosity. As Prime Minister Nawaz Sharif's government scrambled in the days after 13 May to formulate a coherent response to the Indian nuclear tests, opposition leader and former Prime Minister Benazir Bhutto thundered: 'Rogue nations that defy world opinion ought to be taught a lesson. If a pre-emptive military strike is possible to neutralize India's nuclear capability, that is the response that is necessary.'[51] Bhutto went so far as to publicly challenge Sharif's manhood by throwing down her bangles (bracelets), 'suggesting that if he did not authorize a test promptly he was the woman and should wear the bangles'.[52] Sharif was also pressed hard by the hawkish Islamic right wing and a Pakistani military establishment whose views were mixed,[53] but which was demonstrably unsettled by the prospect of India's expanding the Kashmir war under its newly refurbished nuclear umbrella.[54] As it was, Pakistani intelligence officials had 'been put on high alert ever since India's nuclear test. They were told to look out for any attempt to destroy Pakistan's nuclear facilities by methods such as an air strike, a helicopter raid or even a cruise missile attack.'[55] If Sharif took the high road and chose not to test Pakistan's nuclear weapons, would New Delhi doubt Islamabad's deterrent capability? If so, might India then be emboldened to invade Pakistan-held Kashmir and crush the insurgent movement once and for all? In the worst case, would the hardline BJP government be tempted to invade Pakistan and splinter the country yet again, à la the Bangladesh war in 1971?

Indian leaders assiduously stoked these fears in a concerted effort to deny Pakistan the international public relations victory it would have gained from not matching India's nuclear tests. Throughout the fortnight between 13 and 28 May, Indian government officials like home minister Advani and defence minister Fernandes 'issued statement after militant statement chiding Pakistan, and threatening military action in Kashmir'.[56] Other Indian strategic voices suggested that Pakistani restraint would signal to New Delhi that Islamabad's ostensible nuclear-weapon capability had been a bluff all along. Advani provocatively counselled Islamabad to 'realize the change in the geostrategic situation in the region and the world' and 'roll back its anti-India policy, especially with regard to Kashmir'. Moreover, Advani said, India's new nuclear posture had 'brought about a qualitatively new stage in Indo-Pakistani relations' and 'signifies, even while adhering to the principle of no first strike', that 'India is resolved to deal firmly with Pakistan's hostile activities in Kashmir'.[57] India, Advani declared on 25 May, 'would undertake "hot pursuit" to chase insurgents from Kashmir back into Pakistan.'[58]

In the meantime, the US, still reeling from the explosions of 11 and 13 May, and smarting from New Delhi's clever and successful duplicity in hiding its test plans, sought ways to induce Pakistan not to follow suit. Strobe Talbott, President Clinton's confidant and deputy secretary of state, travelled to the region in a carrots-and-sticks attempt to encourage Sharif's government to resist the pressures swirling all around him. Clinton himself urged Sharif by telephone to hang tough, receiving the disconcerting reply that the decision to test was 'out of [Sharif's] hands'.[59] The US president also sent General Anthony Zinni, commander-in-chief of the US Central Command, to meet Pakistan's army chief and 'to offer him a huge conventional arms package in return for a no-test decision'. Washington offered to dramatically reduce Islamabad's foreign debt obligations as well. However, US leverage over Pakistan's nuclear decisionmaking was severely constrained by the fact that the United States had already sanctioned Pakistan's nuclear weapon strides and was, by 1998, providing very little aid to Islamabad, as well as the reality that all promises made by the Clinton administration would have to be approved by a US Congress with which the president's relations were extraordinarily rocky.[60]

By the last week of May, the blustery rhetoric emanating from New Delhi had begun to moderate,[61] but the die was already being cast in Islamabad. On 25 May, Karamat 'met in an urgent session with... Sharif... stating that if Pakistan did not respond quickly with a nuclear explosion of its own, that he believed India could attempt a military solution of the Kashmir crisis as early as... fall, according to civilian and military leaders familiar with the meeting.'[62] As one analyst has observed, 'the "no-holds-barred" nature of Pakistan's still-developing democracy made it virtually impossible for any prime minister to do other than follow the public outcry for a response to India's nuclear blasts... Given the volatile nature of Pakistan's politics, it would have been a tremendous risk for Sharif to resist such pressure.'[63] Ultimately, domestic political pressures, the Clinton administration's weakness, and—most importantly—Pakistani analysts' inability to rule out future Indian nuclear coercion pushed the army and Sharif towards a muscular Pakistani response.

The 1998 crisis came to a head on 27 May. That evening, with Pakistan's first-ever nuclear explosive test slated for the next day, Pakistan's director general of military operations alerted senior civilian and military officials that, according to Saudi intelligence, Israeli fighter-bombers were flying from eastern India towards Pakistan, intent on 'destroying Pakistan's nuclear capability'. Karamat immediately 'scrambled F-16 fighter planes and sent them to protect the test site in Balochistan. Mirage aircraft and ground-based air defence units were tasked with preventing any attack on the Kahuta uranium enrichment plant just outside of Islamabad. Pakistan also dispersed its missile arsenal so as to preserve its nuclear capability in the event of enemy attack.' Ballistic missiles were apparently moved in India, too. Pakistani foreign policy officials went on a diplomatic offensive, frantically contacting other governments and the UN, 'warning of the impending attack'. Sharif, 'backing up the Foreign Office's efforts, personally called President Clinton in Washington and Prime Minister Blair in London and told them that his intelligence reports were clear: Israeli planes were on the way.' Pakistan's permanent representative to the UN appeared on CNN to say that 'the world must understand that Pakistan is ready. The reaction would be massive and dissuasive.'[64]

On 28 May, as governments around the world were ascertaining that Islamabad's fears were ill-founded, Pakistan conducted what it said were five nuclear explosive tests. Sharif told his people that 'today God has given us the power in order to save our kingdom from danger. It was the final solution, which we had to do. In 1974, when India first carried out an atom bomb explosion, we did not have all the know-how then. This nuclear test saved us from a new danger.' Pakistan's prime minister also announced a state of emergency in the country, which Islamabad claimed was for economic reasons—that is, to prepare for the expected rash of international sanctions and other economic penalties. Indicating, however, that the state of emergency was related as much to defence as to economics, Sharif claimed that Pakistan's intermediate-range Ghauri missiles—first tested in April 1998—were already being armed with nuclear warheads. The Ghauri, news reports pointed out, was capable of striking virtually every major city in India.[65] In the days immediately following Pakistan's initial nuclear tests of 28 May, 'senior Pakistani officials' continued to respond to 'rumors of an imminent India attack' by claiming that the Ghauris would be 'immediately armed with nuclear warheads in the face of the manifest Indian threat'.[66] This would appear to have been a direct response to New Delhi's claim, after its own nuclear tests, that it was nuclear-weaponizing its missiles. Pakistan's actions and rhetoric in late May and early June 1998 were its way of trying to announce its strategic parity with India.

Analysis

Yet again in 1998, South Asia endured a crisis and was spared a war. Two nuclear-capable bordering states conducted a series of tit-for-tat nuclear explosive tests in an atmosphere of palpable tension. Unlike in the bipolar past, neither side enjoyed the protection or restraining influence of a superpower ally. Regionally, the Kashmir conflict raged on, with scores of thousands dead and no end in sight. Domestically, India was led by a hawkish—some would say chauvinistic—regime, while in Pakistan a thin veneer of democracy papered over what was still an atavistic, praetorian state. As the crisis intensified in May 1998, both sides moved their ballistic missiles for precautionary purposes, engaged in nuclear-tinted rhetorical outbursts, and generally indulged themselves in a virulent form of brinkmanship. At the height of the crisis, owing either to appallingly bad intelligence or to a desperate hoax by Pakistan's military-intelligence apparatus,[67] Islamabad feared that an Indian-abetted Israeli air strike was about to decapitate its nuclear facilities. 'Altogether, a cacophony of rhetoric and unsubstantiated claims emerged from both India and Pakistan in the month of May, leading the South Asian correspondent of the *Washington Post* to conclude laconically but accurately that "confusion dominates [the] arms race in South Asia."'[68] The retrospective comment of a very senior Pakistani official stands as a symbol of how matters stood as the fog of conflict was thickest on 27 May 1998: 'Our radar stations were on high alert. If some Gulf State Prince had been travelling unannounced in a private jet towards Karachi that night, the results would have been cataclysmic.'[69] In sum, several dire possibilities marked those fateful weeks. Pakistan had reason to fear a preventive air strike that would smash to bits its nuclear test site in Baluchistan, and perhaps its uranium enrichment facility near Islamabad. *Both* sides were caught in what Thomas Schelling long ago termed the 'reciprocal fear of surprise attack',[70] a tornadic spiral whose ultimate outcome—theoretically—is a pre-emptive mindset, in which striking second is seen as the worst option, and striking first is viewed as the second-worst choice.

What was the 'cause' of Indo-Pakistani peace in 1998? Of our three propositions, nuclear deterrence appears to offer the most convincing answer. The conventional deterrence proposition is weak, partly for the same reason it was weak in the 1990 case: in a nuclear-free South Asia in May 1998, India clearly would have had the conventional military capabilities to launch a punishing, blitzkrieg-style attack against Pakistan. Indeed, if anything, the 1990s had brought a significantly *widening* conventional military imbalance between the two countries. After the 1990 cut-off of US security and economic assistance to Pakistan, Islamabad's relative conventional military inferiority grew more pronounced. While New Delhi continued to buy advanced weapon systems from a cash-strapped Russia, Pakistan's purchases were limited mainly to acquisitions of bargain-basement, relatively antiquated Chinese weapons.

Between 1995 and 1999, Indian military expenditures rose by an annual average of 8.8 per cent; in contrast, Pakistan's increased by an annual average of 2.9 per cent. In 1999, India spent $11.3 billion on military expenditures; Pakistan spent $3.5 billion.[71] In addition to India's traditional quantitative superiority in ground forces, the airpower equation shifted from rough parity in 1990 to clear Indian dominance by the end of the decade. Although India still had no aircraft that could match the PAF's F-16s on a one-to-one basis, the condition of those aircraft had declined considerably under the strict US sanctions regime of the 1990s. Michael Krepon wrote in 2003: 'nowhere is the growing disparity in conventional military capabilities more apparent than with respect to airpower. From 1993 to 2002, India received or licensed production of 10 Mirage-2000s, 10 MiG-21s, 10 MiG-29s, 190 SU-30s, 4 TU-22s, 54 MiG-27s, 2 Harriers, and 52 Jaguars. During this period, Pakistan acquired or placed orders for 97 F-7s, 40 Mirage-5s, and 10 Mirage-3s.'[72] All in all, India was well-positioned for a decisive offensive thrust, given sufficient provocation.

Equally suspect is the notion that US intervention was a cause of peace in 1998. Ironically, given that the US was by 1998 the world's definitive 'sole pole', Washington's performance in the May crisis was initially inept and subsequently ineffective. India's strategic enclave utterly blindsided the US intelligence community by concealing its test preparations; 'the day after the tests, it emerged that US satellites had... detected "clear-cut" evidence of test preparations six hours before the devices were detonated. However, CIA satellite intelligence analysts were home sleeping because they had not been put on alert.'[73] George Tenet, the US director of central intelligence, reportedly learned about the Indian tests via the media 'as he sipped coffee at his Langley office'.[74]

Between 11 and 28 May, Washington's main priority was to convince Nawaz Sharif and the Pakistan Army not to rise to India's bait and test Pakistani nuclear devices. The US also failed at this, for a variety of reasons: the generally poor state of US-Pakistani relations; intense resentment among Pakistan's strategic elites for having been 'abandoned' by the Washington after the Soviets left Afghanistan in 1989; Washington's lack of leverage over Pakistani decisionmaking stemming from the stiff nuclear sanctions implemented against Islamabad in the 1990s; and Bill Clinton's inability to extend Pakistan firm economic or security guarantees of any kind, owing to the need for Congressional approval. Having said all that, it is unlikely that even the most generous package of goodies could have swayed Sharif from his ultimate course. Given the balance of political power in Pakistan and the sheer magnitude of popular pro-bomb sentiment, Sharif may well have found himself bounced from power by an army intent on evening the score with India. When all was said and done, the US had to settle for shutting the barn door after the horses had bolted. In June 1998, the Clinton administration imposed upon India and Pakistan the sanctions that were both required by law and acknowledged by most experts to be futile.

Nuclear deterrence provides the best explanation for South Asia's non-war of 1998. As it had done throughout the region's short nuclear history, India refrained from carrying out preventive attacks against

Islamabad's nuclear facilities, because to have done so would have meant certain retaliation in kind. In 1984, Pakistan could protect itself by advertising the possibility of 'boosted' conventional attacks against India's sprawling nuclear infrastructure; by 1998, few people who mattered in New Delhi or Washington doubted that Pakistan could muster at least a crude nuclear response to serious Indian aggression. Indeed, given China's earlier provision of a tested nuclear-warhead design and Pakistan's successful test of the Ghauri missile in April 1998, Pakistan's ability to strike India with nuclear weapons may have been more advanced than India's capability to do the reverse.[75]

Why did the two sides not succumb to the temptations of pre-emption that are so dominant in the nuclear-weapons literature? The answer lies at the opposite end of the nuclear-use spectrum from Schelling's 'reciprocal fear of surprise attack', where resides McGeorge Bundy's notion of 'existential deterrence', as discussed in chapters one and five. Again, the idea behind existential deterrence is that the mere existence of nuclear weapon capabilities imposes its own logic on decision-makers. Faced with the weapons' huge destructive potential, leaders of nuclear powers embroiled in crises look not for ways to use the capabilities at their disposal, but for ways *not* to use them. Unlike Schelling's conception, which is deductively elegant but has no basis in historical fact, Bundy's think was inductively rooted in history. The course of every crisis involving nuclear weapon states[76] (including the Kargil crisis, to be discussed in the next chapter) suggests that, in moments of high international tension, decision-makers tend towards nuclear restraint rather than nuclear pre-emption.

But if India's and Pakistan's exact nuclear prowess was uncertain and open to question in 1998, how is it that nuclear deterrence could have prevailed? Classical nuclear deterrence theory posits that unambiguous, reliable second-strike capabilities are an essential component of the deterrence equation. Such a situation manifestly did not obtain in the South Asia of 1998. As one media account described the situation after Pakistan's response to the Indian tests:

In the nuclear drama unfolding between India and Pakistan, it seems no statement made one day is sacrosanct the next. A series of contradictions and denials by top officials in both governments has created serious doubt about who knows what they're talking about and who is telling the truth... There is no better example of where confusion reigns supreme than in the critical issue of whether India and Pakistan are, as both governments keep saying, 'weaponized' and 'nuclear weapons states'. Top-ranking officials in both governments have made a series of contradictory statements about whether they already have a stockpile of nuclear weapons, and if so, whether the weapons are deployed and trained at each other.[77]

In other words, opacity continued to characterize the Indian and Pakistani nuclear programmes during and even after the 1998 crisis. The bottom line of opacity is not whether a country tests its nuclear weapons; rather, it is how much reliable information each side has about the other's capabilities. How many bombs or warheads have actually been assembled? Where are they? How close are they to delivery systems, and how vulnerable are they? What would be the time lag between tactical warning and response? Is the other side using dummies or other forms of deception? Do we know for sure which system components might be dummies and which are real? As recently as 2001, the dean of American South Asia security analysts could write: 'It is... doubtful that India and Pakistan have good estimates of how many nuclear weapons the other possesses. Guesses based on presumed reprocessing or enrichment facilities may be misleading. It could be that neither country has turned fissile material into metal and metal into warheads, let alone mating warheads to delivery systems.'[78] While Stephen Cohen made this observation in the course of arguing that the South Asian nuclear balance is *unstable*, it could be argued just as powerfully that this uncertainty is what deters. One of the authors has termed this condition '"first-strike uncertainty", or the planting of a seed of doubt in the minds of the potential attacker's leaders about whether it is possible to destroy all of the victim's nuclear weapons before it can retaliate. The same technological backwardness that is said to make new nuclear forces vulnerable also implies that they will be nowhere near sophisticated enough to achieve first strike reliability.'[79] While 'clever briefers' abound as much in the capitals of nuclear weapon states as in other states, political and military leaders—thankfully—tend to shun their advice at critical moments. That this happened in May 1998 is both the main cause of Indo-Pakistani peace that year, and a continuing testament to Bundy's astute strategic analysis.

Notes

[1] This chapter draws on previous work by Hagerty. See his 'The South Asian Nuclear Tests: Implications for Arms Control', in Carl Ungerer and Marianne Hanson (eds), *The Politics of Nuclear Non-Proliferation* (Sydney: Allen and Unwin, 2001), pp. 97–117.

[2] For a detailed overview of India and Pakistan's pre-1998 nuclear capabilities and the mutual perceptions of New Delhi and Islamabad, see Devin T. Hagerty, *The Consequences of Nuclear Proliferation: Lessons from South Asia* (Cambridge, Massachusetts: MIT Press, 1998).

[3] Again, pre-emption differs from prevention. Pre-emption involves the imperative to 'get in the first blow', for fear that the adversary is about to strike first. A preventive strike is one that is carried out for fear of the ongoing augmentation of the adversary's capabilities. Generally speaking, preventive war fears extend over long periods of time, as a stronger country contemplates destroying a weaker enemy's growing capabilities in order to prevent it from eventually gaining the military advantage. In contrast, pre-emptive temptations and fears are usually limited to much shorter time frames, such as crises in which two sides feel that the adversary's first strike may be imminent.

[4] This section discusses the global and regional context of the 1998 crisis. Sections below take account of the domestic political contexts in India and Pakistan.

[5] Devin T. Hagerty, 'Kashmir and the Nuclear Question', in Charles H. Kennedy and Rasul Baksh Rais (eds), *Pakistan: 1995* (Boulder, Colorado: Westview Press, 1995), pp. 167–71.

[6] George Perkovich, *India's Nuclear Bomb: The Impact on Global Proliferation* (Berkeley: University of California Press, 1999), p. 335.

[7] Devin T. Hagerty, 'South Asia's Nuclear Balance', *Current History*, vol. 95, no. 600 (April 1996), pp. 165–70.

[8] Sumit Ganguly, 'India's Pathway to Pokhran II: The Prospects and Sources of New Delhi's Nuclear Weapons Program', *International Security*, vol. 23, no. 4 (Spring 1999), p. 167.

[9] Tellis's analysis is quoted in Neil Joeck, 'Nuclear Developments in India and Pakistan', *Access Asia Review*, vol. 2, no. 2 (July 1999), p. 20.

[10] Ganguly, 'India's Pathway to Pokhran II', pp. 167–71.

[11] Perkovich, *India's Nuclear Bomb*, p. 365.

[12] Devin T. Hagerty, 'Kashmir and the Nuclear Question Revisited', *Pakistan 2000* (Lanham, Maryland: Lexington, 2000), pp. 81–106.

[13] John F. Burns, 'In Brinkmanship's Wake, All Quiet on the Kashmir Front', *International Herald Tribune*, 16 June 1998.

[14] Molly Moore, 'Kashmiri Militants Join the Mainstream', *Washington Post*, 3 July 1998.

[15] For an overview of the scholarly literature in this area, see Devin T. Hagerty, 'Why Do States Acquire Nuclear Weapons?', Paper presented at the Australasian Political Studies Association Annual Conference, Sydney, September 1999.

[16] A fourth argument, prominent in the 1960s and 1970s, has all but passed from the scene today. This is the notion that states which could develop nuclear weapons would develop them. With roughly 50 states theoretically capable of acquiring nuclear weapons and the number of actual nuclear weapon states continuing to hover at ten or fewer, this proposition has steadily lost support.

[17] Jaswant Singh, 'Against Nuclear Apartheid', *Foreign Affairs*, vol. 77, no. 5 (September/October 1998), p. 44.

[18] Perkovich, *India's Nuclear Bomb*, pp. 190–403.

[19] John Zubrzycki, 'Hindu Nationalists Aim for Nuclear Arsenal', *The Australian*, 4 February 1998.

[20] Christopher Kremmer, 'Hindu Right Reaches for the N-Bomb', *Sydney Morning Herald*, 5 February 1998.

[21] Perkovich, *India's Nuclear Bomb*, p. 433.

[22] Robert Lee Hotz, 'Tests Were Exaggerated by India and Pakistan', *International Herald Tribune*, 17 September 1998.

[23] 'India Conducts Three Underground Nuclear Tests', *The Hindu*, 11 May 1998.

[24] Neelesh Misra, 'India Conducts Two More Nuke Tests', *Associated Press*, 13 May 1998.

[25] Kenneth J. Cooper, 'India Says Bomb's Power Surpassed All Estimates', *International Herald Tribune*, 18 May 1998; Robert S. Norris and William M. Arkin, 'After the Tests: India and Pakistan Update', *Bulletin of the Atomic Scientists*, vol. 54, no. 5 (1998), pp. 69–71. A kiloton is equivalent to a thousand tons of TNT. The bombs dropped by the US on Hiroshima and Nagasaki in August 1945 had yields of 15 and 21 kilotons, respectively. By the end of 1945, the Hiroshima bomb had killed 1,40,000 people, out of a pre-bomb population of 3,50,000; the equivalent numbers for Nagasaki were 70,000 out of 2,70,000.

[26] Kenneth J. Cooper, 'India's Atomic Tests Raise Old Fears', *International Herald Tribune*, 12 May 1998.

[27] Narayanan Madhavan, 'India Defiant Over Nuclear Tests', *Reuters*, 12 May 1998. A megaton is equivalent to a million tons of TNT.

[28] 'Weaponisation Now Complete, Say Scientists', *The Hindu*, 18 May 1998.

[29] 'Dueling Abduls: The Men Who Built the Bombs', *Time International*, 30 November 1998.

[30] R. Jeffrey Smith, 'Blasts Create Shock Waves for US Policy', *Washington Post*, 12 May 1998.

[31] Suzanna van Moyland and Roger Clark, 'The Paper Trail', *Bulletin of the Atomic Scientists*, vol. 54, no. 4 (1998), pp. 26–9; Pallava Bagla and Eliot Marshall, 'Size of Indian Blasts Still Disputed', *Science*, vol. 281, no. 5385 (1998), p. 1939.

[32] Terry C. Wallace, 'The May 1998 India and Pakistan Nuclear Tests', *Seismological Research Letters*, vol. 69, no. 5, pp. 386–93. The word 'event' is chosen carefully—to indicate uncertainty about how many devices India actually tested on 11 May. Because the tests were conducted very close together in both time and space, the precise number of tests may always be ambiguous. It should also be noted that wide discrepancies in yield estimates are not uncommon. Indian officials initially claimed that their first nuclear test in 1974 yielded 12 kilotons. Later, Indian estimates put it at 8 kilotons. The actual yield may have been lower than 5 kilotons. See Robert S. Norris and William M. Arkin, 'Known Nuclear Tests Worldwide, 1945–98', *Bulletin of the Atomic Scientists*, vol. 54, no. 6 (1998), pp. 65–7. 'There is some controversy over whether India successfully tested a thermonuclear device, since the yield recorded and analysed by Western seismographers was low, leading many in the scientific community to believe that the boosted-fission primary or the thermonuclear secondary did not function as designed.' Joseph Cirincione, *Deadly Arsenals: Tracking Weapons of Mass Destruction* (Washington, DC: Carnegie Endowment for International Peace, 2002), p. 195.

[33] *Dawn Internet Edition*, 'Some Technical Info', 28 May 1998 (http://www.dawn.com).

[34] Wallace, 'May 1998 India and Pakistan Nuclear Tests', p. 391.

[35] Ibid.

[36] Molly Moore, 'The "Father" of the Islamic Bomb', *International Herald Tribune*, 1 June 1998.

[37] 'Pakistan Drops Missile Alert in Slight Easing of Tensions', CNN, 31 May 1998.

[38] Norris and Arkin, 'Known Nuclear Tests Worldwide, 1945–98', pp. 65–7.

[39] Wallace, 'May 1998 India and Pakistan Nuclear Tests', p. 391.

[40] See, for example, Francois Heisbourg, 'The Prospects for Nuclear Stability Between India and Pakistan', *Survival*, vol. 40, no. 4 (1998–9), pp. 77–92.

[41] See David Albright, 'The Shots Heard "Round the World"', and 'Pakistan: The Other Shoe Drops', *Bulletin of the Atomic Scientists*, vol. 54, no. 4 (1998), pp. 20–5; Norris and Arkin, 'After the Tests: India and Pakistan Update', pp. 69–71.

[42] As Ashley Tellis writes: 'Whether India did in fact stockpile ready nuclear weapons itself prior to May 1998 is anyone's guess. Most official US estimates suggest that India could fabricate complete weapons at short notice, but the safety, efficiency and reliability of such weapons (even in the wake of the May 1998 tests) continue to be the subject of debate both within and outside India.' Ashley J. Tellis, *India's Emerging Nuclear Posture: Between Recessed Deterrent and Ready Arsenal* (Santa Monica, California: RAND, 2001), p. 17.

[43] For a credible analysis of Indian and Pakistani nuclear-delivery aircraft, see Federation of American Scientists, *Nuclear Forces Guide* (http://www.fas.org/nuke/guide).

[44] Raj Chengappa, 'If Government Permits, We'll Sell Our Know-How', *India Today*, 26 April 1999.

[45] 'Pakistan Drops Missile Alert in Slight Easing of Tensions', CNN, 31 May 1998.

[46] Cirincione, *Deadly Arsenals*, p. 148.

[47] For a credible analysis of Indian and Pakistani nuclear-capable missiles, see Federation of American Scientists, *Nuclear Forces Guide* (http://www.fas.org/nuke/guide).

[48] Perkovich, *India's Nuclear Bomb*, pp. 415–6.

[49] Tellis, *India's Emerging Nuclear Posture*, pp. 2–3.

[50] Perkovich, *India's Nuclear Bomb*, p. 420.

[51] Benazir Bhutto, 'A Military Strike Will Teach Rogue India a Lesson', *International Herald Tribune*, 16–17 May 1998.

[52] Joeck, 'Nuclear Developments in India and Pakistan', p. 22.

[53] Owen Bennett Jones, *Pakistan: Eye of the Storm* (New Haven, Connecticut: Yale University Press, 2002), pp. 190–3. Bennett Jones reports that Pakistan Army Chief Jehangir Karamat was 'stung' by Minister for Religious Affairs Raja Zafar ul Haq's suggestion that if Karamat 'did not approve a test, the army rank and file would think they had a leader who lacked the courage to stand up to India.' As Bennett Jones writes dryly, 'no army chief, least of all a Punjabi one, likes to be called a coward.'

[54] John Ward Anderson and Kamran Khan, '5 Tests Are Conducted to Answer India', *International Herald Tribune*, 29 May 1998.

[55] Bennett Jones, *Pakistan*, p. 190.

[56] Praful Bidwai and Achin Vanaik, *New Nukes: India, Pakistan and Global Nuclear Disarmament* (New York: Olive Branch, 2000), pp. 54, 187.

[57] Kenneth J. Cooper, 'India Warns Pakistan over Kashmir', *International Herald Tribune*, 19 May 1998.

[58] Perkovich, *India's Nuclear Bomb*, p. 423.

[59] Samina Ahmed, 'Pakistan's Nuclear Weapons Program: Turning Points and Nuclear Choices', *International Security*, vol. 23, no. 4 (Spring 1999), pp. 194–5.

[60] Bennett Jones, *Pakistan*, pp. 192–3. See also Joeck, 'Nuclear Developments in India and Pakistan', p. 24. For an overview of US policy options, see Richard P. Cronin *et al.*, 'India–Pakistan Nuclear Tests and US Response', *Congressional Research Service Report for Congress*, 9 September 1998.

[61] Michael Ryan Kraig, 'The Political and Strategic Imperatives of Nuclear Deterrence in South Asia', *India Review*, vol. 2, no. 1 (January 2003), p. 5.

[62] Molly Moore and Kamran Khan, 'In Kashmir, The Shooting Never Stops', *Washington Post*, 3 June 1998.

[63] Joeck, 'Nuclear Developments in India and Pakistan', p. 22.

[64] Bennett Jones, *Pakistan*, pp. 187–9.

[65] *The NewsHour With Jim Lehrer*, 28 May 1998.

[66] Tellis, *India's Emerging Posture*, p. 3.

[67] US officials apparently concluded that the Pakistani charges concerning possible air raids were 'false and cooked up by Pakistani intelligence'. Dennis Kux, 'US–Pakistan Relations As the Twentieth Century Ends', in Charles H. Kennedy and Craig Baxter (eds), *Pakistan 2000* (Lanham, Maryland: Lexington, 2000), p. 79.

[68] Tellis, *India's Emerging Nuclear Posture*, p. 3, quoting John Ward Anderson, 'Confusion Dominates Arms Race', *Washington Post*, 1 June 1998.

[69] Bennett Jones, *Pakistan*, p. 189.

[70] Thomas C. Schelling, *The Strategy of Conflict* (New York: Oxford University Press, 1963), pp. 207–29.

[71] Michael Krepon, *The Stability–Instability Paradox, Misperception, and Escalation Control in South Asia* (Washington, DC: Henry L. Stimson Center, 2003), pp. 8–9.

[72] Krepon, *Escalation Control in South Asia*, p. 9.

[73] Perkovich, *India's Nuclear Bomb*, p. 418.

[74] Raj Chengappa, *Weapons of Peace: The Secret Story of India's Quest to Be a Nuclear Power* (New Delhi: HarperCollins, 2000), p. 17.

[75] As Ashley Tellis writes, 'on balance... India's capabilities prior to the May 1998 tests seem to justify the conclusion that New Delhi possessed a "nuclear option" in the form of latent and, in some areas, rudimentary capabilities but had no effective nuclear arsenal.' Tellis, *India's Emerging Nuclear Posture*, p. 18.

[76] These would include the 1962 Cuban missile crisis, the 1969 Sino-Soviet border clash, the 1973 Arab–Israeli war, and the 1990 Kashmir crisis.

[77] John Ward Anderson, 'Doubt Dominates South Asia Arms Race', *Washington Post*, 1 June 1998; see also John F. Burns, 'In Nuclear India, Small Stash Does Not an Arsenal Make', *New York Times*, 26 July 1998.

[78] Stephen Philip Cohen, *India: Emerging Power* (Washington, DC: Brookings Institution, 2001), p. 194.

[79] Devin T. Hagerty, 'Nuclear Deterrence in South Asia: The 1990 Indo-Pakistani Crisis', *International Security*, vol. 20, no. 3 (Winter 1995/96), p. 85.

7

The Road to Kargil

Between early May and mid-July 1999, India and Pakistan fought the fourth war in their independent history. The war ensued during the first week of May shortly after local herdsmen alerted Indian security forces about a Pakistani military incursion near the village of Garkhun in the Kargil region of Kashmir. Despite initial scepticism about this report, Indian military authorities did send out a military patrol on 4 May that confirmed the presence of possible intruders.[1] Other infiltrators were soon detected in adjoining sectors in short order.[2] Shortly thereafter, to confirm the presence of Pakistani forces, a series of patrols were launched to assess the extent and scope of the incursions. However, it was not until about the last week of May that the Indian Army had a full appreciation of the Pakistani incursions. Almost immediately thereafter, the Cabinet Committee on Security (CCS) made a decision that the Pakistani intruders would be militarily evicted.[3]

Even though there was no formal declaration of war, this conflict proved to be among the costliest of the Indo-Pakistani war in terms of both men and materiel. While estimates of casualties vary it is believed that India lost 1,714 military personnel and Pakistan lost 772.[4] The conflict also saw the extensive use of heavy artillery at high altitudes and India resorted to the use of its air force against Pakistan for the first time since their 1971 war. This was also the second war that had ensued between two nuclear-armed states. (The first such conflict had taken place along the Ussuri River between the People's Republic of China and the then Soviet Union in 1969.)

This conflict again provides an opportunity to test the proposition about the role that nuclear weapons may play in containing the prospects of a full-scale war between two nuclear-armed adversaries. At the outset, it is important to underscore that unlike in previous conflicts, especially the 1965 war, on this occasion India chose not to resort to horizontal escalation. It carefully confined its military response to those areas where Pakistani forces had made incursions across the LoC. Such restraint calls for an explanation.

In this chapter we will explore three alternative explanations. First, we will examine the proposition that India was inhibited from expanding the scope of conflict because it lacked the requisite military capabilities. Second, we will assess the possibility that external powers, especially the US, played a critical role in limiting the conflict. Third, we will discuss the possible role of nuclear weapons in containing escalation. Our analysis of the available evidence suggests that, in all likelihood, the Pakistani possession of nuclear weapons played a crucial role in inhibiting India from opening a second front to draw away Pakistani forces from their points of incursion in Kashmir. We will also argue that India decided to limit all air operations to its side of the LoC for fear of provoking Pakistani misgivings about a larger, more protracted conflict designed to carry the war into Pakistani-controlled Kashmir and possibly beyond.

The International and Domestic Contexts

The Pakistani incursions cannot be understood without some attention to the larger political and strategic backdrop in the region. Key military and strategic developments between India and Pakistan that transpired during the 1980s profoundly influenced the genesis of this conflict. India's willingness to forcefully defend what it deemed to be its territorial integrity had dramatically increased in the 1980s. Simultaneously, India's military capabilities came to gradually match such resolve. Finally, an understanding of the significance of the Siachen Glacier conflict, which had its genesis in 1984, is vital to a discussion of the forces that led up to the Kargil war.

The Siachen Glacier lies in the Karakoram Range in the disputed state of Jammu and Kashmir.[5] The glacier is 75 kilometres long, 2 to

8 kilometres wide, and 300 metres deep. The total area covered by the glacier is about 10,000 square kilometres and at particular points the glacier rises to heights of nearly 24,000 feet.

As discussed in Chapter Three, the roots of the controversy can be traced to the demarcation of the CFL in the Karachi Agreement of 1949, and subsequently in the aftermath of the Simla Agreement of 1972. At bottom, the dispute over the glacier stems from competing interpretations of some ambiguous language embodied in both agreements. In the Karachi Agreement, the last demarcated grid point was NJ 9842 near the Shyok River at the base of the Saltoro mountain range. Beyond this grid point, the agreement states that the CFL runs 'thence north to the glaciers'. Neither side sought to demarcate the line fully because the adversaries had no civilian or military assets in the region, and demarcating this line at such high altitudes was not worth the effort. The Simla Agreement of 1972 also did not lead to an attempt to delineate the grid point beyond NJ 9842.

The legal–technical problem about the control of the glacier stems from the interpretation of the crucial phrase 'thence north to the glaciers'. The Indian side, based upon its experiences of border negotiations with China insists on adherence to the watershed principle. India relies on this principle because it holds that boundaries, to the extent possible, should conform to natural topographic features. This formulation places much of the glacier in Indian hands. Pakistan, of course, disputes this interpretation and contends that the line should run in a northeasterly direction all the way to the Chinese border and the Karakoram Pass. The significance apparently lies in its strategic location abutting a trijunction of Pakistani, Indian, and Chinese territory.

Indian and Pakistani accounts of how the glacier became the subject of a dispute, quite understandably, vary. From this morass of claims and counter-claims, it is possible to make the following reconstruction. It is quite clear that India did deploy troops first on the glacier in 1984 to establish its formal claim. On the other hand, there is also evidence that the pre-emptive Indian action in April 1984 stemmed from its awareness that Pakistan had been issuing mountaineering permits to foreign nationals interested in scaling the heights leading to the glacier. Specifically, intelligence reports that the Pakistani military was planning a similar operation to establish a presence on the glacier prompted the Indian operation, 'Operation Meghdoot' (Cloud Messenger). Faced with the Indian military occupation of the glacier, Pakistan launched its own military operation, 'Abadeel' (Swallow) shortly thereafter. However, they were unable to dislodge the Indian troops who were already well-entrenched and commanded certain strategic salients. There have been pitched artillery duels at Siachen ever since, especially in 1989.[6]

It is widely believed in Indian military circles that the periodic Pakistani attacks on Kargil in subsequent years were closely related to efforts to cut off the Srinagar–Leh Highway, a vital link for supplying the Indian troops at Siachen. While other factors were undoubtedly significant, one of the goals of the Pakistani incursion in Kargil in April 1999 was to disrupt the Indian control of Siachen.

Containing the Insurgency

Apart from the Siachen Glacier conflict, Indo-Pakistani relations were also deeply strained as a consequence of the outbreak of an indigenous, ethno-religious insurgency in the Indian-controlled portion of Kashmir in December 1989. The origins of the insurgency in Kashmir have been discussed at length elsewhere.[7] Suffice to say that its origins were indigenous, and can be traced to the processes of political mobilization and institutional decay in Kashmir. Shortly after its genesis in December 1989, however, Pakistan became quickly involved in shaping the direction, scope, and intensity of the insurrection. Pakistani involvement in support of the insurgents is not a matter of speculation but a matter of fact.

Pakistan's goals in supporting the insurgents were manifold. Its politico-military leadership, unable to take on India since the latter's decisive victory in 1971 and its subsequent clear-cut military superiority, seeks to impose a 'war of a thousand cuts' through support for the insurgents. Thus far, Pakistan's leadership, whether civilian or military, has deemed that the risks associated with this strategy are both calculable and controllable.[8]

The insurgency in Kashmir, which continues apace, has been quite sanguinary. While estimates of its lethality vary, it is widely accepted that more than 40,000 individuals have perished since its onset. This figure exceeds the total number of battle deaths that occurred in all the four Indo-Pakistani conflicts combined.[9] The attempt to quell the rebellion has also tied down a significant number of Indian Army and paramilitary units. Though the exact numbers are unavailable, it is widely believed that as many as 250,000 troops are involved in this counter-insurgency operation, making it the largest of its kind in India's post-independence history.

Prelude to Lahore

As the 1990s drew to a close, the Indian state had succeeded, through a variety of military and political measures, in bringing about a degree of order, if not law, to Kashmir. How did it accomplish this task? In the military realm, contrary to the expectations of many of the insurgent groups, India's application of force proved to be steady, unwavering, and increasingly calibrated. India deployed security forces that proved to be less panicky and less trigger-happy, its intelligence-gathering apparatus improved, and it managed to turn a number of surrendered insurgents against their erstwhile compatriots. Simultaneously, the insurgency itself underwent a profound transformation by the mid-1990s. One of the principal insurgent groups, the Jammu and Kashmir Liberation Front (JKLF), which had arguably commanded the greatest degree of support among Kashmir's disaffected populace, chose to dispense with the use of force in the quest for an independent Kashmir, their putative and stated goal. The JKLF's exit from the field of battle largely stemmed from the losses that it had suffered both at the hands of the Indian security forces as well as at the hands of the Pakistan-supported groups, most notably the Hizb-ul-Mujahideen (HUM). In part because of the departure of the JKLF, but also because of the increasing presence of 'mehamaan mujahideen' ('guest insurgents') from Afghanistan, Pakistan, and even parts of the Arab world, local support for the insurgency started to wane. Unlike the home-grown JKLF, many of these latter-day entrants into the Kashmiri fray had few, if any, blood-soil ties to Kashmir. Consequently, they exhibited scant scruples in their harsh dealings with the local population. Since all insurgent movements necessarily depend upon the largesse and succour of the indigenous population this decline in support from native Kashmiris cost the insurgents dearly, and enabled India's security forces to increasingly seize the upper hand.

The government in New Delhi also sought to start discussions with any militant groups who appeared willing to forswear the violence. In mid-March of 1996, the Indian Home Minister, Shankarrao Chavan, initiated talks with a group of breakaway insurgent leaders. The talks were aborted. However, the mere willingness of both the national government and a range of insurgent groups to engage in discussions in New Delhi suggested that elements of the insurgency were losing steam.[10]

Beyond the military dimension, the Indian state had also scored a minor political victory when it held a state-level election in September 1996. The previous election for the national parliamentary seats, held in May–June 1996, had been characterized by widespread charges of coerced voting.[11] The September voting, however, was remarkably free of such accusations and taint. The National Conference, the long-dominant regional political party, led by Farooq Abdullah, won a decisive victory, securing as many as fifty-seven out of a possible eighty-seven seats in the state assembly. Within the Valley itself, the National Conference won forty out of a possible forty-four seats. A new government was sworn in in early October with Farooq Abdullah as the chief minister. This election and the emergence of a popularly elected regime raised considerable hopes for a return to some semblance of normalcy within the state. The military weakening of the insurgents, their internecine battles, and the declining support among the local populace for the insurgency had made the election possible.

Two critical questions remained in abeyance. Would the Indian state use this opportunity to seize the diplomatic initiative with Pakistan? And would the Farooq Abdullah regime succeed in addressing the genuine grievances of a violence-fatigued population? Almost immediately after taking office, Farooq Abdullah raised the prospects of increased autonomy for Kashmir.[12] For informed observers of Kashmir such a demand was unexceptional. Many of India's problems in Kashmir had stemmed from the steady erosion of the state's autonomy since the dismissal of Farooq's father, Sheikh Mohammed Abdullah, in 1953 on dubious grounds.[13]

Apart from calling for a restoration of autonomy, the Farooq Abdullah regime also sought to obtain substantial financial assistance from the central government in New Delhi to address a variety of economic woes that besieged the state.[14] Among other matters, the regime was keen on generating new employment in the state, renewing the tourist industry, and addressing the continuing shortfalls of electrical power generation. Apart from these new initiatives, the regime also boldly called upon the insurgent groups to surrender while holding out the promise of amnesty and rehabilitation. This offer, not surprisingly, did not evoke an overwhelming response. However, some insurgents did avail themselves of this opportunity.[15] Also, early in 1997, in an attempt to address rampant charges of human rights violations on the part of local and central security forces, the Farooq regime appointed a local human rights commission designed to examine and address these charges.[16] The presence of a regime with a modicum of legitimacy and with an apparent willingness to address deep-seated grievances seemed to restore elements of normalcy in the Valley. Yet the problems of that had besieged the state for the past several years could not be easily addressed within a few short months. Problems continued to plague the state in terms of revenue collection, the reconstruction of damaged infrastructure, and the activities of former insurgents turned state-sponsored guerillas.[17]

At a bilateral level, hopes for some renewed movement on the Kashmir question emerged in mid-1997. This willingness to grasp this nettlesome issue stemmed from a meeting of the two newly elected Prime Ministers, Nawaz Sharif of Pakistan and Inder Kumar Gujral of India, at the annual meeting of SAARC in Male, the capital of the Maldives in early 1997. Sharif had won a landslide victory in a national election in Pakistan and thereby could afford to pursue a more cordial relationship with India. Gujral, on the other hand, had enunciated a doctrine of 'non-reciprocity' in the conduct of India's foreign policy towards its neighbours. Pared to the bone, the doctrine held that India would not immediately demand reciprocal concessions from its neighbours when it made cooperative gestures to try and improve relations.[18] Consequently, it was not surprising that at this meeting the two leaders chose to initiate foreign secretary-level talks.

It was sign of the Gujral regime's determination to proceed with an attempt to improve relations with Pakistan that the foreign secretary-level talks actually transpired. In the aftermath of the Male meeting in late April and early May the Pakistan Army started intensive shelling in the Kargil sector. Though the Indian Army responded with vigour, the shelling remained confined to this sector.[19]

Despite this untoward set of incidents the foreign secretaries of India and Pakistan, Shamshad Ahmed and Salman Haider, respectively, met in Islamabad in late June.[20] Little of substance was agreed to at this initial meeting beyond creating a milieu more conducive for tackling some of the most vexing issues in the relationship. Shortly after these bilateral talks, Prime Minister Gujral travelled to Kashmir and extended an unconditional offer for talks with the insurgent groups in Kashmir. The initial reaction to his unprecedented proposal was not encouraging.[21]

The desultory course of infiltration across the LoC continued throughout the year despite the diplomatic initiatives of the Gujral regime. Later in the year, as the Himalayan passes closed with snow and infiltration petered out, there was a resumption of cross-border shelling once again in the Kargil sector. In early October, in particular, an artillery barrage near Kargil resulted in a large number of civilian casualties.[22] The bonhomie that had been generated in Indo-Pakistani relations as a consequence of Gujral's diplomacy proved short-lived. The resumption of large-scale shelling, particularly against vulnerable civilian targets led Indian analysts to argue that despite Nawaz Sharif's significant majority in parliament, he was not in complete control over Pakistan's Kashmir policy. Instead, it appeared that the Pakistan Army, unhappy with the diplomatic efforts to normalize relations with India, was seeking to undermine the process.[23] Ironically, the situation in the Kashmir Valley in late 1997 appeared somewhat more peaceful. One key indicator of a return of some semblance of normalcy to the Valley was the resumption of tourism, a staple of the state's economy.[24]

Under the Nuclear Shadow

In May 1998, India and Pakistan both crossed the nuclear Rubicon by carrying out nuclear tests. The overt nuclearization of the region had no direct impact on the conditions prevailing in the Kashmir Valley. The insurgency, which had started to flag, showed few signs of gathering renewed strength or dramatically abating. What did change, however, was the international climate. India and Pakistan encountered widespread disapprobation from the global community and the United States in particular. Faced with such a barrage of criticism, it made sense for the two national leaders, Nawaz Sharif of Pakistan and Atal Behari Vajpayee of India, to make some attempts at reconciliation. Prime Minister Vajpayee, who in the mid-1970s as India's foreign minister in another coalition government had sought to improve relations with Pakistan, took the initiative. In February 1999 he chose to visit the historic Pakistani city of Lahore, the capital of the Pakistani state of Punjab, to inaugurate a new bus service linking it with the Indian city of Amritsar. The journey was fraught with symbolic and material significance. It was symbolically significant because Vajpayee, the leader of a hyper-nationalist party, chose to initiate this attempt at reconciliation. It was also symbolically charged because during the visit he paid his respects at the *Minar-e-Pakistan*, a monument that commemorates the call for the creation of the Pakistani state. This gesture on the part of an Indian leader signified India's acknowledgement of the legitimacy of the Pakistani state. The visit also had significant material consequences. The two sides issued the Lahore Declaration, which among other matters called for a series of nuclear-related confidence-building measures and reaffirmed the two sides' wish to resolve the Kashmir dispute through peaceful means.

The Lahore Summit, however, despite its magnanimous goals, failed to contribute to a significant amelioration of Indo-Pakistani tensions. Even as discussions of the possible benefits and pitfalls of the summit were underway, the two countries became embroiled in a fourth war in Kashmir after Pakistani forces crossed the LoC in late winter or early spring 1999.

Did Prime Minister Sharif willfully deceive his Indian counterpart at Lahore or was he simply not privy to the Pakistani military's war planning about Kargil? It is impossible to definitively assess Sharif's commitment to the Lahore peace process in light of the Pakistani incursions in Kargil only a few months later. There is some evidence that suggests the prime minister and the Chief of Staff of the Pakistan

Army, General Pervez Musharraf, cared little about reaching an accord with India. Some analysts have argued that General Musharraf was working at odds with the effort that the prime minister had undertaken to improve relations with India, and thereby secretly revived and implemented an existing plan for military action against India.[25]

The Pakistani military, no doubt, was able to undertake such an enterprise as a consequence of the changed security dynamics in the region in the wake of the mutual, overt acquisition of nuclear weapons. They had now realized that India would be loath to dramatically expand the scope of a conflict for fear of escalation to the nuclear level.[26] Consequently, the military became more risk-acceptant in planning a 'limited probe' to challenge Indian conventional deterrence.[27] More to the point, the emerging situation in Kashmir was clearly intolerable to the Pakistani politico-military establishment that had invested considerable blood and treasure in supporting the insurgency in Kashmir. Since the insurgency was flagging and a frontal military assault on India was all but suicidal, the strategy they fashioned sought to 'design around' Indian deterrence.[28]

One other key factor emboldened the Pakistani military. In the aftermath of the Lahore peace process, the Indian political leadership had come to believe that there was little likelihood of renewed Pakistani military malfeasance across the LoC in Kashmir. As a result, they had reduced routine surveillance flights near the LoC, had ignored reports of Pakistani military activities near the LoC, and had not entertained the prospect of a Pakistani pincer movement near National Highway One A.[29]

It is therefore hardly surprising that the Pakistani military designed a strategy to infiltrate both regular and irregular forces across the LoC in a region where Indian forces were at a tactical disadvantage, and where Indian inattention made the initial incursions easy. The Pakistani strategy was to present India and the world with a fait accompli. In turn, the Pakistani leadership had hoped that the renewed international attention would focus on the Kashmir question as a consequence of Western fears about the possibilities of a nuclear war in the region. These calculations, which had worked well in the past, went completely awry on this occasion. The US, which had previously equivocated on assigning blame to a particular party for having initiated a crisis, squarely condemned Pakistan's incursions across the LoC.

What were the more proximate factors that contributed to the Kargil incursion? Specifically, four factors, both domestic and regional, set the stage for the conflict. First, India had increasingly managed, through an amalgam of repression and co-optation, to bring about a degree of order if not law in the disputed state of Jammu and Kashmir. Second, as a consequence of India's limited success in suppressing the decade-old insurgency, there was growing concern in Pakistan's politico-military establishment that the Kashmiri cause was losing its international salience. Third, in the aftermath of the Indian and Pakistani nuclear tests of May 1998, many Indian decision-makers had assumed that the possibility of Pakistani military malfeasance was extremely low. They had convinced themselves that the mutual possession of nuclear weapons had rendered the likelihood of war extremely small. Finally, Prime Minister Vajpayee's decision to try and improve relations with Pakistan, culminating in his historic bus trip in February 1999 to Lahore, had directly contributed to Indian complacency about Pakistani intentions. This complacency, in turn, led to a lapse of military alertness along remote areas of the Indo-Pakistani border.

The Onset of Conflict

The events unfolded as follows. The initial report of possible Pakistani intrusions came from some villagers in the remote border hamlet of Garkhun. Accordingly, the Indian Army sent a patrol out on 6 May in the Batalik sector. This small party was ambushed and lost a soldier. Soon thereafter, subsequent patrols were launched and quickly came into contact with other Pakistani intruders.

Shortly thereafter, 121 Brigade made an assessment that there were some 100 or so intruders near Kargil. They also concluded that the brigade had sufficient capabilities to dislodge them. By 15 May, their numerical assessment was dramatically revised upwards to some 800 intruders. The military authorities soon realized that these groups had also breached the LoC in Mushkoh Valley, Kaksar, and Batalik.[30] However, it was not until the last week of May that the Indian Army realized that Pakistani regular forces and Kashmiri insurgents had come to occupy as many as seventy positions along the LoC.

The initial Indian reaction was clumsy and lacked tactical and strategic sense. Indian troops attempted to push their way up to heights of 16,000 feet and beyond. Due to the lack of ground cover, they became easy targets for Pakistani snipers and gunners. After taking substantial casualties, the Indians realized that they needed considerably greater firepower to dislodge the Pakistani intruders. On 18 May, to obtain a better sense of the exact dispositions of the Pakistani forces, Lieutenant General Chandra Shekhar, the Vice-Chief of the Army Staff (in the absence of General Ved Prakash Malik, but in consultation with him), sought the assistance of the IAF and the permission of the CCS to use attack helicopters. Air Marshal A.Y. Tipnis, however, recommended against the use of airpower for two compelling reasons. First, the helicopters would not perform well at those high altitudes. Second, that the use of airpower could escalate and enlarge the scope of the conflict. Accordingly, the CCS refused to grant such permission.

When Malik returned from Poland on 20 May, he promptly visited Northern Command's Headquarters in Udhampur and 15 Corps Headquarters in Srinagar. (He was unable to go to Kargil because of inclement weather.) Based upon briefings that he received at both posts, he came to the conclusion that the use of airpower was essential to dislodge the intruders. Late on the afternoon of 23 May, Malik held a meeting with his counterparts from the Navy and the Air Force under the aegis of Chiefs of Staff Committee, and convinced them of the critical need to utilize airpower. Having successfully persuaded them of the necessity of using airpower, he then sought the permission of the CCS on 24 May. The CCS granted such permission but issued a categorical injunction that the air force refrain from crossing the LoC in pursuit of its goals.[31] During the same meeting of the high-powered CCS, a decision was taken to induct as many as three brigades into the region.[32]

Accordingly, the IAF carried out the first air strikes on 26 May. On 27 May, the IAF launched a second round of air strikes with the objective of dislodging the intruders from Batalik, Turtuk, and Dras. Indian authorities insisted that all air attacks were confined to areas that India deemed to be on its side of the LoC. Pakistani officials, however, claimed that the IAF planes had crossed the LoC and had struck targets within 'Azad Kashmir'.[33] In conducting these air operations, the IAF relied on Mirage-2000s, Mig-23s and MiG-27s.[34] During 'Operation Vijay' (literally, 'operation victory'), the IAF carried out as many as 550 sorties. This decision to permit the use of air power marked a significant departure from past Indian attempts to deal with Pakistani incursions along the LoC. Indeed, not since the 1971 war had air power been used in support of military operations in Kashmir.[35]

With the air strikes underway, the Indian Army moved post-haste to dislodge the intruders from the salients that they had come to occupy. Though 'Operation Vijay' was eventually successful, it proved to be extraordinarily costly in both human and materiel terms.[36] Logistical, organizational, and topographic limitations significantly hobbled military operations. In the initial stages of the conflict, troops deployed in counter-insurgency operations in Kashmir were hastily moved to significantly higher altitudes, seriously threatening their health. At another level, the drawing down of troops engaged in counter-insurgency operations left other parts of the state vulnerable to terrorist actions. Finally, the topography of the terrain along the LoC favoured the Pakistani forces.[37] The Indians had to assault bunkers and redoubts while facing punishing fire from well-entrenched, fortified positions at considerable heights.[38]

It was only around 14–16 June that the Indian forces managed to re-take the two key positions near Dras and Batalik. These two positions were deemed to be of considerable importance because they overlook the principal supply route for the Indian military to the Siachen Glacier.[39] Subsequently, around 20 June, they fully managed to re-establish control over Batalik.[40] Some 539 Indian men and officers perished in this conflict, and at least two IAF aircraft and one helicopter were shot down.

As the hostilities showed few signs of abating, in the last week of June, General Anthony Zinni, the commander-in-chief of the US Central Command, visited Pakistan and categorically told Prime Minister Sharif to call off his troops.[41] In the aftermath of Zinni's visit, Gordon Lanpher, a US deputy assistant secretary of state for South Asia, visited New Delhi to apprise his Indian counterparts of the substance of General Zinni's message to Islamabad, and also to counsel restraint in New Delhi. According to a well-known Indian journalist and commentator, Lanpher informed the Indians that Zinni had told his Pakistani counterparts to start a prompt withdrawal of their forces from the Kargil region. More to the point, Zinni had refused to entertain Pakistan's efforts to link the Kargil question to the broader Indo-Pakistani dispute over Kashmir.[42]

Despite Zinni's message, the conflict continued into early July. No doubt surprised by the intensity of the Indian attacks and the inability to persuade the US and other powers to back Pakistan, Prime Minister Nawaz Sharif visited Washington, DC on 4 July seeking a face-saving device. By not accepting the Pakistani version of the origins of the Kargil crisis, namely that it was inseparable from the broader Kashmir dispute, the US helped hasten its end.[43] Also, unlike in the past, the US also refused to mediate between the two parties.[44]

The US' unwillingness to mediate stood out in marked contrast to the Clinton administration's propensity to intervene in a variety of regional disputes. Two factors mostly explain the American unwillingness to invest significant time and resources in mediating an end to this conflict. At one level, even in the post-Cold War era, South Asia still remains a fairly low priority for most American administrations. At another, the US, while keen on preventing a full-scale conflagration in South Asia, does not have any vital interests in the region. Consequently, it remains loath to step into a region riven by a long-standing dispute lacking any prospect of easy or quick resolution.

By the second week of July, the Pakistani forces were facing relentless artillery barrages and air attacks from the Indian military. A more sympathetic American response to Sharif might have emboldened him and allowed the Pakistani military to continue on with their plans. However, in the face of escalating losses and a paucity of international diplomatic support for its position, Sharif was forced to reconsider the value of continuing military operations.[45] By 9 June, Pakistan was expressing a willingness to send a special envoy to New Delhi to discuss a de-escalation of the crisis. Initially, India expressed little interest in talks but later agreed.[46]

On 12 July, Prime Minister Sharif gave a nation-wide television address where he called for the withdrawal of the mujahideen from the mountain redoubts. It should be noted that Sharif carefully avoided making a public statement about altering any deployments of the

Pakistani Army.[47] In effect, he was keen on maintaining the fictive position that the mujahideen had scaled these heights and seized the redoubts of their own accord. By 14 July, the first set of infiltrators started to withdraw from their positions and ceded them to the advancing Indian forces.[48] It was in mid-July that the conflict finally came to a close.

In India, which was in the midst of a national election campaign, the Pakistani climb-down was played up as a major military success. It remains an open question whether or not the Indian victory in Kashmir shaped the electoral outcome. The failure to anticipate and accordingly respond to the Pakistani incursions, however, did lead to some self-assessment on the part of the Indian leadership. In the aftermath of the crisis, the Vajpayee regime appointed a high-level committee headed by K. Subrahmanyam, a well-known political commentator and former bureaucrat, to examine the causes of this colossal intelligence failure.

Explaining the Pakistani Incursions and the Indian Responses

Why did the Pakistani Army embark on this risky enterprise? What were its proximate and longer-term goals? Were these incursions tied to a larger political strategy, or were they merely opportunistic? Simultaneously, what factors explain the Indian failure to anticipate the possibility of such intrusions and take steps to forestall them? Finally, what factors constrained Indian decision-makers from expanding the scope of the conflict and eschewing the option of horizontal escalation? The answers to these questions are complex. A number of factors can be adduced to explain the Pakistani enterprise. Some of these are firmly based upon available evidence, while others can be substantiated only on the basis of inference and attribution.

The explanations for the crisis have to be sought from two different perspectives. One perspective deals with Islamabad's decision to attempt an infiltration across the LoC along a most difficult terrain. The other focuses on India's failure to anticipate the possibilities of Pakistani infiltration, and respond in a timely and appropriate fashion.

Why did Pakistan embark on this enterprise? At a tactical level, the incursion along the LoC had all the characteristics of what is referred to, as a 'limited probe'.[49] This involves making a small, calibrated incursion to test and clarify the adversary's willingness to fight and defend its territory. The ability to reverse course is one of the distinguishing features of a limited probe. In effect, if the thrust runs into firm opposition, its course is reversed. The party making the probe believes that the risks associated with the probe are both calculable and controllable.

The timing of this action was not insignificant. Since the late 1990s, the Pakistani-aided insurgency was increasingly on the wane. The Indian security forces had the bulk of the insurgents on the run. With the insurgents at bay, India had held three elections in the state for state-level and national offices. Turnout in these elections had varied but had resulted in a popular, elected government. By 1997–8, while pockets of resistance continued to wreak occasional havoc in Kashmir, a semblance of normalcy had been restored to the Valley.[50] Though most of the Muslim inhabitants of the Valley remained disaffected from the Indian state, they also lived in abject fear of the more virulent insurgents groups, such as the Al-Faran, the Laskhar-e-Taiba, the Harkat-ul-Ansar (later named the Harkat-ul-Mujahideen) and the Al-Badr.[51] The Pakistani leadership feared that this emergent normalcy in the Valley, if consolidated, would foreclose the possibility of further incitement to the insurgency. Already due to India's diplomatic and military strategies, the international community's interest in the Kashmir issue had dramatically declined. If Pakistan still wished to remain a relevant player in the Kashmir problem, it had to jump-start the insurgency. With the normal routes of infiltration closed and with the increased alertness and deployments on the part of the Indian security forces, it had to choose a more remote and unlikely region to mount a serious incursion.

In making this incursion, the Pakistani leadership simply assumed that the US as well as other major states would step in to prevent an escalation of the crisis.[52] They also believed that these states would bring concerted pressure on India to desist from undertaking any compellent action.[53] As in various past episodes, recounted in previous chapters, *false optimism* was at work because there is little or no evidence that the leadership had any tangible basis for this belief. Even Pakistan's traditional ally, China, had distanced itself from Pakistan after 1996.

Pakistan's overt nuclearization had also bolstered this sense of *false optimism*.[54] Pakistani decision-makers had convinced themselves that their achievement of rough nuclear parity with India now enabled them to probe along the LoC with impunity. In their view, the Indian leadership, cognizant of Pakistan's nuclear capabilities, would desist from using overwhelming force and also avoid a dramatic escalation or expansion of the conflict.[55] The Pakistani behaviour in precipitating this conflict conformed closely to the expectations of the 'stability–instability paradox'.[56] This proposition holds that nuclear weapons do contribute to stability at one level for fear of nuclear escalation. Simultaneously, they also create incentives for conventional conflicts in peripheral areas as long as either side does not breach certain shared thresholds.

Certain Indian actions, which sought to alleviate the acute tension in Indo-Pakistani relations in the wake of the 1998 tests, also strengthened the Pakistani resolve to provoke a crisis. These Indian moves constituted an effort to deflect pressure from the United States as well as other major powers on the festering Kashmir question. To this end, India had initiated a dialogue designed to tackle the underlying sources of hostility. These pressures had been brought to bear because of a widespread and shared belief that Indo-Pakistani border tensions in the wake of the nuclear tests had made the region a 'tinderbox' or a 'flashpoint'.[57] With the overt nuclearization of the region after May 1998, these fears were further exacerbated.

No doubt as a consequence of these anxieties and with a clear-cut interest in addressing them, Prime Minister Vajpayee chose to visit Pakistan in February 1999. In the wake of this historic visit, many in the defence and foreign policymaking bureaucracies in New Delhi assumed that relations with Pakistan would now be on the mend. As a consequence, the routine gathering of intelligence on Pakistan's force deployments, movements, and likely actions were slackened. Moreover, many senior officials became caught up in the heady 'spirit of Lahore', and were unwilling to countenance the prospect of Pakistani malfeasance in Jammu and Kashmir.

Within Kashmir, the ebbing of the insurgency and the return of a modicum of normalcy had an ironic consequence; they led to a significant slackening of the vigilance operations that had taxed the resources of the army as well as the paramilitary forces over the better part of the decade. Few individuals in the higher realms of political authority believed that large-scale infiltration could again resume from Pakistan to boost the flagging insurgency.[58] More to the point, they believed that no Pakistani decision-maker would contemplate infiltrating soldiers and insurgents at altitudes of over 16,000 feet. In the same vein, they had also correctly assessed that the Pakistani intruders could find little succour from the largely Shia and Buddhist population of these regions who do not harbour significant grievances against the Indian state. Finally, they had concluded that India's overt nuclear status would nullify the possibilities of conventional conflict with Pakistan.[59] These inferences and judgments proved to be fatally flawed.

Finally, what explains India's unwillingness to expand the scope and dimensions of the conflict? In 1965, a far weaker Indian Army with untested political leadership lost little time in resorting to horizontal escalation when Pakistan launched 'Operation Gibraltar' in Kashmir.[60] As discussed in Chapter Two, within a week of the Pakistani attack in Kashmir, India had opened a second front in the Punjab threatening significant Pakistani civilian and military assets. In 1999, important elements of the Indian ruling elite were known for their unyielding stance on defence and security issues, and their long-standing hostility towards Pakistan. It was the BJP-led regime that had finally crossed the nuclear rubicon in May 1998. The prime minister, despite his attempt to improve relations with Pakistan, had long been known for his intransigent views about Pakistan. One of the key members of his Cabinet, Home Minister L.K. Advani, had an even more bellicose stance towards Pakistan.

Yet the Indian armed forces displayed considerable restraint in the conduct of military operations. Specifically, the IAF did not cross the LoC. Such a decision made little strategic or military sense. Crossing the LoC would have enabled the air force to interdict Pakistani lines of communications and logistics, and thereby hastened an end to the conflict.[61] Nor for that matter, did India seek to open a theatre of operations elsewhere.

Was India inhibited from widening and deepening the scope of the conflict because of the paucity of conventional forces, timely American intercession, or the mutual possession of nuclear weapons? The first proposition, namely American intercession, can easily be dismissed. According to General Ved Prakash Malik, the then Chief of Staff of the Indian Army, about ten hours before Prime Minister Sharif met with President Clinton in Washington, DC, the Indian Army had already achieved one of its key strategic objectives, the capture of Tiger Hill. For all practical purposes, the re-capture of Tiger Hill meant that the tide had turned inexorably in India's favour. It needs to be underscored that this happened some *ten hours before* Nawaz Sharif met with President Clinton.[62] Consequently, a critical objective of the war had been accomplished before President Clinton exerted any pressure on Prime Minister Sharif at Blair House.

Contrary to popular belief, India did possess adequate army formations to widen the scope of the war. Specifically, India possessed three strike corps, each consisting of 60,000 soldiers broken down into three divisions each. According to a reliable military source, force constraints were hardly a problem in expanding the Kargil war.[63] Nevertheless, there were compelling reasons for not extending the scope of the war. Widening the scope of the conflict, it was believed, would play into the hands of the Pakistanis, who were intent on dramatizing the danger of a large-scale war in the region, designed to attract international attention. More to the point, the politico-military elite in India had not fully come to terms with the interactive effects of nuclear and conventional capabilities. For example, they had not, yet fashioned the operational dimensions of a 'limited war' in a nuclearized environment.[64] In the absence of the Pakistani possession of nuclear weapons, these considerations inhibiting Indian behaviour would simply have not arisen.

In effect, the mutual possession of nuclear weapons was the critical determinant in controlling both vertical and horizontal escalation. The Indian politico-military elite was now acutely cognizant of Pakistan's status as an overt nuclear weapons state, and therefore realized it would have to act with considerable restraint. Consequently, India could ill-afford to press Pakistan militarily in ways that might provoke a threat to resort to nuclear weapons.[65] Clearly, the mutual acquisition of nuclear weapons could not prevent low-level incursions in peripheral areas. However, their existence did ensure that the status quo state chose not to expand the ambit of conflict for fear of generating uncontrollable escalation.[66]

Notes

[1] Major General Ashok Kalyan Verma, *Kargil:Blood on the Snow* (New Delhi: Manohar, 2002), pp. 95–6.

[2] One of the most detailed accounts of the war can be found in Lieutenant General Y.M. Bammi (retd), *Kargil 1999: The Impregnable Conquered* (Noida: Gorkha Publishers, 2002).

[3] Major General Ashok Krishna (retd), 'The Kargil War', in Major General Ashok Krishna (retd) and P.R. Chari (eds), *Kargil: The Tables Turned* (New Delhi: Manohar, 2001).

[4] Amarinder Singh, *A Ridge Too Far: War in the Kargil Heights* (Patiala: Motibagh Palace, 2001).

[5] For an account sympathetic to Pakistan see Robert Wirsing, *Pakistan's Security Under Zia, 1977–1988: The Policy Imperatives of a Peripheral Asian State* (New York: St Martin's Press, 1991); two Pakistani perspectives can be found in General K.M. Arif, *Working With Zia: Pakistan's Power Politics, 1977–1988* (Karachi:Oxford University Press, 1995); Iqbal Akhund, *Trial and Error: The Advent and Eclipse of Benazir Bhutto* (Karachi: Oxford University Press, 2000); for Indian views see Air-Commodore Jasjit Singh (retd), 'Battle for Siachen: Beginning of the Third War', in Jasjit Singh (ed.), *Kargil 1999: Pakistan's Fourth War for Kashmir* (New Delhi: Knowledge World, 1999); also see Major General Ashok Krishna (retd), 'The Military Dimensions of Kargil', in Major General Ashok Krishna (retd) and P.R. Chari (eds), *Kargil: The Tables Turned* (New Delhi: Manohar, 2001); also see Lieutenant General M.L. Chibber, 'Siachen—The Untold Story (A Personal Account)', *Indian Defence Review*, (January 1990), pp. 146–7.

[6] Lieutenant General V.R. Raghavan, *Siachen: Conflict Without End* (New Delhi: Viking, 2002).

[7] Sumit Ganguly, *The Crisis in Kashmir: Portents of War, Hopes of Peace* (Cambridge: Cambridge University Press and Washington, DC: Woodrow Wilson Center Press, 1999).

[8] On this point see Anthony Davis, 'The Conflict in Kashmir', *Jane's Intelligence Review*, vol. 7, no. 1 (1995), pp. 41–6; also see Peter Chalk, 'Pakistan Role in the Kashmir Insurgency', *Jane's Intelligence Review*, vol. 9, no. 1 (2001).

[9] Sumit Ganguly, *Conflict Unending: India-Pakistan Tensions Since 1947* (New York: Columbia University Press and Washington, DC: Woodrow Wilson Center Press, 2001).

[10] Tarun Basu and Binoo Joshi, 'Ground-Breaking Talks With Militants,' *India Abroad*, 22 March 1996, p. 6.

[11] See the reports of voter coercion in Harinder Baweja, 'Exercise in Opportunism', *India Today*, 30 April 1996, pp. 70–1, Ajith Pillai, 'Vote Marshalled', *Outlook*, 5 June 1996, pp. 10–15 and Shiraz Sidhwa, 'Guns and Votes', *Frontline*, 14 June 1996, pp. 122–5.

[12] Binoo Joshi, 'Farooq Tells of Tasks Ahead', *India Abroad*, 11 October 1996, p. 4.

[13] Amitabh Mattoo, 'Past and Present', the *Telegraph*, 28 October 1997, p. 11.

[14] Staff Writer, 'New Economic Package for Jammu and Kashmir', the *Asia Observer*, 8 November 1996, p. 7.

[15] Binoo Joshi, 'Poor Response to Surrender Call', *India Abroad*, 28 November 1996, p. 20.

[16] Binoo Joshi, 'Rights Body Seen as Effort to Blunt Criticism', *India Abroad*, 17 January 1997, p. 15.

[17] Ramesh Vinayak, 'Sliding Into Gloom', *India Today International*, 31 January 1997, pp. 32–4.

[18] For an important statement on the role of reciprocity in international relations see Robert Axelrod, *The Evolution of Cooperation* (New York: Basic Books, 1984).

[19] Manoj Joshi, 'Hardball, Diplomacy', *India Today International*, 15 May 1997, pp. 40–3.

[20] John F. Burns, 'India and Pakistan Plan Kashmir Talks', the *New York Times*, 24 June 1997, A6.

[21] Associated Press, 'Indian Leader Proposes Talks on Kashmir', the *Washington Post*, 27 July 1997, A28.

[22] Neelesh Mishra, 'Pakistani Shelling Ravages Border Town,' *India Abroad*, 10 October 1997, p. 4.

[23] Manoj Joshi and Ramesh Vinayak, 'War on Peace', *India Today International*, 13 October 1997, pp. 18–23.

[24] Harinder Baweja, 'Out of the Mists', *India Today International*, 1 December 1997, pp. 12–14.

[25] For a discussion of the differences in perspectives see Owen Bennett Jones, *Pakistan: Eye of the Storm* (New Haven, Connecticut: Yale University Press, 2002).

[26] Lieutenant General Talat Masood (retd) as quoted by Bharat Bhusan, 'In Enemy Country', in *Guns and Yellow Roses* (New Delhi: Harper Collins, 1999), p. 101.

[27] The concept of a 'limited probe' is discussed in Alexander George and Richard Smoke, *Deterrence in American Foreign Policy: Theory and Practice* (New York: Columbia University Press, 1974).

[28] For a discussion of the concept of 'designing around' deterrence, see George and Smoke, *Deterrence in American Foreign Policy*.

[29] The reasons for Indian complacency in the aftermath of the Lahore Summit see Ganguly, 2002; also see the discussion in Praveen Swami, *The Kargil War* (New Delhi: Leftword, 1999).

[30] Ranjit Bhushan, Nitin A. Gokhale, and Ajith Pillai with Murali Krishnan, 'Kargil, Post Mortem', as downloaded from http://www.outlookindia.com/issue3/affairs.htm.

[31] Press Release of General Ved Prakash Malik, 15 June 2004.

[32] Cover Story, 'The War in Kargil', *Frontline*, vol.16, no.12, 5–18 June 1999 from http://www.the-hindu.com/fline/fl1612/16120040.htm.

[33] Arthur Max, 'Pakistan Charges India With Bombing', Associated Press, 26 May 1999 as downloaded from America Online, www.aol.com.

[34] See Barry Bearak, 'India Jets Strike Guerilla Force Now in Kashmir', the *New York Times*, 27 May 1999, p. A1. Also see Special Correspondent, AIAF strikes supply base in Batalik, the *Hindu* (online), 27 June 1999 from http://www.the-hindu.com/stories/01270002.htm.

[35] This, of course, does not include the air dropping of supplies and equipment to the Indian soldiers encamped on the Siachen Glacier along the Saltoro Range. For a detailed account of the origins, evolution, and current status of the conflict on the Siachen Glacier see Barry Bearak, 'Frozen in Fury on the Roof of the World', the *New York Times*, 23 May 1999, p. A1.

[36] Agence France Presse, 'Delhi's battle bill: $6.8 a day', the *Straits Times* (Singapore), 16 June 1999, p. 9.

[37] For early Indian assertion that challenged Pakistan's claim that its security forces were not involved in the Kargil operation see Shujaat Bukhari, 'Clear Proof of Pak. Role', the *Hindu*, 6 June 1999, from http://www.hinduonline.com/today/stories/01060003.

[38] Dinesh Kumar, 'Death stalks Jawans at Every Step in Kargil', the *Times of India*, 9 June 1999, from http://www.timesofindia.com/today/09home2.htm.

[39] Agence France Presse, 'India Retakes Two Key Peaks in Kashmir', the *Straits Times*, 16 June 1999.

[40] Associated Press, 'India Reports Major Highway Recaptured From Rebels', the *New York Times*, 21 June 1999, p. A7.

[41] Farhan Bokhari and May Louise Kazmin, 'US Ggeneral Presses Pakistan on Kashmir', *Financial Times*, 25 June 1999.

[42] C. Raja Mohan, 'Pak. Must Pull out Troops', the *Hindu*, 28 June 1999 from http://www.the-hindu.com/stories/001280001.htm.

[43] See 'Joint Statement By President Clinton And Prime Minister Sharif of Pakistan', The White House, Office of the Press Secretary, 4 July 1999.

[44] C. Raja Mohan, 'US Opposed to Mediation on Kashmir', the *Hindu*, 27 September 1999 downloaded from http://www.hinduonline.com/today/stories/01280008.htm.

[45] See the analysis in Steven R. Weisman, 'Kashmir: A Story of "Blowback" in Paradise', the *New York Times*, 17 July 1999, Section 4, p. 8.

[46] Stephen Kinzer, 'India and Pakistan to Discuss Flare-Up in Kashmir', the *New York Times*, 9 June 1999, p. A10.

[47] Barry Bearak, 'Pakistani Makes Case For a Halt to Fighting', the *New York Times*, 13 July 1999, p. A6.

[48] Celia W. Dugger, 'Pakistan-Backed Force Leaves Indian Kashmir', the *New York Times*, 15 July 1999, p. A9.

[49] For a discussion of the concept of a 'limited probe' see George and Smoke, *Deterrence in American Foreign Policy*.

[50] Murali Krishnan, 'The Forgotten War', *Outlook*, 14 June 1999, p. 24.

[51] Manoj Joshi, *The Lost Rebellion: Kashmir in the 1990s* (New Delhi: Penguin, 1998).

[52] Naveen S. Garewal, 'Post-Kargil: Trying Times for India and Pakistan', ASIANaffairs, August 1999, no.34, pp. 16–18.

[53] The concept of 'compellence', which involves getting an aggressor to undo an act. For a discussion of the concept see Thomas Schelling, *Arms and Influence* (New Haven: Yale University Press).

[54] For a discussion of the concept of 'false optimism' see Stephen Van Evera, *The Causes of War: Power and the Roots of Conflict* (Ithaca: Cornell University Press, 1999).

[55] M.B. Naqvi, 'Looking Beyond Kargil', ASIANaffairs, August 1999, no.34, pp. 14–16.

[56] For the initial discussion of the 'stability–instability paradox' see Glenn Snyder, 'The Balance of Power and the Balance of Terror', in Paul Seabury (ed.), *The Balance of Power* (San Francisco: Chandler, 1965); for an application

of the concept to the South Asian context see Sumit Ganguly, 'Indo-Pakistani Nuclear Issues and the Stability/Instability Paradox', *Studies in Conflict and Terrorism*, vol. 18, no. 4, 1995, pp. 325–34.

[57] Interview with senior US Department of Defense official, Stanford University, 3 December 1999.

[58] On this point see Praveen Swami, 'Trouble Ahead in Kashmir', *Frontline*, vol. 18, no. 6, 13–26 March 1999, pp. 5–8.

[59] Waheguru Pal Singh Sidhu, 'Of Myths and Realities: The Kargil Experience', in Kanti Bajpai, Afsir Karim, and Amitabh Mattoo (eds), *Kargil and After: Challenges for Indian Policy* (New Delhi: Har Anand, 2001).

[60] For details see Russell Brines, *The Indo–Pakistani Conflict* (New York: Pall Mall, 1968).

[61] D.N. Ganesh, 'Indian Air Force in Action', in Air-Commodore Jasjit Singh (retd) (ed.), *Kargil 1999: Pakistan's Fourth War for Kashmir* (New Delhi: Knowledge World, 1999).

[62] Sumit Ganguly, personal communication with General Ved Prakash Malik (retd), 7 August 2003.

[63] Personal correspondence between Sumit Ganguly and Major General Dipankar Banerjee (retd), 7 August 2003.

[64] Ibid.

[65] Singh, *A Ridge Too Far*.

[66] For a useful discussion of the role of nuclear weapons in this conflict and specifically in Pakistani calculations see Major General Ashok Krishna (retd) 'Lessons, Precepts and Perspectives', in Krishna and Chari (eds), *Kargil*.

8

The 2001–2 Indo-Pakistani Crisis

Exposing the Limits of Coercive Diplomacy

In the early morning of 24 March 2003, a group of men dressed in Indian Army uniforms and equipped with small arms entered the tiny hamlet of Nadimarg outside the city of Jammu in the Indian-controlled portion of the disputed state of Jammu and Kashmir. Within hours, they had killed twenty-four out of the fifty-two villagers, all of them Hindu, including a number of women and children. This massacre came in the aftermath of an almost year-long lull in such acts of wanton terror in Jammu and Kashmir, where Indian security forces have been battling an ethno-religious insurgency that erupted in 1989.[1] The attack carried a significance beyond the tragedy at its surface, however: it revealed that India's pursuit of a strategy of coercive diplomacy to end Pakistan's support for various terrorist organizations had failed.

About a year prior to this incident, in a determined effort to stop the infiltration of potential terrorists from Pakistan, India had inaugurated a strategy of coercive diplomacy. One episode in particular triggered India's resort to forceful persuasion. On 13 December 2001, six individuals believed to be members of the Lashkar-e-Taiba attacked the Indian parliament building in New Delhi after easily penetrating a lax security cordon. As they sought to assault the parliament's sanctum, the Central Hall, an unarmed but alert security guard sounded the tocsin, and quickly a gun battle began between the would-be assailants and the building's security forces.[2] In the ensuing exchange, all six of the attackers were killed along with eight members of the security forces.

This assault was the most brazen in a series of attacks that the Lashkar-e-Taiba and a similar group, the Jaish-e-Mohammad, both based in Pakistan, had carried out against India. Earlier these groups had confined their acts of terror and mayhem to the Indian-controlled portion of the disputed state of Jammu and Kashmir.[3] But in the months following the terrorist attacks against the US on 11 September 2001, these and other groups had undertaken a series of vicious and increasingly bold acts of terror against non-military targets in Indian-controlled Kashmir and beyond, such as an attack on the Jammu and Kashmir state legislature on 1 October 2001, which killed twenty-six people.[4]

Within a day after the attack on the Indian national parliament, Indian officials linked the attackers to the Lashkar-e-Taiba. They also contended that the group had acted at Pakistan's behest.[5] In an attempt to induce Pakistan to stop these insurgent groups from carrying out similar attacks, Indian officials spelled out a series of demands and simultaneously began a significant military mobilization. The demands made of Pakistan were quite explicit: ban the two groups, the Jaish-e-Mohammed and the Lashkar-e-Taiba, implicated in the attacks on the Jammu and Kashmir state legislature and the national parliament, respectively; extradite twenty individuals whom India accused of having carried out terrorist attacks on its soil; and put an end to the infiltration of insurgents into Kashmir.

After a six-month ratcheting of tensions by each side via a series of bellicose statements and continued military mobilizations, India started to demobilize its forces in late October 2002. Indian spokespersons publicly justified the demobilization on the grounds that the purposes of the general mobilization had been served. They contended that the international community had taken cognizance of Pakistan's involvement with terror and so India could now afford to return its military units to their peacetime stations. Such an argument, however, was mostly self-serving; India had, in fact, failed to accomplish the stated goals of its dramatic military mobilization.

The interesting aspect of this most recent flare-up of tensions between these two long-term South Asian adversaries is why, after mobilizing its troops and publicly threatening military action, and despite this extraordinary attack on Indian soil by Pakistan-based insurgents, did

India not resort to war against Pakistan? At one level India's self-restraint appears puzzling. Indian decision-makers had long been arguing publicly that Pakistan was surreptitiously supporting terrorist groups and their acts against India. In the aftermath of the 11 September 2001, terrorist attacks on the US, key Indian decision-makers had sought to depict Pakistan as a state that was actively harbouring terrorist organizations and thereby providing a breeding ground for terror in South Asia and beyond. Against this backdrop it made eminent military, political, and strategic sense for India to consider and resort to the use of force against Pakistan in an attempt to suppress its continuing support for terror. Yet, even after the brazen attack on their national parliament, India's decision-makers refrained from going to war against Pakistan, instead pursuing a strategy of forceful persuasion to induce Pakistan to end its support for terror in Kashmir and beyond.

This chapter will examine this crisis and India's strategy in detail and will show that as with the previous crises, India's choice of actions (coercive diplomacy) was driven primarily by the fear of escalation to the nuclear level.

The Strategy of Coercive Diplomacy

The concept of coercive diplomacy evolved during the Cold War. The US and the Soviet Union each used this strategy frequently, leading to a number of confrontations with distinctly mixed results.[6]

Pared to the bone, the strategy seeks to induce an adversary to desist from ongoing hostile actions by threatening to resort to force (but never actually doing so) if the adversary fails to comply with the stated demands. It also offers the adversary possible rewards for compliance and holds in reserve the possibility of increasing the costs of noncompliance. In any of its variants, the strategy offers important advantages over pure diplomacy or resort to war.[7] It is more compelling than diplomacy alone, for it carries with it the explicit threat of the resort to war if compliance is not forthcoming within a specified time span. On the other hand, it also avoids the rapid resort to war, the consequences of which may not be calculable or controllable. The latter concern is especially salient when the adversary in question possesses nuclear weapons.

The likely success of this strategy depends in considerable measure on two closely related variables: what exactly is demanded of the adversary and how strongly disinclined the adversary is to comply with these demands.[8] If the target state perceives that the demands being made on it are extraordinarily great and the threatened costs not sufficiently credible, the strategy is unlikely to succeed. Unlike a strategy of pure intimidation, it calls for combining positive inducements with threats, under the assumption that an adversary may prove to be more tractable if the demands and threats are paired with possible rewards for compliance.

Searching for Explanations

Why India chose to pursue a strategy of forceful persuasion rather than resort to war or even a set of carefully calibrated surgical strikes against Pakistan-aided terrorist training camps within Pakistani territory is an interesting question. Certainly India possessed the requisite mobile and airborne attack units to carry out a decisive and effective strike against these encampments. More to the point, it had access to the requisite intelligence to locate these camps. Yet, even after full-scale mobilization of its forces, which took until the end of January 2002, India did not resort to a conventional military strike against Pakistan designed to degrade its adversary's war-making capabilities. Was it deterred from doing so because of the prevailing conventional military balance? Or was it inhibited from carrying out such an attack because of the fear of escalation to the nuclear level? Was it also constrained by concerns about losing the moral high ground or fear of inadvertently attacking American civilian and military personnel deployed in Pakistan? How crucial was American intercession in the avoidance of full-scale war as the crisis continued to evolve through late June of 2002?

Our analysis suggests that India chose not to launch a large-scale conventional attack on Pakistan principally because of the fear of escalation to the nuclear level. At a lower level of conflict, India did have the requisite military formations to have carried out short, sharp raids across the LoC (the *de facto* Indo-Pakistani border in Kashmir). It was constrained from carrying out such an operation, however, for fear of conventional retaliation against which it had inadequate defences. Subsequently, in the second phase of the crisis (May–June 2002), when confronted with similar constraints, India's successful manipulation of the US fear of nuclear war in the region brought American intercession and provided Indian decision-makers a face-saving means of defusing the crisis.

Despite a significant display of military clout, and the seeming willingness to use it if necessary, the Indian strategy of coercive diplomacy failed. Pakistan did not comply with India's immediate demand to hand over the twenty individuals sought for terrorist acts in India. Furthermore, despite several promises to the contrary, including those made at the highest level to American officials, Pakistani authorities failed to stop the infiltration of terrorists into Indian-controlled Kashmir. Although India's strategy, as formulated and implemented, met many of the expectations of the theory and practice of coercive diplomacy, it failed to achieve these stated aims for a number of cogent reasons.

In the aftermath of the attack on the parliament, Indian decision-makers were highly motivated to induce Pakistan to change its behaviour. They were also clear in terms of what they sought to accomplish and conveyed these goals in unequivocal terms to their Pakistani counterparts. They enjoyed considerable domestic support in pursuit of these goals and also possessed the requisite conventional military capabilities, once they were mobilized, to impose significant costs on Pakistan.

On the other hand, it is far from clear that the asymmetry of motivation favoured India. The Kashmir dispute, especially since the outbreak of the insurgency in 1989, has been a central focus of Pakistani foreign and security policy.[9] The Pakistani military, which is *primus inter pares* within Pakistan, had made support for the Kashmir insurgency an almost non-negotiable issue.[10] Additionally, India found it quite difficult to manipulate Pakistani fears of unacceptable escalation. Pakistani decision-makers were cognizant that India would not resort to full-scale war for fear of escalation to the nuclear level. Consequently, the expected fears that a failure to comply with the demands of the initiator of coercive diplomacy should have engendered in the mind of the adversary really did not enter Pakistani calculations.

Indeed, Pakistan had few incentives to at all comply with the Indian demands. Domestic politics within India, for the most part, constrained Indian decision-makers from offering any meaningful incentives or rewards. Furthermore, a purely contingent factor also helped Pakistan avoid complying with India's expectations. Namely, its role in aiding the US in the war against the remnants of Al Qaeda and the Taliban gave Pakistan significant bargaining leverage with the US. The US, dependent on Pakistan's cooperation for the pursuit of its anti-terrorist goals, was loath to pressure Pakistan heavily to alter its behaviour towards India.[11]

The Evolution of the Crisis

The First Phase

In the aftermath of the attack on the parliament building Indian decision-makers acted with alacrity. They had three distinct audiences in mind when they set forth their demands. The first and most important of these was the military dictatorship of General Pervez Musharraf in Pakistan. The second target audience was Indian public opinion, especially its 'attentive public'. The third audience was the US in particular, and the global community in general. The immediate task at hand for the Indian political leadership was to demonstrate a seriousness of purpose in pressing Pakistan to end its support for terrorism in India.

The messages that the Indian leadership wanted to convey to these audiences had important overlapping features but also had important differences. It wanted to dissuade Pakistan from carrying out any further attacks with the threat of a possible resort to war; it was keen on reassuring the Indian public that sufficient steps were being taken to deter Pakistan from abetting such attacks in the future; and it sought to induce the US to bring pressure on Pakistan to end its support for the insurgents. As this analysis will show, the Indian leadership was prepared to manipulate the American fear of a possible nuclear war to bring about heightened American concern and pressure on Pakistan.

In pursuit of these ends, the Indian government issued a stern warning to Pakistan on 18 December 2001, making clear that its patience was rapidly running out. Rising domestic pressures within parliament for tough action against Pakistan necessitated such a public stance.[12] Despite India's seemingly unyielding position, Pakistani decision-makers denied any complicity in the attacks. The US, however, took a more serious view of the attacks and on 20 December chose to freeze the assets of the Lashkar-e-Taiba, the group that Indian authorities had blamed for the parliament attack.[13]

Matters in the subcontinent continued to worsen, however, as India recalled its ambassador from Pakistan as a gesture of its displeasure with Musharraf's response. Simultaneously, it chose to suspend bus and train services to Pakistan and indicated that it was sharing information about Pakistan's complicity in the attack with the US, France, and the UK, among other countries.[14] Shortly thereafter, India's exercise in coercive diplomacy was put into motion. Having made a series of explicit demands on Pakistan it now launched military manoeuvres to demonstrate its willingness and ability to coerce Pakistan. India significantly mobilized its army, moved key military formations to forward deployments, and permitted its air force to carry out repeated sorties near the border. Pakistan, in response, cancelled all leave for its army personnel and asserted that its medium-range missiles were on alert.[15] A retired Indian general aptly summed up the Indian strategy:

Soon India will go on an extended diplomatic offensive, the kind Indira Gandhi launched on the eve of the 1971 war. The manifestation of outrage, high-octane political rhetoric, diplomatic forays and the threat of war are all part of coercive diplomacy, which will sooner than later, force the US to put breaks on Pakistan.

It was Madeleine Albright who told [Indian foreign minister] Jaswant Singh that diplomacy works better when backed by force. Double standards aside, the last thing the US wants at this time is a war either by design or accident between nuclear India and nuclear Pakistan while its own war with Afghanistan is still being fought.[16]

The mutual troop movements and other military deployments caught the attention of the US and other major global powers. No doubt to assuage India's acute sense of anger and frustration with Pakistan, the US announced that Pakistan had rounded up some fifty individuals connected with the Lashkar-e-Taiba and the Jaish-e-Mohammed. Despite this assurance from President George W. Bush, India continued its troop build-up along the Indo-Pakistani border, bringing seven new divisions into attack positions.[17] India continued these deployments on the grounds that Pakistan had failed to demonstrate sufficient sincerity and resolve in cracking down on the militants operating from within its territory.[18]

Faced with significant American diplomatic and Indian military pressure, Pakistani authorities arrested Maulana Masood Azhar, the founder of the Jaish-e-Mohammed, and Hafiz Mohammed Saeed, the leader of the Lashkar-e-Taiba, in quick succession. India's reactions to these arrests varied from the muted to the dismissive. Indian authorities took advantage of this opening to formally hand over the list of twenty accused terrorists that it wanted Pakistan to arrest and turn over to India.[19] Although Pakistan continued its crackdown against the two militant groups, it refused to extradite these individuals to India. Indian intelligence sources continued to insist that General Musharraf had done little to dismantle terrorist training camps in Pakistan-controlled Kashmir in such places as Barakot, Bhimber, Kotli, Chilas, Astor, Gilgit, Skardu, and Muzaffarabad.[20] Even a meeting of Indian Prime Minister Atal Behari Vajpayee and General Musharraf in Kathmandu during the annual summit of the SAARC proved to be distinctly frosty, despite the latter's efforts at bonhomie.

India's decision to maintain sustained military pressure on Pakistan was evident in a forceful statement from General Padmanabhan, the Chief of Staff of the Indian Army. On 11 January 2001, he stated in an uncharacteristically blunt fashion at a press conference in New Delhi that any country that was 'mad enough' to initiate a nuclear strike against India would be 'punished severely'. Some Indian commentators argued that his remarks were directed not only towards Pakistan, but also towards the US in a deliberate attempt to signal the possible danger of nuclear war on the subcontinent.[21] Padmanabhan's sharp remarks to the press were of considerable significance in a country where the uniformed military rarely makes public statements about the higher direction of war.[22]

Against this backdrop of rising tensions, General Musharraf gave an important speech on Pakistani national television on 12 January 2002. In this speech, he promised to prevent Pakistani territory from being used to carry out acts of terror against India or other foreign countries. However, he also categorically refused to end Pakistan's support for the

Kashmiri cause, stating, 'Kashmir runs in our blood. No Pakistani can afford to sever links with Kashmir.'[23]

Musharraf's speech was viewed with considerable circumspection in New Delhi. India's leaders, while pleased with his seeming desire to crackdown on Islamic extremists, nevertheless expressed the need to assess the changes that would come about, as part of this renewed commitment on the part of the Pakistani leader to curb the growth and export of religious extremism and terror.[24] Within two weeks of Musharraf's speech, however, it became apparent that the Indian authorities still believed a 'gradual turning of the screw' was necessary.[25] The next step in their strategy of forceful persuasion was the testing of a new missile with a range of 400 miles, and capable of delivering a nuclear warhead. Not surprisingly, the former Chief of Staff of the Indian Army, General Ved Prakash Malik, on this occasion openly stated, 'The message is part of the strategy, call it coercive diplomacy, or whatever.'[26]

Indian military pressures continued throughout the winter months of early 2002, despite American statements that progress was being made to curb religious extremism within Pakistan.[27] Levels of infiltration across the LoC in Kashmir during this period routinely taper off because of the heavy snowfall that closes off most mountain passes in the Himalayas. Infiltration and, therefore, significant attacks on Indian positions become nearly impossible during the winter, and the pattern of insurgent activity in 2002 mostly conformed to this norm.

The Second Phase

The seasonal lull proved to be short-lived, however (see Table 8.1). On 14 May, a set of suicide bombers launched an attack on an Indian Army base in Kaluchak, near Jammu, killing thirty-three individuals, mostly the wives and children of army personnel. The Lashkar-e-Taiba initially claimed responsibility for this attack but subsequently denied any responsibility for it.[28] The timing of this attack was not insignificant, coming just as Christina Rocca, the US Assistant Secretary of State for South Asian affairs, was in New Delhi to discuss the state of Indo-Pakistani relations.

TABLE 8.1 The India–Pakistan Confrontation, 2001–2

Indices of Violence	January		February		March		April		May		June		Total	
	2001	2002	2001	2002	2001	2002	2001	2002	2001	2002	2001	2002	2001	2002
Violent Incidents	249	241	210	168	236	263	320	208	342	290	296	239	1653	1409
Attacks on Security Personnel	135	132	118	79	116	138	169	102	164	165	182	121	884	737
Attacks on Civilians	59	54	47	49	63	58	74	55	79	67	52	67	374	350
Security Personnel Killed	23	35	42	12	48	43	55	37	33	40	49	28	250	195
Civilians Killed	76	67	74	51	60	82	80	74	96	98	59	84	445	456
Terrorists Killed	81	166	92	110	90	163	99	109	157	162	223	109	742	819
Infiltration	149	33	104	60	115	132	94	141	179	202	263	30	904	598
Exfiltration	25	2	46	2	10	6	9	13	54	–	40	63	184	86

Source: Compiled by Praveen Swami; data from the Union Ministry of Home Affairs; used with permission.

Tensions, which had somewhat subsided during the preceding few months, once again soared. Reports from New Delhi again suggested that the Indian authorities were planning attacks on terrorist training camps in Pakistan.[29] Despite these warnings, matters continued to worsen. On 21 May, terrorists shot and killed Abdul Ghani Lone, a prominent Kashmiri separatist leader who had expressed some willingness to enter into talks with the government of India.[30] The crisis that had started with the terrorist attack on the parliament on 13 December now entered a new and more intense phase. It was apparent to decision-makers in New Delhi that despite his repeated promises, General Musharraf was either unwilling or unable to expend the necessary political and military resources to rein in the insurgents. Consequently, New Delhi began to ratchet up the military and diplomatic pressure on Pakistan again to demonstrate its resolve. In a speech to Indian troops deployed along the Indo-Pakistani border, for example, Prime Minister Vajpayee called for a 'decisive fight'.[31]

The escalation of bellicose rhetoric from India certainly reached one of its target audiences. The US reacted with alacrity to the prime minister's truculent words. Secretary of State Colin Powell promptly called General Musharraf to reiterate the importance of reining in the terrorists who were again striking at will in Kashmir. Simultaneously, other State Department representatives urged Indian authorities to eschew military options and seek a diplomatic resolution to the escalating crisis.[32] But US efforts to dampen the spiralling tensions in the region bore little fruit. Pakistan announced that it would move army units from its western border with Afghanistan to its eastern border with India. These troops had been assisting American special forces in their hunt for Al Qaeda operatives and the remnants of the Taliban regime.[33] Worse still, far from backing down, General Musharraf delivered a belligerent speech in which he accused the ruling regime in New Delhi of perpetrating terrorist acts against its country's own minorities.[34]

Towards the end of May war appeared imminent. India started to move key military assets into position, and senior, well-connected military officers publicly expressed growing irritation with Pakistan's intransigence. The IAF moved several squadrons of fighter aircraft to forward bases, the navy rushed five of its most sophisticated warships from the eastern to the western fleet, and the navy's only operational aircraft carrier, the INS Viraat, was taken out of dry dock and placed on alert off the coast of Mumbai.[35]

These military manoeuvres, the increasingly heated rhetoric emanating from New Delhi, and Islamabad's seemingly feckless behaviour generated considerable misgivings in Washington. On 30 May 2002, President Bush sent Secretary of Defense Donald Rumsfeld back to the region and publicly upbraided General Musharraf, stating, 'He must stop incursions across the Line of Control. He must do so. He said he would do so. We and others are making it clear to him that he must live up to his word.'[36]

Despite Rumsfeld's visit to the region, however, tensions continued to mount, and in an effort to signal its increasing fears of the outbreak of a full-scale war between India and Pakistan, the US issued a travel advisory urging all Americans to leave the country, even as Deputy Secretary of Defense Paul Wolfowitz was meeting with the Indian Defence Minister, George Fernandes, at a conference in Singapore in an effort to break the impasse.[37] A number of other countries including the UK, Japan, and Germany, decided to issue travel advisories to their citizens in the wake of the American announcement. Finally, faced with these multiple pressures, the military dictatorship in Pakistan took heed and at least temporarily changed course. In early June, Indian authorities stated that they had detected the first signs that insurgent activity in Kashmir was abating.[38] The US nevertheless kept up the diplomatic pressure on both states, insisting that Pakistan desist from supporting the insurgents and that India exercise military restraint.[39] By mid-June, the crisis showed further signs of easing as hostile statements from both sides drew to a close and further military manoeuvres along the tense border ceased. By the last week of June, tensions had subsided to the extent that India removed its ban on Pakistani overflights of Indian territory and stood down its warships from aggressive patrolling in the Arabian Sea.[40] By early July, the crisis had come to a close. However, not until October of 2002 would India finally pull back the bulk of its forces from their deployments along the Indo-Pakistani border.

Exploring Competing Explanations

Why did India opt to pursue the strategy of forceful persuasion and why did it ultimately fail? In answering these questions, the two phases of the crisis as outlined above must be considered separately. The first phase came in the immediate aftermath of the 13 December 2001 attack on the parliament in New Delhi. The second phase emerged after the 14 May 2002 attack on the Indian Army base in Kaluchak.

Shortly after the attack on parliament, Indian decision-makers assessed the military and diplomatic options available to deal with this new, brazen, Pakistani-abetted terrorist strategy. They chose to adopt a policy of forceful persuasion only after carefully weighing the available options. One important alternative was a series of air strikes against insurgent training camps in Pakistan-controlled Kashmir. Within two weeks of the 13 December attack, the IAF was ready to carry out strikes against some fifty to seventy-five insurgent training bases.[41] A second wave of helicopter-borne commandos would then attack these camps. Shortly thereafter, helicopter gunships would ferry these troops back to Indian territory.[42] This strategy, of course, was not without important drawbacks. At best, even if the attacks were successful and the Indian forces successfully airlifted out of hostile territory, the Pakistanis could once again reconstitute the camps in neighbouring areas without great effort.

At a meeting of the apex CCS, Prime Minister Vajpayee was prepared to approve the execution of these plans. His colleagues, however, cautioned against their immediate implementation, largely on the advice of top-level army officers. Senior army commanders cautioned against the implementation of this strategy because they feared that Pakistan would retaliate in a series of armoured counter-thrusts in Punjab and Rajasthan at a time of its choosing, and probably at night. Since Indian forces were not equipped with night-vision equipment they would be acutely vulnerable to any such well-orchestrated Pakistani attacks. (There is some debate about whether or not such constraints actually existed.)[43]

A second option that was discussed was resort to full-scale war. Such an option, obviously, was not immediately available in the aftermath of the 13 December attack. Much of the Indian Army was in its peacetime

stations, ammunition and other logistics had not been appropriately
stocked, and hospitals in forward bases had not been adequately prepared
to deal with substantial casualties. The military build-up that followed
over the next month and half was a prerequisite for launching a large-
scale war.[44] However, as the retired Chief of Staff of the Indian Army,
General Ved Prakash Malik has argued, the military requirements of
coercive diplomacy and those of large-scale war are quite different. The
twenty-day process of gearing up for threatening Pakistan with a major
assault contributed to the loss of both strategic and tactical surprise.[45]

However, India remained unwilling to resort to large-scale war once
it had the requisite forces in place, even after yet another brutal terrorist
attack on 14 May 2002. Although it possessed a respectable overall
advantage in terms of its conventional military arsenal (even though the
Pakistani Army may have had a few, specific qualitative advantages),
India chose not to go to war.[46] What ultimately inhibited India was
Pakistan's possession of nuclear weapons.[47] The fear of Pakistan's resort
to a possible nuclear threat was paramount in the minds of Indian
decision-makers, thereby inhibiting a resort to all-out war.[48]

Under these circumstances, the most viable strategy was the resort
to forceful persuasion. Unfortunately for India, from the very outset the
likely success of that strategy was compromised. To begin with, the central
Indian demand—the end to all infiltration into Indian-controlled
Kashmir—set an extraordinarily high standard for Pakistani compliance.
Such a demand was entirely understandable in the light of Indian public
opinion in the aftermath of the 13 December attack. The government
could ill afford to seem weak in responding to this direct attack on the
Indian parliament. On the other hand, in terms of its bilateral relationship
with Pakistan, such a demand was simply unviable. A Pakistani military
dictator, lacking popular legitimacy, could himself ill afford an about-
face on an issue of such mammoth proportions.[49] Consequently, the
Pakistani motivation for non-compliance was exceedingly high.

More to the point, Indian decision-makers were both unable and
unwilling to offer any tangible rewards for Pakistani compliance with
their demands, other than some significant concession on the contentious
and all-important Kashmir dispute. Even if they had meaningful
incentives at hand, the Indian public, already outraged after the attack

on the parliament, would not have countenanced any concessions to Pakistan on the Kashmir issue. Such concessions would have been construed as tantamount to caving in to terrorist acts.

Thus, the Indian strategy violated two of the key tenets of the successful pursuit of coercive diplomacy: the demands made on the adversary far exceeded its willingness and motivation to comply, and the status quo power had few, if any, rewards to proffer for the adversary's compliance.

Furthermore, India's threats to escalate the conflict militarily were not really credible. Pakistan's possession of nuclear weapons had not only emboldened it to embark on the Kargil invasion of 1999, but also persuaded India to keep its response to that invasion limited to the area of infiltration.[50] India's unwillingness to expand the scope and dimensions of the Kargil conflict had convinced Pakistani decision-makers that their country's overt acquisition of nuclear weapons had effectively neutralized India's conventional military superiority. Pakistan's diplomats, including its permanent representative to the UN, Munir Akram, had made clear that if Pakistan felt militarily beleaguered, it would resort to the use of nuclear weapons.[51]

The Indian inability to credibly threaten escalatory action against Pakistan thus violated a third important principle of a successful strategy of coercive diplomacy: that threats must be sufficiently strong and credible. If India chose to resort to a large-scale conventional attack against Pakistan, the consequences would be neither controllable nor calculable. Pakistani decision-makers, if they felt that their country was in mortal danger from an Indian attack, could always threaten to resort to nuclear weapons, thereby preventing India from keeping the conflict limited in scope or intensity. Even evidence from Indian sources indicates that key individuals in Indian national security circles believed that Pakistan's nuclear arsenal neutralized India's threats and plans to resort to large-scale conventional conflict, even after the 14 May massacre. As an Indian diplomat stated at the peak of the crisis, 'The idea that Pakistan will cooperate in a conflict and comply with India's wishes to fight a limited war is ridiculous. It will be naturally in their interest to keep any conflagration as unlimited as possible.'[52]

So what exactly did India's massive military mobilization in the wake of the 13 December 2001 attack accomplish? For the most part, India won a pyrrhic victory. The large-scale military mobilization cost India dearly in wear and tear on its military equipment. The mobilization, which failed to achieve a genuine resolution of the crisis, undermined the morale of the armed forces. Significant numbers of Indian troops and other military personnel had to withstand considerable physical hardship over an extended time span, while coping with extreme fluctuations in climatic conditions in a situation of high alert. Most important, India was unable to stop Pakistan from continuing infiltration into Kashmir. The only meaningful accomplishment of this Indian exercise of coercive diplomacy was to draw the US into the fray as a significant player to try and curb Pakistan's continuing support to the insurgency and to acts of terror.[53] And even this achievement came at the cost of abandoning India's long-standing aversion to the involvement of the US as an actor in subcontinental affairs.[54]

Our analysis of this case again confirms our hypothesis of the robustness of nuclear deterrence in South Asia. Despite extraordinary provocation and the possession of adequate conventional forces, India resorted to a strategy of coercive diplomacy rather than undertake a war against Pakistan. Even this strategy of coercive diplomacy proved to be of limited utility against Pakistan, a nuclear-armed adversary. Finally, while American diplomacy may have played an ameliorative role in this crisis, it was hardly decisive in shaping its final outcome. The mutual possession of nuclear weapons was the most significant factor in bringing the crisis to a close.

Notes

[1] Amy Waldman, 'Kashmir Massacre May Signal the Coming of Widespread Violence,' the *New York Times*, 25 March 2003, p. A8.

[2] Celia Dugger, 'Pakistan's Arrest of Militant Is "Step Forward" India Says', the *New York Times*, 22 December 2001, p. A1.

[3] See Sumit Ganguly, *The Crisis in Kashmir: Portents of War, Hopes of Peace* (Washington, DC: Woodrow Wilson Center Press; Cambridge: Cambridge University Press, 1999).

[4] Barry Bearak, '26 Die as Suicide Squad Bombs Kashmir Legislative Building', the *New York Times*, 1 October 2001, p. B3.

[5] Economist Global Agenda, 'Terror in India', 19 December 2001, available at www.economist.com.

[6] There is a small but significant body of literature on this subject. The classic statement of coercive diplomacy can be found in Alexander L. George, David K. Hall, and William E. Simons, *The Limits of Coercive Diplomacy* (Boston: Little, Brown, 1971); also see Alexander L. George, *Forceful Persuasion* (Washington, DC: United States Institute of Peace Press, 1991). For applications of this concept to a number of Cold War crises, see Barry M. Blechman *et al.* (eds), *Force without War: US Armed Forces as a Political Instrument* (Washington, DC: Brookings Institution, 1978); Stephen S. Kaplan, *Diplomacy of Power: Soviet Armed Forces as a Political Instrument* (Washington, DC: Brookings Institution, 1981); Kenneth Roberts, 'Bullying and Bargaining: The United States, Nicaragua, and Conflict Resolution in Central America', *International Security*, vol. 15, no. 2 (1990), pp. 67–102; and Bruce W. Jentleson, 'The Reagan Administration and Coercive Diplomacy: Restraining More Than Remaking Governments', *Political Science Quarterly*, vol. 106, no. 1 (1991), pp. 57–82.

[7] The two variants of this strategy are 'the-try-and-see approach' and the 'tacit ultimatum variant'. See George, Hall, and Simons, *The Limits of Coercive Diplomacy*, p. 27. In a later work, George also discusses a third variant, 'the gradual turning of the screw', which calls for the steady, increased application of pressure on the adversary as his compliance with the demands are found wanting over an extended span of time. See George, *Forceful Persuasion*, p. 8.

[8] George, Hall, and Simons, *The Limits of Coercive Diplomacy*, p. 22.

[9] Sumit Ganguly, 'From Aid to the Civil to the Defense of the Nation: The Army in Contemporary India', *Journal of Asian and African Affairs*, vol. 26 (1991), pp. 1–12.

[10] On the Pakistani military's involvement in the Kashmiri insurgency see Victoria Schofield, *Kashmir in Conflict: India, Pakistan and the Unfinished War* (London: I.B. Tauris, 2000).

[11] The American difficulty of courting Pakistan while still addressing India's concerns is nicely discussed in Aziz Haniffa, 'Musharraf's Turnaround May Make India Talk', *India Abroad*, 25 January 2002, p. 32.

[12] Celia W. Dugger, 'India Raises the Pitch in Criticism of Pakistan', the *New York Times*, 19 December 2001, p. A14.

[13] David E. Sanger and Kurt Eichenwald, 'Citing India Attack, US Aims at Assets of Group in Pakistan', the *New York Times*, 21 December 2001, p. A1.

[14] Celia W. Dugger, 'India Recalling Pakistan Envoy over Delhi Raid', the *New York Times*, 22 December 2001, p. A1.

[15] Howard Witt and Uli Schmetzer, 'Missile Alert in Kashmir', *Chicago Tribune*, 27 December 2001, p. 1.

[16] Major General Ashok K. Mehta (retd), 'More Bark than Bite', 31 December 2001, available at www.rediff.com.

[17] John F. Burns, 'Pakistan Moves against Groups Named by India', the *New York Times*, 29 December 2001, p. A1.

[18] John F. Burns and Celia W. Dugger, 'India Builds Up Forces as Bush Urges Calm', the *New York Times*, 30 December 2001.

[19] Celia W. Dugger, 'Pakistan's Arrest of Militant Is "Step Forward" India Says', the *New York Times*, 1 January 2002, p. A8.

[20] Paul Watson and Siddhartha Barua, 'Camps Thrive in Pakistan, India Charges', *Los Angeles Times*, 11 January 2002, p. 1.

[21] The *Hindu*, 'We Are Prepared: Army Chief', 12 January 2001; also see Celia W. Dugger, 'Indian General Talks Bluntly of War and Nuclear Threat', the *New York Times*, 12 January 2002, p. A1.

[22] Ganguly, 'From Aid to the Civil to the Defense of the Nation'.

[23] Pervez Musharraf, text of speech, 12 January 2002, reproduced at www.outlookindia.com.

[24] Press Trust of India, 'Full Text of Statement Issued by the Ministry of External Affairs', 13 January 2002.

[25] George, *Forceful Persuasion*, pp. 8–9.

[26] Celia W. Dugger, 'India Tests Missile, Stirring a Region Already on Edge', *New York Times*, 26 January 2002, p. A2.

[27] Todd S. Purdum and Celia W. Dugger, 'Powell Now "Very Encouraged" on Kashmir', the *New York Times*, 19 January 2002, p. A5.

[28] Edward Luce and Farhan Bokhari, 'Bombers Kill 33 in Kashmir as US Envoy Visits India', *Financial Times*, 15 May 2002, p. 4.

[29] Edward Luce, 'India Prepares for Strike on Camps', *Financial Times*, 17 May 2002, available at www.ft.com.

[30] Edward Luce, 'Kashmir Killing Seen as Talks Warning', *Financial Times*, 22 May 2002, available at www.ft.com.

[31] Reuters, 'Indian PM Calls for "Decisive Fight"', 22 May 2002.

[32] Barry Schweid, 'Powell Confers with Musharraf as Bush Administration Turns Up Heat on Pakistan to Curb Extremists', Associated Press, 23 May 2002.

[33] Howard W. French, 'Pakistan Prepares to Shift Troops from Afghan Border to Kashmir', the *New York Times*, 24 May 2002, p. A10.

[34] Celia W. Dugger, 'India Reacts Angrily to Pakistani's Speech', the *New York Times*, 26 May 2002, p. A24.

[35] Josy Joseph, 'The Mood Is for War', *India Abroad*, 31 May 2002, p. 3.

[36] Elisabeth Bumiller and Thom Shanker, 'Bush Presses Pakistan on Kashmir and Orders Rumsfeld to Region', the *New York Times*, 31 May 2002, p. A1.

[37] Thom Shanker and Elisabeth Bumiller, 'Citing Tensions US Advises Americans in India to Leave', the *New York Times*, 31 May 2002, p. A1.

[38] Raymond Bonner, 'India Believes Pakistan Restrains Militants', the *New York Times*, 6 June 2002, p. A12.

[39] Edward Luce and Richard Wolffe, 'US Makes Headway Calming Antagonists', *Financial Times*, 7 June 2002, available at www.ft.com.

[40] Josy Joseph, 'India Removes Overflight Ban on Pakistani Aircraft', *India Abroad*, 21 June 2002, p. 15.

[41] A detailed discussion of India's capabilities and advantages in air assets over those of Pakistan see Anthony H. Cordesman, *The India–Pakistan Military Balance* (Washington, DC: Center for Strategic and International Studies, May 2002), p. 5.

[42] For a discussion of Indian capabilities see 'Para Commandos', available at www.bharat-rakshak.com/LAND-FORCES/Special-Forces/para.html.

[43] Rahul Bedi, 'A Strike Staunched', *Frontline*, 8–21 June 2002. It should be noted that in interviews conducted with mid-level serving officers in the Indian and US armies, the claim about India's lack of night vision capabilities was openly questioned. At least two knowledgeable individuals indicated that Indian forces do indeed possess *limited* if not *extensive* night vision capabilities.

[44] On this point see Lieutenant General V.K. Sood (retd) and Pravin Sawhney, *Operation Parakram: The War Unfinished* (New Delhi: Sage Publications, 2003).

[45] General Ved Prakash Malik, 'Lessons From Operation Parakram', *The Tribune*, 13 December 2002.

[46] Rahul Bedi, 'The Military Dynamics', *Frontline*, 8–21 June 2002.

[47] In the past, especially during the 1965 war, when Pakistan attacked in Kashmir, India quickly resorted to horizontal escalation. Within a week of the initial Pakistani attack in Kashmir, Indian forces had crossed the international border in the state of Punjab, and were threatening the key regional capital city of Lahore. Of course, in 1965 neither side possessed even incipient nuclear capabilities. For a discussion of Indian military strategies and objectives in the

1965 war see Russell Brines, *The Indo-Pakistani Conflict* (New York: Pall Mall, 1968).

[48] V. Sudarshan and Ajith Pillai, 'Game of Patience', *Outlook*, 27 May 2002, pp. 34–9.

[49] For a discussion of the tenuous legitimacy of the Pakistani regime of General Pervez Musharraf see Sumit Ganguly, 'Pakistan's Never Ending Story: Why the October Coup Was No Surprise', *Foreign Affairs*, vol. 79, no. 2 (2002), pp. 2–7.

[50] Praveen Swami, *The Kargil War* (New Delhi: LeftWord Books, 2000).

[51] Rahul Bedi, 'The Military Dynamics', *Frontline,* 8–21 June 2002.

[52] V. Sudarshan and Ajith Pillai, 'Game of Patience', *Outlook*, 27 May 2002, pp. 34–9.

[53] C. Raja Mohan, interview by author, January 2003.

[54] On the Indian aversion to the presence of a third part in the affairs of the subcontinent see J.N. Dixit, *India–Pakistan in War and Peace* (New Delhi: Books Today, 2002).

9

Lessons, Implications,
and Policy Suggestions

In this study, we set out to explain why India and Pakistan have avoided a major war over the past two decades, despite deep mutual mistrust, chronic political tensions, an intractable conflict over Kashmir, a recent history of three major wars, and the inexorable refinement of both sides' nuclear weapon and delivery capabilities—factors which together suggest to many analysts that South Asia has been ripe for major war over the last twenty years. We undertook to examine this puzzle in a way that—unlike previous studies—would be comprehensive in the sense of covering all of the crises, major and minor, that have erupted between New Delhi and Islamabad since both countries became nascent nuclear weapon states in the 1980s. All but one of these six crises were resolved peacefully, and the 1999 Kargil war was purposefully contained by both sides within the disputed territory of Kashmir. What, other than providence or sheer dumb luck, accounts for such a remarkable record of mutual military restraint in the face of near-constant hostility?

We readily acknowledge that there can be no powerful monocausal explanations for the myriad of complex decisions attending matters of war and peace; however, we feel equally strongly that, especially over time, patterns can emerge that begin to transcend mere description and come to enjoy the status of theoretical generalizations—generalizations that can be subjected to further logical and empirical scrutiny by other scholars. Our methodological approach was, at the outset, to articulate three propositions that seemed potentially to explain why no major Indo-Pakistani wars were fought during the period under consideration. As detailed in Chapter One, these propositions speculated that, in each case, crisis resolution was attributable to one or more of the following factors: (1) timely and forceful US intervention; (2) mutual fears that war might escalate to the nuclear level; (3) one or both sides' lack of sufficient conventional military superiority to pursue a successful blitzkrieg strategy. We also explained why we rejected other propositions that seemed theoretically plausible but empirically irrelevant to the Indo-Pakistani crises between 1984 and 2002.

Our overall conclusion is that the nuclear-deterrence proposition best explains the absence of major war in the region over the last twenty years, especially during the crises beginning with 1990. US crisis management occasionally played a secondary role—particularly in 1990, 1999, and 2001–2. The US was most significant in the 1999 Kargil war, when the Clinton Administration essentially forced Nawaz Sharif's government into pulling out of Indian Kashmir. At other times, US policies were actually counterproductive, as in 1984. The weakest proposition was the one concerning conventional deterrence, not because its underlying theory is flawed, but because India nearly always had sufficient conventional military capabilities to inflict a blitzkrieg defeat on Pakistan and consistently chose a different policy. This suggests that nuclear deterrence generally trumped conventional deterrence as a source of crisis resolution.

One of the main values of theoretically driven research is that it can yield serendipitous insights; in the cases we have studied, the process of analysing the influence of nuclear and conventional capabilities on Indian and Pakistani behaviour generated the notion that, at least in the 1984 crisis, a form of 'boosted conventional deterrence' prevailed. It is likely, too, that this hybrid type of deterrence quietly influenced New Delhi and Islamabad's decision calculus in each subsequent crisis. The idea that there exists a grey area between nuclear and conventional deterrence is not a new one,[1] but its relevance is enhanced by its demonstrable prominence in South Asian thinking over the past twenty years. This area of study demands greater attention in the future, especially considering that one of the US' main national security challenges is devising effective policies towards aspiring and new nuclear weapon states, such as Iran and North Korea, respectively.

The remainder of this concluding chapter unfolds in the following way. In the next section, we recapitulate why each of the six crises was ultimately resolved short of major military conflict. In section three, we assess current India–Pakistan nuclear dynamics, paying particular attention to capabilities, doctrines, and the issue of deterrence stability. In the final section of the book, we make recommendations for US policy based on our research and analysis. Our central conclusion is that the US has a limited degree of influence on Indian and Pakistani nuclear decision-making, but that Washington can better address Indo-Pakistani political conflicts, especially over Kashmir.

The Six Crises: Why No Major Wars?

In the early 1980s, Indian civilian and military planners seriously considered launching preventive air strikes against Pakistan's evolving, but disaggregated, nuclear capabilities. In turn, worried Pakistani leaders warned the Indian government that they would respond to such an attack by ordering their own air strikes against New Delhi's nuclear facilities, thereby spreading lethal radioactive materials into densely populated Indian cities. Islamabad's fears reached their apex in 1984, when two squadrons of Indian Jaguar fighter-bombers seemingly went missing. Pakistani officials feared that the undetectable Jaguars had been moved by the Indians in preparation for a preventive strike against the Kahuta uranium enrichment facility, and they repeatedly called on their then US ally for protection. Ultimately, India and Pakistan restrained themselves from fighting. In the 1984 crisis, none of our three propositions fared very well. Instead, the main source of Indo-Pakistani peace seems to have been 'boosted conventional deterrence'—the mutual fear of the adversary striking one's own nuclear facilities with advanced conventional weapons. This conclusion is strengthened by the fact that, in the immediate aftermath of the crisis, India and Pakistan reached an agreement not to attack each other's nuclear sites, the first of its kind in the nuclear era.[2]

In 1986–7, New Delhi and Islamabad endured a long crisis emanating from India's 'Brasstacks' military exercises, the largest in South Asia's history. Brasstacks set off a process of competitive mobilization— and nearly a war—between Indian and Pakistani military forces that faced off all along the border in a chain reaction of military moves and countermoves. The two sides backed down from their war footings in early 1987. India and Pakistan's nascent nuclear weapon capabilities had little discernible impact on the outcome of the crisis, which was resolved peacefully mainly because India lacked the requisite conventional military capabilities to launch confidently a blitzkrieg-style invasion of Pakistan. Islamabad, in 1987, was at the height of its conventional military sophistication, given the inflow of weapons and technology stemming from the US preoccupation with supporting the anti-Soviet guerrilla forces in Afghanistan. Moreover, while India enjoyed overall conventional military advantages vis-à-vis Pakistan, many of its best army divisions were pinned down on the Himalayan frontier, where Indian forces had skirmished with China's in 1986. The US role in the Brasstacks crisis was minimal, consisting mainly of providing information and reassurance to both sides in an attempt to counteract the mutual mistrust and appallingly bad intelligence that structured the crisis.

In 1990, India and Pakistan engaged in an intense, months-long crisis over the emerging Islamist insurgency in Indian Kashmir. As Islamabad dramatically stepped up its support for the Muslim militants across the LoC in Kashmir, New Delhi ordered a brutal crackdown on the insurgents. National temperatures rose, and the Indian and Pakistani militaries were partially mobilized, moved towards sensitive border areas, and put on high alert. Goaded by the public outcry over Kashmir and opportunistic opposition politicians across the political spectrum, both governments issued shrill nuclear-tinged rhetoric in the spring of 1990. US officials became so alarmed by the situation in April and May that President George H.W. Bush tried to calm tempers by sending a senior foreign policy team to both countries. Ultimately, the two sides backed away from the brink of war, owing to the twin restraints of nuclear deterrence and timely and forceful US intervention. New Delhi and Islamabad had already determined by the time of the US crisis management initiative that the stakes of a war in 1990 were simply too high due to the existential deterrent effects of their mutual nuclear weapon capabilities. Resolute US diplomacy both reinforced that realization and facilitated face-saving steps back from the brink of war.

In 1998, New Delhi sparked another crisis by conducting a series of nuclear explosive tests on 11 and 13 May. A few weeks later, after considerable external pressure and internal debate, Islamabad followed suit. For much of the time between the Indian and Pakistani tests of 1998, Pakistani officials worried—as they had in 1984—about the possibility of an Indian preventive strike. The tit-for-tat South Asian nuclear tests then created a spiral of alarm that raised mutual fears of pre-emptive nuclear strikes, put the two sides' military forces on high alert, and generated an atmosphere of extremely bellicose rhetoric. Again, however, military hostilities were avoided. We argue that this result was the outcome of existential nuclear deterrence: neither side could have had confidence in carrying out an effective, decapitating first strike against the other side's nuclear assets. The conventional deterrence explanation fails with respect to 1998, because by that time India had regained and was widening its conventional military advantages over Pakistan. Our US intervention proposition is weak in explaining Indo-Pakistani restraint in 1998; indeed, the US role appears to have been ineffective, largely due to the inflexibility of US laws in 1998.

The years 1998 and 1999 brought an empirical playing-out of the stability–instability paradox, as described in Chapter One. Pakistan covertly infiltrated soldiers into the remote Kargil region of Indian Kashmir, in a surprise initiative that sparked a robust Indian military response—but one carefully limited to the Indian side of the disputed territory. Kargil was, in fact, a war, and thus represents the second exception to the theoretical law that nuclear weapon states do not engage in direct military conflict (the first being the Sino-Soviet border clashes of 1969). Why did the Kargil war not spread and develop into a major Indo-Pakistani war? First, New Delhi studiously avoided expanding its military operations beyond the Kargil area, due to its fear that escalation might ultimately create a situation in which nuclear weapons could be used. This is a point that bears reiteration: *despite severe provocation, India limited its war-fighting operations not only to the disputed territory of Kashmir, but to its* own *side of the LoC in Kashmir.* Absent nuclear weapons, Pakistan would probably not have undertaken the Kargil misadventure in the first place; but absent nuclear weapons, India would likely have punished Pakistan much more severely for violating the LoC in such a blatant and duplicitous fashion. A secondary but very important war-inhibiting factor in 1999 was the Clinton administration's strong pressure on Islamabad to cease and desist in Kargil.

In late 2001 and 2002, New Delhi responded to an audacious Pakistani-supported terrorist attack on the Indian Parliament by fully mobilizing its military forces along the international border and the LoC in Kashmir. After Islamabad responded with its own massive troop build-up, an estimated one million Indian and Pakistani soldiers were poised on high alert along the entire Indo-Pakistani frontier. Both sides' armoured formations stood ready to launch offensive strikes deep into the opponent's territory, and short-range ballistic missiles were moved to border areas. By the time it was defused in autumn 2002, this latest crisis had generated the largest South Asian military build-up since the 1971 Indo-Pakistani war. After nearly a year of crisis-grade tension, however, India and Pakistan once again eased themselves away from the brink of war. Nuclear deterrence again seems to provide the best explanation for that outcome. With Pakistan now an established, unambiguous nuclear weapon state, Indian decision-makers were loath to undertake attacks—either in Kashmir or across the international border—that might provoke Pakistani escalation to the nuclear level. Absent nuclear weapons, India by 1999 was clearly in a position of sufficient conventional superiority that it could have ordered a successful blitzkrieg attack against Pakistan. The US role, as in previous crises, was that of a facilitator of peace, providing both sides with the political cover they needed to stand down while still saving face.

South Asian Nuclear Dynamics in 2005

After navigating a treacherous, decades-long transition to mutual nuclear weapon status, India and Pakistan have arrived at a threshold of sorts. Both countries are now—and are now acknowledged to be—nuclear weapon states. This is so notwithstanding the fact that they, like Israel, remain outside the regime centred upon the NPT. Any discussion of South Asia's nuclear dynamics needs to begin by recognizing that, despite the crisis-strewn path they have traversed, New Delhi and Islamabad have managed to confound Western non-proliferation analysts, the vast majority of whom predicted that the spread of nuclear weapons to conflict-prone regions would have disastrous outcomes. To pick a single example, one of the two or three most prominent American non-proliferation analysts wrote in 1982 that the 'heightened stakes and lessened room for manouevre in conflict-prone regions, the volatile leadership and political instability of many of the next nuclear powers, and the technical deficiencies of many new nuclear forces all threaten the first decades' nuclear peace.'[3] According to this analyst, whose views were and are shared by nearly all of his Western counterparts, Third World countries' territorial integrity, independence, and national survival may ride on the outcome of conflicts with adversaries; consequently, 'some of these countries' leaders may be ready to risk nuclear confrontation, if not even to *accept a surprisingly high level of nuclear damage*, in pursuit of their objectives.'[4] A decade later, this analyst argued that 'many of the political, technical, and situational roots of stable nuclear deterrence between the US and the Soviet Union may be absent in South Asia, the Middle East or other regions to which nuclear weapons are spreading. *There is a high risk of nuclear weapons being used.*'[5] The point of recounting this stream of thought is not to be complacent, to suggest that all is well when it comes to the nuclear element of Indo-Pakistani relations. Rather, as with this book in general, the point is to recognize where we have been, so as to chart the best way forward.

In terms of their actual nuclear weapon capabilities, India and Pakistan appear to remain in a state of non-deployed non-weaponization. They are no longer opaque proliferants in the classic sense: that is, countries that covertly acquire nuclear weapon capabilities, but do not test nuclear explosive devices, do not acknowledge the possession of nuclear weapons, do not make direct nuclear threats against adversaries, do not publicly enunciate nuclear doctrines, do not allow open nuclear debates, do not deploy nuclear weapons, and insulate their nuclear weapon programmes from routine national security activities. In other words, India and Pakistan have moved on from the situation that continues to characterize Israel, the prototypical opaque nuclear weapon state.[6] However, neither New Delhi nor Islamabad has apparently moved with dispatch into the more transparent proliferation universe of the five NPT-recognized nuclear weapon powers—the US, the Soviet Union (now Russia), the UK, France, and China. While India and Pakistan are, no doubt, refining and enhancing their nuclear weapons and delivery capabilities, and while both have articulated skeletal nuclear doctrines, they also continue to be notably reticent when it comes to revealing their nuclear force levels and configurations. This situation—which we might call 'veiled proliferation'—could be due to the fact that their capabilities continue to be quite rudimentary, which Indian and Pakistani leaders would naturally be reluctant to advertise. It could also be due to the perception among South Asian nuclear decision-makers that the fewer quantitative and qualitative details they reveal publicly, the lower the likelihood that the other side would be tempted to undertake a decapitating first strike. Either way, India and Pakistan have opened the closet door, but they are not quite out of the closet.

The veiled nature of both countries' nuclear weapon programmes suggests the need for a huge degree of modesty in speculating about their extant nuclear forces. One credible source suggests that:

India possesses the components to deploy a small number of nuclear weapons within a few days and has produced enough weapons-grade plutonium to produce between 50 and 90 nuclear weapons... Yet three years after India's... nuclear tests, the most striking aspect of the country's weapon program has been its deliberate pace. No nuclear weapons are known to be deployed among active military units or deployed on missiles, and India's nuclear arsenal is believed to be routinely maintained as separate components.

As for delivery systems,

India has developed several types of ballistic missiles capable of carrying and delivering a nuclear payload. These are the short-range Prithvi and the medium-range Agni... Despite its pursuit of ballistic missiles, India's most likely delivery platforms are its fighter-bomber aircraft. These probably include the MiG-27 and Jaguar and potentially the Mirage 2000, MiG-29, and Su-30 aircraft. In a classified internal memo, the Indian Air Force reportedly determined that the country's fighter-bomber aircraft remains the only feasible delivery system until the end of this decade.

Pakistan, suggests this source,

...possesses the components and material to assemble a small number of nuclear weapons in a matter of hours or days and has produced enough weapons-grade uranium to produce between 30 and 50 nuclear weapons... Pakistan's nuclear weapons are reportedly stored in component form, with the fissile material core separated from the non-nuclear explosives. It is unclear where Pakistan stores its fissile material and warheads.

Pakistan's delivery systems include:

...nuclear-capable missiles with ranges from 280 kilometers to 2,000 kilometers. Pakistan has acquired the bulk of its missile capabilities from China and North Korea. Its missile arsenal includes the Chinese-built and supplied M-11, the liquid-fuel Hatf short-range series, the Ghauri medium-range missiles, and the solid-fuel Shaheen series... The F-16 could be Pakistan's primary nuclear-capable aircraft, capable of delivering a 1,000 kilogram bomb to a distance of 1,400 kilometers. Other delivery vehicles include the French Mirage III fighter-bombers and the Chinese A-5 Fantan.[7]

It is vital to note in this context that these represent broad estimates of *potential* nuclear weapon capabilities. 'From all that we know publicly,' another credible source states, 'India and Pakistan are yet to deploy their missiles and bombers with nuclear warheads.'[8]

Several other observations can be made about the nuclear equation in South Asia today.[9] First, measured on a continuum with operational nuclear weapon deployments at one end and unassembled, nondeployed nuclear-weapon capabilities at the other, Pakistan is apparently closer than India to having ready-to-use nuclear weapons. In India, the military is generally kept out of the nuclear loop, meaning that the political and operational uses of nuclear weapons have not been appreciably integrated. This comparative decision context is hardly surprising, given that Pakistan's nuclear weapons are controlled by the Pakistan Army, while India's are under the strict control of civilian authorities. Second, Pakistan's nuclear forces are more heavily geared towards delivery by ballistic missiles than are India's, which will, as noted above, rely on delivery by aircraft for some years to come. Pakistan's ground-based air defences are weak, and its air force capabilities are limited, aged, and primarily defensive. Most analysts believe that in a future war, the IAF would quickly achieve dominance of the air. Also, India is a more target-rich country than Pakistan, but its air- and ground-based defences are significantly stronger, which bolsters the Pakistani reliance on ballistic missile delivery systems. Pakistan's strengths in this regard are mainly due, of course, to China's nuclear and missile beneficence in the 1980s and 1990s,[10] as well as to Pakistan's acquisition of North Korean missiles in the 1990s.

In the aftermath of their 1998 nuclear explosive tests, both New Delhi and Islamabad enunciated bare-bones nuclear doctrines. In the spirit of McGeorge Bundy's analysis of the nuclear condition, alluded to in previous chapters,[11] we believe that these should be regarded as *hints* of how Indian and Pakistani decision-makers view the possible uses of their nuclear weapons, but not as *guides* to what would actually transpire in a conflict. That having been said, any discussion of South Asian nuclear dynamics must make some reference to Indian and Pakistani nuclear-use doctrines.

India's evolving nuclear doctrine would appear to rest on two pillars. The first is what Indian officials refer to as 'minimum credible nuclear deterrence'.[12] This means that India will strive for an assured, second-strike nuclear capability vis-à-vis China (and thus, by implication, Pakistan), without seeking to match China's nuclear arsenal in quantitative terms. As Prime Minister Vajpayee said shortly after India's 1998 nuclear tests, 'we have no intention of engaging in a nuclear arms race and building huge arsenals as we have seen other nuclear weapons states do.' Furthermore, Vajpayee declared, 'India's nuclear doctrine is qualitatively different from that of other nuclear weapons states... we do not need to, or intend to, replicate the kind of command and control structures which they required. Our approach is to have a credible deterrent, which should prevent the uses of these weapons... India's nuclear policy is not predicated on war but its avoidance.'[13] New Delhi's long-term goal is to have a sufficiently abundant and diverse nuclear force structure that neither Beijing nor Islamabad can have a reasonable hope of launching a successful first strike against India's nuclear weapons. As the August 1999 'Draft Indian Nuclear Doctrine' puts it, 'any nuclear attack on India and its forces shall result in punitive retaliation with nuclear weapons to inflict damage unacceptable to the aggressor.'[14]

The second pillar of India's nuclear doctrine is its pledge never to be the first party in a dispute to resort to nuclear weapons.[15] This 'no-first-use' posture reflects India's ample strategic depth and Indian decision-makers' concomitant lack of anxiety about the prospects of a conventional invasion by either Pakistan or China. On paper, India's nuclear weapons exist primarily to deter military-nuclear aggression and political-nuclear blackmail; if they also deter conventional attacks, that is all to the good, but India does not threaten nuclear reprisal in the face of a conventional invasion. It bears noting here that India's 'no-first-use' pledge is mainly a rhetorical device aimed at making its peacetime nuclear stance appear unthreatening to its potential adversaries. In the extremely unlikely event that India were to be the victim of a massive conventional assault by China or Pakistan, there can be little doubt that New Delhi's no-first-use pledge would go by the boards. No-first-use is a tool for reassurance in a conflict-free context, not a recipe for national suicide during war.

Pakistan's nuclear doctrine involves a more straightforward, last-resort deterrent to aggression of all kinds. Unlike New Delhi, Islamabad has limited strategic depth. As a result, it rejects no-first-use pledges and implicitly threatens nuclear reprisals for nuclear *or* conventional aggression. With a rapidly developing intermediate-range missile deterrent, Pakistan's basic, counter-city nuclear deterrent needs are well on their way to being met. Pakistan may already be capable of hitting any important target in India with atomic warheads. Islamabad would perhaps be content to achieve a very small, survivable second-strike nuclear force, but for one problem: the harder India strives to attain a secure nuclear deterrent against China, the more severe will be the Indian challenge to Pakistan's assured destruction capabilities, and the more Pakistan will be compelled to match India's nuclear strides. In other words, India's perceived threat from China has the effect of exacerbating South Asia's nuclear-arms competition. Absent the China factor, India and Pakistan could conceivably settle into a relatively modest, counter-city nuclear-deterrent relationship; but China's inevitable involvement in the South Asian nuclear equation significantly increases the complexity of Indo-Pakistani nuclear dynamics.

Analysts sharply disagree about one central question: how stable is nuclear deterrence in South Asia today?[16] For some observers, India–Pakistan nuclear dynamics today constitute a creaky, delicate form of deterrence that remains vulnerable to breakdown by design, by accident, or by inadvertence.[17] For others, India and Pakistan have, over the past two decades, settled into a more stable nuclear-deterrent balance.[18] On the whole, we tend towards the latter view.[19] The main danger, obviously, is that India or Pakistan might actually *use* the weapons they claim to have developed for purely deterrent purposes.[20] Most observers believe that the India–Pakistan nuclear balance is different in important respects from the US-Soviet balance during the Cold War. Those differences, many analysts believe, inhibit the realization of stable nuclear deterrence in South Asia. Unlike the US and the Soviet Union, India and Pakistan share a long, hotly disputed border, not to mention Kashmir's always-tense LoC. Over time, this reasoning goes, Washington and Moscow developed command-and-control arrangements that buffered their nuclear infrastructures against the use of nuclear weapons, intended or otherwise. In contrast, little is known about the Indian and Pakistani command-and-control systems, which are assumed to be rudimentary. If missile flight times of 20–30 minutes provoked enormous anxiety in the US–Soviet case, flight times of 5–10 minutes in South Asia are even more worrisome. These considerations cause many analysts to fear that pre-emptive pressures may some day lead to an Indo-Pakistani nuclear war. One influential American report sums up this conventional wisdom: 'The presence of nuclear forces in the arsenals of two adjacent and often quarrelling countries increases the likelihood that nuclear weapons could be used in a conflict—and dramatically raises the human and financial costs of any armed confrontation should deterrence fail... No one should be sanguine about the prospects for regional stability.'[21]

We believe there is reason to be more confident about South Asian nuclear-deterrence stability than the prevailing perspective would suggest. For purposes of clarity, the subcontinent's nuclear challenges can be divided into three scenarios: purposive, inadvertent, and accidental use of nuclear weapons. The first scenario evolves like this: India grows impatient with the Kashmir insurgency, which has killed some 60,000 people, pinned down hundreds of thousands of Indian troops, generated increasingly audacious terrorist operations on Indian soil, and wasted 15 years' worth of scarce resources. New Delhi orders search-and-destroy operations across the LoC, hoping to disrupt the militants' and terrorists' supply routes. Faced with the possibility that Indian forces will crush the insurgency once and for all, the Pakistan Army grows alarmed. Unable to turn the tide in the remote northern region, the army resorts to its traditional strategy of 'offensive defence'—that is, taking the fight to the enemy across the Punjab plains, in order to neutralize India's gains in Kashmir and create the circumstances for an advantageous political settlement. In response, India launches a conventional counterattack across the Punjab border, which soon threatens to engulf Lahore, Pakistan's second-largest city. At this point, Pakistani options narrow to one: resorting to nuclear weapons to prevent the country from being overrun.

While superficially compelling, this scenario begs one vital question: why would any Indian or Pakistani leader order a strike corps across the international border in the face of possible nuclear retaliation? Indian counter-insurgency forces might indeed attack the supply lines and assembly points of the insurgents based in Pakistan-held Kashmir. After all, this option was intensely debated by senior Indian leaders during the 1999 Kargil war.[22] But why would Islamabad respond by invading India proper, when the very success of such an assault might render Karachi or Lahore a smoking ruin? And why would New Delhi repeat its 1965 offensive, knowing that every yard of territory gained would increase the possibility of a nuclear reprisal against densely populated Indian cities? Furthermore, why would *either* side use nuclear weapons against the other when their close proximity means that radioactive fallout could drift back over the attacker's territory and cause widespread illness and loss of life? This scenario implies a degree of irrationality that has been wholly absent in South Asia's post-independence international relations.

A second scenario suggests that a South Asian nuclear war might erupt inadvertently.[23] This is the idea that, during a future crisis, India and Pakistan could stumble into a conflict that neither side purposefully seeks. In this scenario, miscalculation of the adversary's intentions by one or both sides leads inexorably to conventional war. At this point, faulty Pakistani intelligence estimates suggest that India is preparing to launch a pre-emptive nuclear strike against Pakistan's small nuclear arsenal. Islamabad fears that its last-resort nuclear insurance— painstakingly bought at huge expense over decades—is about to be destroyed. Instead of risking such an outcome, Pakistani decision-makers choose to use rather than lose their precious nuclear stockpile. Pakistan launches a pre-emptive strike of its own, in an attempt to decapitate Indian nuclear forces.

This scenario, too, defies logic. None of the Indo-Pakistani wars has begun inadvertently; indeed, all of the major international wars since the end of World War II have been premeditated. It is even less likely that two *nuclear* powers would slide down the slippery slope into inadvertent war, given the additional margin of caution induced by nuclear weapons. Even if Pakistani (or Indian) planners bucked the historical trend, how could they launch a pre-emptive nuclear strike with any hope of success? How many deliverable nuclear warheads does the other side possess? Have they been mated with delivery systems? Which are deployed on aircraft and which on ballistic missiles? Where are these delivery systems located? Are the missiles mobile or concealed? Which weapon systems are real and which are dummies? These and many other questions severely inhibit planning for a pre-emptive nuclear strike. Military planners' inability to answer them with confidence creates first-strike uncertainty. In nuclear matters, even 99 per cent certainty is insufficient to rule out the possibility of a punishing response in kind. To assume that Indian and Pakistani leaders do not understand this simple equation is to indulge in ethnocentrism.

The third scenario is most disturbing. The main nuclear danger in South Asia today is accidental nuclear war. Although there is no evidence that this possibility has posed problems during the region's short nuclear history, neither is there any guarantee that this record will stand indefinitely. Washington and Moscow have decades of experience with the command and control of large nuclear forces. They developed a variety of protections against the accidental use of nuclear weapons, including, at various times, non-mating of warheads with delivery systems; Permissive Action Links (PALS); and elaborate human controls. They also trained thousands of military personnel in the safe handling of nuclear weapons. New Delhi and Islamabad have no such experience on which to draw; they are basically starting from scratch. And, while there is no reason to believe that Indian and Pakistani scientists and military officers could not eventually devise and implement reliable command and control systems, that process will likely take years. Recent history suggests that more crises may erupt before India and Pakistan implement such command and control practices. During another crisis, if Islamabad or New Delhi were to make preparations for possible nuclear use, 'any one of a number of shocks (fire, unintentional drops, or stray electrical charges)' could 'directly or indirectly detonate the high explosive sphere surrounding a weapon's fissile core. Depending on the weapon's design, this could lead... to a full nuclear detonation.'[24] Once the first nuclear weapon explodes, anything can happen. This possibility—not purposive or inadvertent nuclear war—is South Asia's most daunting nuclear challenge.[25]

Implications for US Policy[26]

The most fundamental US goal with respect to Indo-Pakistani relations should be strategic stability: a relationship between two adversaries where the likelihood of crises is low, the likelihood of crises escalating to war is low, and, in the event that war *does* erupt, the fighting is as limited as possible in duration and destruction. Strategic stability can be enhanced by a variety of policies known collectively as conflict management. In turn, conflict management takes three main forms: conflict resolution, or the settling of international political disputes; arms control, which aims at reducing states' armed forces, configuring those forces in non-threatening modes, and/or deploying them in non-provocative postures; and CBMs, which are intended to increase transparency, political-military communication, and mutual reassurance.[27]

Conflict management policies can be conceptualized in terms of three concentric circles. At the core, symbolizing its greatest efficacy in the conflict management process, is conflict resolution. In the second ring, symbolizing its lesser—but not negligible—efficacy is arms control. In the outer ring, symbolizing their even lesser—but still not negligible—efficacy are CBMs. For any adversarial relationship, conflict resolution is the preferred type of conflict management; after all, if the underlying political conflict between two countries can be resolved, that would mitigate the need for acutely militarized security postures, and thus for arms control and CBMs. Absent conflict resolution, arms control is the preferred method of conflict management; if the respective armed forces can be deployed at the lowest possible levels, in the least threatening configurations, and in the least provocative postures, the potential for war will be minimized. Absent either conflict resolution or arms control, CBMs are of limited usefulness, but better than nothing.

This concentric-circles conceptualization of conflict management illustrates not only the *fact* of different conflict-management policies, but also the *relationship* between them. Conflict resolution is an inherent sub-set of both arms control and confidence building: in other words, to resolve an underlying political conflict is also, in a sense, to control arms and build confidence. In turn, arms control is an inherent sub-set of confidence-building: to control arms is also to build confidence. This is not to say, of course, that the three types of conflict-management policies we have identified are mutually exclusive. In practice, a strategically stable relationship will exhibit elements of all three types of policies, and the relationship's custodians—diplomats, military officers, politicians, etc.— will scarcely be aware of which ones they are following. The ideal-type strategically stable relationship would be one in which a seamless web of conflict management policies ensures political-military harmony. The ideal-type strategically unstable relationship would be one in which conflict management policies are either non-existent or so under-developed as to be ineffective. In such a situation, the main hopes for avoiding major war rest on crisis management, which is the least comforting tactic of all.

Unfortunately, US policy with respect to the India–Pakistan relationship has tended over the last twenty years to emphasize CBMs and arms control, while at the same time favouring crisis management over conflict resolution. In other words, Washington has chosen to pursue policies to constrain and stabilize the South Asian nuclear arms competition, but has shied away from taking bolder initiatives to help resolve the Kashmir dispute. When it comes to Kashmir, the US has tended to be reactive rather than proactive, which stands in stark contrast to its more resolute pursuit of conflict resolution in other chronic disputes, such as in West Asia, Northern Ireland, the Korean peninsula, South Africa, and the Balkans. If the US hopes to spur an enduring resolution to the India–Pakistan conflict over Kashmir, it must abandon its crisis-management orientation.

Two broad avenues conceivably lead towards conflict resolution. In the first, the US decides to engage the diplomatic impasse with all its resources, devises a tentative blueprint for resolution, and begins to work doggedly with India and Pakistan to realize the aim of a just and lasting peace. In the second, the US continues to use its 'good offices' and minimal diplomatic pressure to nudge the two sides into bilateral discussions whose destination is uncertain. Washington has chosen the latter approach for decades, and it has manifestly failed.

The situation as it stands today is unsustainable over the long term. Neither New Delhi nor Islamabad can unilaterally impose a military solution in its favour. Even with intensive cross-LoC conventional military operations, India will never be able to stem the flow of enough arms and terrorists into its part of Kashmir to prevent a weaker but tenacious Pakistan from bleeding India indefinitely. And, in attempting such an aggressive solution, New Delhi would run the risk of Pakistani escalation to nuclear weapons, either purposeful, inadvertent, or accidental. For its part, Pakistan is no better placed to achieve a military solution to the conflict than it has been for the last half-century, short of triggering a nuclear war that would lay waste to much of the subcontinent and render the Kashmir dispute moot. If a military resolution of the conflict is out of the question, the prevailing status quo—chronically low-grade but occasionally explosive hostility—is less and less palatable. Nuclear weapon states have a special responsibility to the international community to act circumspectly when it comes to matters of war and peace. How many times can India and Pakistan walk the 1990, 1998, 1999, and 2001–2 tightropes without falling into the abyss?

If politics is the art of the possible, why has conflict resolution proved so elusive in Kashmir? A 'mini-max' analysis—identifying each side's most- and least-preferred outcomes—demonstrates the fundamental nature of the quandary. In mini-max terms, each side's minimum aim is to retain what it has today, and each side's maximum goal is to become sovereign over all of the former princely state of Jammu and Kashmir. As one of the authors wrote in 1998, neither side has been willing to countenance the other side's achieving its maximum aim:

partly for strategic reasons, but also because to do so would be to deny the legitimating ideology on which each state was founded. Pakistan's two-nation theory held that the subcontinent's Muslims could safeguard their political rights only through the formation of a separate country. For Pakistanis, the idea of a Muslim-majority state falling within Indian borders is anathema, as it repudiates the two-nation theory and thus the entire basis for the creation of Pakistan.

Indian leaders' secular ideology rests on the successful incorporation of all minorities, including Muslims, into the Indian political order. A Pakistani Kashmir would be an insult to Indian secularism. If Muslims' rights cannot be protected in Kashmir, they are subject to doubt throughout India. Kashmir is a zero-sum test for each state's legitimating ideology: one's validity invalidates the other.[28]

In sum, neither side can give up the part of Kashmir it controls today, yet neither side can acquire all of Kashmir. Is there, between these two ends of the continuum, a 'midi' position, a mid-range outcome that would fall short of each side's maximum, but not force it to forsake its minimum? The most logical mid-range outcome is a formalized status quo, minus the chronic tension that creates instability in Indo-Pakistani relations and sucks up an enormous amount of resources on both sides.[29] How feasible would it be, then, to make the LoC a permanent, internationally recognized border between India and Pakistan?

From the Indian perspective, turning the LoC into a formal international boundary would solve the Kashmir problem—at least in its international dimension. New Delhi would retain Hindu Jammu, the Muslim Valley, and Buddhist Ladakh, thereby reinforcing India's preferred identity as a secular country composed of many diverse, but relatively harmonious, nations. In comparison, the parts of Kashmir administered by Pakistan—referred to by Islamabad as the 'Northern Areas' of Gilgit and Baltistan, and 'Azad Kashmir' in the western part of the state—are much less integral to India's self-identity. From Pakistan's perspective, the best midi solution would be to hold the statewide plebiscite called for by the UN Security Council resolutions that ultimately ended the first Indo-Pakistani war. But this process would threaten to yield an outcome that endangers India's minimum objective of retaining at least the part of Kashmir that it controls today. Viewed in mini-max terms, a Kashmiri plebiscite is a dead letter, as the international community increasingly recognizes.

Non-experts have a hard time understanding why India and Pakistan cannot simply agree to partition Kashmir permanently, along lines close to if not identical with today's LoC. After all, by the terms of the 1972 Simla Agreement, the two countries are resolved to settle their differences through bilateral negotiations or by any other peaceful means mutually agreed upon between them. Why not use this diplomatic mechanism to formalize what is already, for all intents and purposes, an informal border between the two countries?

The answer goes deeper than Pakistan's legalistic response that the relevant UN resolutions call for a plebiscite. More fundamentally, Islamabad resists transforming the LoC into an international border because that, in effect, would *resolve* the Kashmir dispute. In turn, conflict resolution would rob important political interests of their thin claims to legitimacy within the Pakistani polity. Even under civilian rule, democracy in Pakistan is only skin-deep. Political power remains, by and large, in the hands of traditional, largely conservative interests: the Pakistan Army, neo-feudal landowners, big business houses, and Islamists of various sociopolitical hues. These elite constituencies have a vested interest in the domestic status quo, because a wider distribution of political and economic power would threaten their privileged positions in Pakistani society. Chronic conflict in Kashmir provides these interests with the only non-coercive way to preserve their power. It allows them to portray India's control of predominantly Muslim Kashmir as an insult to both Pakistan and Islam. They shout to their downtrodden countrymen, 'Pakistan's *raison d'être* is Islam; if Kashmiri Muslims can live contentedly in secular India, what is the *purpose* of Pakistan?' The best—perhaps only—way for conservative Pakistani interests to maintain their grip on power is to stoke the flames of discontent in Indian Kashmir, a tactic that, it must be admitted, has too often been abetted by New Delhi's own malfeasance in the state. As long as Kashmir is rent by turmoil, Pakistan's power brokers can depict themselves as defenders of the nation and the faith. Without this distraction, the political attention of Pakistan's miserable masses might instead shift dramatically to the country's deep economic inequalities, its profoundly venal politics, and the rampant corruption infecting every aspect of Pakistani society. In short, actually resolving the Kashmir dispute would threaten the dominance of the entrenched powers-that-be in Pakistan.

For this reason, Islamabad resists transforming the LoC into an international boundary. Thus, because no other solution is availing, conflict resolution is—alas—exceedingly unlikely in Kashmir. Is there a way forward? Yes, but only if both sides make fundamental concessions

in the service of mutually acceptable, midi objectives. Turning the LoC
into an extension of the international border between India and Pakistan
would satisfy that criterion. It is the potential basis—perhaps the *only*
potential basis—for constructive discussions. US policy-makers
concerned with South Asia should seriously consider presenting to New
Delhi and Islamabad a 'road map' towards conflict resolution based on
the following guidelines:

- As a first step, India and Pakistan should reaffirm the letter
  and spirit of the Simla Agreement: the two sides will resolve
  the Kashmir dispute peacefully and bilaterally.

- Second, Pakistan should make a permanent, good-faith effort
  to end the flow of *jihadi* militants into both Indian Kashmir
  and India proper. Islamabad will be unable to stop all such
  infiltrations, but Washington and New Delhi will be able to
  distinguish between inability and unwillingness. The United
  States can provide monitoring and surveillance technologies
  to verify Pakistan's compliance.

- In response to a significantly diminished flow of militants across
  the LoC, India should begin to thin out its military presence
  in Kashmir. This would constitute a good-faith demonstration
  that New Delhi is serious about resolving the conflict. Forces
  sufficient to ensure law and order should, of course, be allowed
  to remain in the state. Pakistan, in response, should then thin
  out its own military presence in the part of Kashmir it controls.
  Again, Washington can help to verify compliance.

- Once these actions have been taken, and the situation on the
  ground has stabilized, India and Pakistan should sign a treaty
  making the LoC—perhaps with minor adjustments—a
  permanent international border between the two countries.

- India and Pakistan should then negotiate the further
  demilitarization of the areas of Kashmir over which they would
  now be sovereign. Security forces should be capped at the
  lowest possible levels, and in the least-threatening modes,
  consistent with ensuring internal security.

- In terms of process, Washington needs to be steady in its engagement with New Delhi and Islamabad. US leaders should indicate clearly and repeatedly that this is a long-term commitment, not a one-shot deal. Indian and Pakistani officials have ample historical justification for doubting US stamina in this regard.

- Washington should be low-key with its 'road map'. Domestic political winds could easily blow away the initiative. Negotiators must be given the political space to exercise leadership.

We readily acknowledge that the prospects for settling the Kashmir dispute are slim. However, the possibility that another crisis will erupt and perhaps escalate to cataclysmic proportions, dictates a more proactive posture on the part of US policy-makers. Like it or not, the US is the 'sole pole'[30] in a unipolar world. With respect to the world's most difficult international political disputes, it can either lead or sit on the sidelines and ultimately bear the brunt of its own passivity. Leadership involves more than devising policies that are guaranteed to work; it also involves taking risks on bold initiatives that may fail, but whose success may produce greater stability in a tense and fluid international system. In today's South Asia, a failed US policy thrust would have minimal costs; at the same time, the benefits of a successful subcontinental *rapprochement* would be enormous. The people of Kashmir could live in peace for the first time in 15 years. Social and economic development could resume in an area that is among the least developed in all of India and Pakistan. New Delhi and Islamabad could break the pattern of mutual acrimony that too often degenerates into war-threatening crises. Both sides could stop wasting precious resources on defending their positions in Kashmir. Over the longer term, a Kashmir settlement would almost certainly spark a generalized Indo-Pakistani *detente* that could well bring tangible economic and social benefits to over a billion people. For India, Pakistan, and the US, resolving the conflict would help to prevent what appears to be an increasingly ominous development: the relocation from Afghanistan to the subcontinent of Al Qaeda's terrorist epicentre. A final benefit would accrue for the world as whole: a decreased likelihood of nuclear weapons being used in warfare for the first time since 1945.

With respect to South Asia's nuclear weapons themselves, the experience of the last two decades suggests that American influence on Indian and Pakistani decisionmaking is severely limited. Whether in the 1980s with respect to Islamabad, or in the 1990s with respect to New Delhi, the US has utterly failed to inhibit either government from doing what it wishes in the nuclear realm. Neither carrots, in the form of security guarantees, nor sticks in the form of sanctions, have had much impact on two states who see their respective security predicaments as perilous. Washington should, of course, continue to urge the two sides to refrain from further nuclear tests, limit their production of fissile material, resist the political, strategic and technological imperatives to deploy at-the-ready nuclear forces, and work together to develop CBMs like the recent agreement to establish a nuclear-related hotline between the Indian and Pakistani foreign secretaries.[31] The US should also, within the bounds of international legal obligations and US law, help India and Pakistan to ensure that their nuclear weapon capabilities are maintained as securely as possible.

Most important, Washington should inform Islamabad—quietly but in no uncertain terms—that further transfer of nuclear weapons technology to other states will seriously damage US-Pakistani relations. We are still learning about the extent of Pakistani bomb-maker A.Q. Khan's provision of nuclear knowledge and materials to Libya and North Korea over the past decade. At a bare minimum, Pakistan transferred to North Korea raw uranium hexafluoride, uranium enrichment centrifuges, and 'one or more warhead designs', in 'what now appears to be one of the largest nuclear proliferation networks in the past half-century'.[32] Khan's activities, almost certainly abetted by the Pakistan Army, if not the country's political leadership, give the lie to Islamabad's claim that it has always been a responsible custodian of nuclear materials. At the highest levels of government, the US should tell Pakistan that further nuclear weapons exports will result in the termination of American military and economic assistance to Islamabad.

But mere words will not bring strategic stability to South Asia. After all, India and Pakistan—like the US—have the right as sovereign states to acquire, for deterrent purposes, the ultimate weapon. If a country protected by two vast oceans and the world's most sophisticated conventional military technologies still requires the security insurance provided by nuclear weapons, why should India and Pakistan—with their more vulnerable geopolitical positions and technological inferiority—be expected to give up their nuclear aspirations? It is mainly Washington's attitude towards nuclear weapons, not India's or Pakistan's, that promotes the continuing legitimacy of nuclear weapons as an international currency of power. In the final analysis, the only truly effective non-proliferation tools Washington has in South Asia are meaningful US action in the form of denuclearization and a serious commitment to helping India and Pakistan resolve the Kashmir dispute, once and for all.

Notes

[1] See Bennett Ramberg, *Nuclear Power Plants as Weapons for the Enemy: An Unrecognized Military Peril* (Berkeley: University of California Press, 1984).

[2] George Perkovich, *India's Nuclear Bomb: The Impact on Global Proliferation* (Berkeley: University of California Press, 1999), pp. 276–7.

[3] Lewis A. Dunn, *Controlling the Bomb* (New Haven, Connecticut: Yale University Press, 1982), p. 75.

[4] Ibid., p. 70 (emphasis added).

[5] Lewis A. Dunn, *Containing Nuclear Proliferation, Adelphi Paper No. 263* (London: International Institute for Strategic Studies, 1991), p. 4 (emphasis added). Although it may appear as if we are picking on one particular analyst, it should be remembered that his assessments squarely reflect the predominant analytical thinking of the nuclear nonproliferation community. On this point, see Devin T. Hagerty, *The Consequences of Nuclear Proliferation: Lessons from South Asia* (Cambridge, Massachusetts: MIT Press, 1998), pp. 9–37. Indeed, we chose to cite Dunn's analysis because it reflects the highest standard of thinking about the spread of nuclear weapons.

[6] Hagerty, *Consequences of Nuclear Proliferation*, pp. 40–5.

[7] Joseph Cirincione, *Deadly Arsenals: Tracking Weapons of Mass Destruction* (Washington, DC: Carnegie Endowment for International Peace, 2002), pp. 191 (India) and 207 (Pakistan). For additional details, see pp. 191–219.

[8] R. Rajaraman, M.V. Ramana, and Zia Mian, 'Possession and Deployment of Nuclear Weapons in South Asia: An Assessment of Some Risks', *Economic and Political Weekly* (Mumbai), 22 June 2002.

[9] These are derived from the authors' discussions with knowledgeable analysts at a variety of scholarly and policy gatherings over the past three years.

[10] In this regard, see the discussion in Cirincione, *Deadly Arsenals*, pp. 147–53.

[11] To repeat Bundy's argument: 'It is one thing for military men to maintain our deterrent force with vigilant skill, and it is quite another for anyone to assume that their necessary contingency plans have any serious interest for political leaders. The object of political men—quite rightly—is that these weapons should never be used. I have watched two Presidents working on strategic contingency plans, and what interested them most was simply to make sure that none of these awful events would occur.' McGeorge Bundy, 'To Cap the Volcano', *Foreign Affairs*, vol. 48, no. 1 (October 1969), p. 12.

[12] 'Opening Remarks by National Security Adviser Brajesh Mishra at the Release of Draft Indian Nuclear Doctrine', New Delhi, 17 August 1999. <http://meadev.gov.in/govt/opstm-indnucld>.

[13] Kenneth J. Cooper, 'India Warns Pakistan Over Kashmir', *International Herald Tribune*, 19 May 1998.

[14] National Security Advisory Board, 'Draft Report of National Security Advisory Board on Indian Nuclear Doctrine', New Delhi, 17 August 1999. <http://www.meadev.gov.in/govt/opstm-indnucld>.

[15] C. Raja Mohan, 'India Offers Nuclear "No-First-Use"', the *Hindu*, 5 August 1998.

[16] See Michael Ryan Kraig, 'The Political and Strategic Imperatives of Nuclear Deterrence in South Asia', *India Review*, vol. 2, no. 1 (January 2003), pp. 1–48; Scott D. Sagan and Kenneth N. Waltz, *The Spread of Nuclear Weapons: A Debate Renewed* (New York: Norton, 2003), especially pp. 88–124; Michael Krepon, *The Stability–Instability Paradox, Misperception, and Escalation Control in South Asia* (Washington, DC: Henry L. Stimson Center, 2003); Ashley J. Tellis, *India's Emerging Nuclear Posture: Between Recessed Deterrent and Ready Arsenal* (Santa Monica, California: RAND, 2001), pp. 725–65; and Neil Joeck, 'Maintaining Nuclear Stability in South Asia', *Adelphi Paper no. 312* (London: International Institute for Strategic Studies, 1997).

[17] From the previous note, this group includes Sagan, Krepon, and Joeck.

[18] From note 16, this group includes Waltz and Tellis.

[19] See Sumit Ganguly, *Conflict Unending: India-Pakistan Tensions since 1947* (New York: Columbia University Press and Washington, DC: Woodrow Wilson Center Press, 2001), pp. 108–10; Devin T. Hagerty, 'The South Asian Nuclear Tests: Implications for Arms Control', in Carl Ungerer and Marianne Hanson

(eds), *The Politics of Nuclear Nonproliferation* (Sydney: Allen and Unwin, 2001), pp. 110–13.

[20] The remainder of this section is a slightly revised version of arguments made by Hagerty in 'The South Asian Nuclear Tests', pp. 110–13.

[21] The Brookings Institution and The Council on Foreign Relations, *After the Tests: US Policy Toward India and Pakistan* (New York: Council on Foreign Relations Press, 1998), pp. 2–3.

[22] One analyst makes the startling claim that the Kargil war 'destroyed any illusion that the overt nuclear postures of [India and Pakistan] would act as a restraint on military conflict'. Cirincione, *Deadly Arsenals*, p. 210. To the contrary, it was nuclear deterrence that impelled India to limit its military operations to *its own side of a disputed territory*. For a long discussion about why nuclear deterrence of low-intensity conflicts is inherently problematic, see Hagerty, *Consequences of Nuclear Proliferation*, pp. 60–2.

[23] See the discussion in Francois Heisbourg, 'The Prospects for Nuclear Stability Between India and Pakistan', *Survival*, vol. 40, no. 4 (Winter 1998–99), pp. 82–6.

[24] Gregory F. Giles, 'Safeguarding the Undeclared Nuclear Arsenals', *Washington Quarterly*, vol. 16, no. 2 (1993), p. 173.

[25] One hopes that this analysis, which traces back to Hagerty's earlier work— *Consequences of Nuclear Proliferation*—lays to rest once and for all the mistaken notion that 'deterrence optimists... presume that "Murphy's Law" does not apply to nuclear weapons—at least not to the extent that an accident or a chain reaction of miscalculation, error, chance, or misuse of authority would lead to a crossing of the nuclear threshold'. Krepon, *Escalation Control in South Asia*, p. 8.

[26] This section draws extensively on arguments first made in Devin T. Hagerty, 'US Policy and the Kashmir Dispute', *India Review*, vol. 2, no. 3 (July 2003), pp. 89–116.

[27] It might be argued that a fourth type of policy—crisis management— could be added to this typology of conflict management policies. However, if crises erupt routinely between two states, those states are already and inherently in a situation of strategic instability. Crisis management is properly understood as a last-ditch tactical, rather than strategic, goal.

[28] Hagerty, *Consequences of Nuclear Proliferation*, p. 67.

[29] From this mini–max perspective, an independent Kashmir is out of the question, because it would fail to meet either side's minimum requirement.

[30] The term is William C. Wohlforth's 'The Stability of a Unipolar World', *International Security*, vol. 24, no. 1 (Summer 1999), p. 40.

[31] Amy Waldman, 'India-Pakistan Talks Make No Specific Gains on Kashmir', the *New York Times*, 29 June 2004.

[32] David E. Sanger, 'US Sees More Arms Ties Between Pakistan and Korea', the *New York Times*, 14 March 2004.

Index

Printed in the United States
52249LVS00006B/1-126